WHERE DID IT ALL GO RIGHT?

Andrew Collins

EBURY
PRESS

Heaven is a place where nothing ever happens.
Talking Heads, 'Heaven' (1979)

To Mum, Dad, Simon and Melissa.
It's a family affair.

3 5 7 9 10 8 6 4

Copyright © 2003 Andrew Collins

Andrew Collins has asserted his moral right to be identified as the author of
this work in accordance with the Copyright, Designs and Patents Act 1988.

First published 2003 by Ebury Press,
An imprint of Random House,
20 Vauxhall Bridge Road, London SW1V 2SA
www.randomhouse.co.uk

Random House Australia (Pty) Limited
20 Alfred Street, Milsons Point, Sydney,
New South Wales 2061, Australia

Random House New Zealand Limited
18 Poland Road, Glenfield, Auckland 10, New Zealand

Random House South Africa (Pty) Limited
Endulini, 5a Jubilee Road, Parktown 2193, South Africa

The Random House Group Limited Reg. No. 954009

www.randomhouse.co.uk

Printed and bound in Great Britain by Mackays of Chatham plc, Kent

A CIP catalogue record for this book is available from the British Library.

Cover designed by Keenan
Interior by seagulls

ISBN 0 09188 667 8

contents

acknowledgements

Everyday People

It's not practical to thank all those who have written miserable memoirs about their terrible childhoods, but collectively they inspired me to write this book with their redemptive and more importantly best-selling tales of woe: abuse, death, deprivation and the search for love among the wreckage. The aim of *Where Did It All Go Right?* is not to belittle their suffering, or to mock the therapeutic qualities of externalisation, but simply to provide an alternative view.

Shit happens. But sometimes it doesn't.

The degradation endured by the young Dave Peltzer (*A Boy Called 'It'* and numerous sequels) may in fact be the polar opposite of my childhood, but I started to think in mid-2000 that, hey, perhaps my voice should be heard too. Then I read Paul Morley's elegant book *Nothing* and my mind was made up. Perhaps then I should single out Paul Morley for sincere appreciation above all the other whingers.

It almost seems indulgent to thank my family when the book is dedicated to them, but clearly I could not have told my story without their blessing, as it is their story too. While writing and researching it, I spent valuable quality time with them, sorting through boxes of memorabilia in Mum and Dad's loft and sorting through events in our minds. Of all my grandparents, it was only Pap Reg who looked likely to see the book's publication but sadly he died while I was writing it. That's a mortal watershed for any grandchild, and it was for me, but it made the book seem more important to finish. I hope I have done a halfway decent job. I like to think that my late father-in-law, Sam Quirke, would have enjoyed it too.

I read two very different autobiographies during the writing of this one that fed directly into it: *Experience* by Martin Amis and *Frank Skinner* by Frank Skinner. One gave me the conviction to run footnotes on the page, the other made me feel a lot better about the occasional coy reference to a teenage girlfriend (if you've read it you'll know exactly what I mean). I also found inspiration in the first published diary (1660) by Samuel Pepys – the guv'nor! – and in Gavin Lambert's memoir *Mainly About Lindsay Anderson*, in which he quotes from the great British director's first diary (1942), aged 19. 'Its purpose is both to remind me in after years how I felt and what I did, [and] to give me literary exercise.'

Two people were instrumental in helping me treat a labour of love as a literary exercise: firstly my agent Kate Haldane, who read the sample chapters and laughed (I can't believe it – I've just thanked my agent!), and secondly the man who turned out to be my publisher, Andrew Goodfellow at Ebury. He phoned Kate seemingly out of the blue and asked if certain of her clients were interested in writing a book. I was; she quickly arranged the lunch at a restaurant that stupidly serves wine but not beer, and thanks to Andrew's long-sighted vision – and his Seventies childhood – a deal was struck.

Only one person read the book before these two did, and that is Julie Quirke, who wisely kept her own name when she married me. I have taken her advice on style and ethics throughout, and do nothing without seeking her approval, except buy John Wayne DVDs.

Life would have been a lonely writer's hell were it not for the good people who continue to populate the rest of my life: Frank Wilson, Stephen Hughes, Sarah Roome, Gary Bales, Adam Smith, Antonia Quirke, Stuart Maconie, David Quantick, John Aizlewood, Lorna Aizlewood, John Harris, Alex Walsh-Taylor, Simon Day, Eileen Quirke, Mary and Steve Rowling, Rob Mills and Jessie Nicholas, the combined Quirkes, Collinses, McFaddens and Joneses; all at Amanda Howard; Jim, Sarah, Miles, Tom, Jupitus, Wilding, Julie, Mark, Mike, John, Helen, Mad Dog, Lauren, Jon,

ACKNOWLEDGEMENTS

Antony and everyone else who knows me at the mightly 6 Music;
Paul, Toby, Mo, all the Johns, Zahid, Mark, Francine and all at BBC
Radio Arts; Fat Bloke; *Q*; Colin, Jeremy, Sue, Shem, Gill and all
at *Radio Times*; Sarah, Jo, Di, Polly and all at Ebury; and John Yorke
and Mal Young, without whom I might not even be writing this
interminable list.

Name dropping: thanks to Richard Coles for geographical
support, Billly Bragg for setting me up, and to Mark Radcliffe and
Marc Riley for recognising the comedy potential of my diaries on
late-nite Radio 1: you are honorary 'dirt collectors'.

Hats in the air for Friends Reunited, the website that became
fashionable just at the right time for a book about old school-
friends, and to all those who got in touch: Paul Milner, Paul Bush,
Anita Barker, Catherine Williams, Alan Martin, Dave Griffiths,
Craig McKenna, Kevin Pearce, Wendy Turner, Sue Stratton, Lis
Ribbans, Louisa Dominy, Gavin Willis, Ricky Hennell, Mark Crilley,
Rebecca Warren (via Tim Clubb), Andrew Sharp, Jo Flanders and
Andrew Hoskin.

Goodnight, sweet Tessie. We should all have such spirit.

This book was brought to you in conjunction with Twinings,
Able & Cole, Ingmar Bergman and The Temptations.

Andrew Collins
November 2002

introduction

Ask the Family

We shipped 'em in all the way from Northampton – the Collins family!
Noel Edmonds, *Telly Addicts* (1990)

Who went from the Hotel du Lac to the Bangkok Hilton?
Come on, I'll have to hurry you

My family, the Collins family, appeared as contestants on *Telly Addicts* in 1990. We managed to reach the dizzy heights of the semi-finals and took home a *Telly Addicts* board game and four fleecy-lined *Telly Addicts* sweatshirts. This brush with the limelight may seem like the wrong place to start a book about being *normal*, but as much as anything it's a sign of the times. It's more *normal* to have been on a TV quiz show than not. I knew someone when I was working at the *NME* who'd been on *Fifteen to One* (as had his girl-friend), and I later worked under a bloke who'd been on *Blockbusters*. My sister-in-law was close enough to *Who Wants to Be a Millionaire* to have recruited me as one of her phone-a-friends (they callously disqualified her for taking more than the allotted time to answer the qualifying phone question about the length of the Golden Gate Bridge, which she gallingly got right). Further, my brother was on *Crimewatch* (as an officer of the law, I might add), my future wife could be seen dancing to Hall & Oates' 'Maneater' on a 1982 edition of *Top of the Pops*, her brother was an extra on *Grange Hill*, and you could see my Uncle Allen's head in the crowd when *Jeux sans Frontières* came to Northampton. (This

8

was *after* he'd lost his rag with some noisy Europeans in the row behind and thrown a pair of their dustbin-lid cymbals on to the field of play.)

So – hold the front page – Warhol was right. Tragically, the 15 minutes of fame granted by contestanthood on a TV quiz show quickly fades (even in Northampton where nothing ever happens). But let us not lump *Telly Addicts* in with all the other quiz shows: in those days it was special. It was about families. Most quiz or game shows want you in ones or pairs – or in meritocratic school groups for things like *Beat the Teacher* and *University Challenge*. At that time only *Telly Addicts* and *Family Fortunes* traded in the nuclear unit, and you have to admire their commitment to a dying currency.

Of course there used to be the eugenic *Ask the Family* with Robert Robinson, open exclusively to the families of university lecturers, and only then if they had two sons. It wasn't until the Eighties, when the American show *Family Feud* was translated back into English, that the proletariat were invited to leave the sofa *en famille* and flaunt *their* knowledge on TV. Knowledge aptly accumulated not from reading books but from watching TV – literally so in the case of *Telly Addicts*, where families were put on a prop sofa and given a prop remote control, to make them feel at home.

Telly Addicts moved with the times in 1994 and relaxed the rules to allow workmates and friends to join in: tantamount to a requiem for the family unit in this country. Back in 1990 though it was still a place for mums and dads and sons and daughters, and we were right there, on display in the petri dish of early evening BBC1: a happy, normal family of addicts. The point is – and how unlike television as a rule – this was no façade, no lie. Although I'd left home by then and had my own sofa and telly in London, we *were* a happy, normal family.

Mum, Dad, my younger sister Melissa and I really did get on famously, and when I occasioned to visit Northampton at weekends, we really might sit on a sofa together and watch telly. (It would have been a fine thing if the show had accepted five-person teams and our brother Simon could have joined us there in front of that studio audience at Pebble Mill, but he was in Germany with the army at the time, and unable to take the day off for such frippery, despite the fall of the Berlin Wall on 9 November 1989 and the reduced likelihood of the Russians invading.)

I was 25, and wore the same white, oversized, partially laced hip hop trainers on all three editions of *Telly Addicts*, letting the side down below the ankle but otherwise very much a team player. In the first round we beat the Young family from Stevenage by a whisker, 18 points to 16. ('There's an atmosphere of relief, mingled with a little surprise,' said Noel Edmonds at the end of the show.)

In the quarter finals, we were up against the Gawthrops (Nick, Deb, Chris and Russ, all jumpers and cardigans). Another close-run, low-scoring clash, the *Hotel du Lac* was the last of my three individual questions in the Spotlight Round. I'd actually 'passed' on the first: Who presents *The Late Late Show*? (the roguish Gay Byrne, as any addict *not* under the studio lights could tell you), but I'd salvaged my reputation by correctly naming Dr Who's robot dog from a library shot (eas-y!): K-9.

Then ...

Who went from the Hotel du Lac to the Bangkok Hilton?

A pretty upmarket question for a light early evening BBC1 quiz show I trust you'll agree, and I fluffed it. They had to hurry me. 'Don't know,' I said – college boy! – scoring one lousy point out of a possible three, bringing the family's total for that round up to an anorexic four points.[1] You have to bear in mind that for this decisive round the studio lights are dimmed, a clock ticks in the corner of the screen and there's no conferring. Suddenly it's not like sitting at home on the sofa with Mum, Dad and Melissa any more. We were neck and neck before the Spotlight, and now, having gone first, we were on 17. The stoic Gawthrops were on 13. They only needed five points – out of a possible 12! – to win.

As you can imagine, we were willing them from the darkness to blow it. They did. The Collins family from Northampton scraped through to the next round, where we would be defeated by the Allmans. Still, it wasn't the winning, it was the being on

---

1. It was Denholm Elliott.

television three times. It made Mum, Dad and Melissa locally famous for a while, with people coming up to them in shops and everything.[2]

I went back to London, having quietly enjoyed playing a family again. I never wore the sweatshirt, not even in irony. The lining was too hot.

* * *

I don't hold with the convention of biographies that says you must trace the subject's ancestry back to at least the Reformation. What use is it – I mean really – to know that Clint Eastwood's great-great-great-great-grandfather owned a tannery in Long Branch, New Jersey?[3] It's largely a fact for fact's sake about someone long dead. Our family goes way back in Northampton – it is our heartland – but I don't know how far back. One day I will actually use the Internet to trace my family tree and find out if I really am distantly related to Bootsy Collins (let's hope so), but for now, here's all you need to know.

The *Telly Addicts* team:

My dad is John William Collins.[4] A voluble, witty, kind-hearted conservative with more than one chin, a fine head of hair for a sixty-year-old and a *c'est-la-vie, que-sera-sera,* could-be-worse-could-be-raining attitude to life, fortified by forty years in insurance, which is to my mind his greatest attribute. If I have anything undiluted of Dad in me it's this.

My mum is Christine Anne Collins née Ward, a small woman on a permanent voyage of discovery whose lack of academic colours at school never held her back (she is the very essence of

---

2. In the local paper, Mum, Dad and Melissa got 'Telly watching family become screen stars' (6 October 1990), with a hopelessly posed picture in which they are *pointing at a telly*. I was recognised once in the immediate aftermath. A man came to fix the boiler in my flat and looked me up and down. 'You were on *Blind Date*,' he said, confidently. No, *Telly Addicts*. 'That's it!' he said. I then had to tell him what Noel Edmonds was like in real life (a consummate professional, actually).

3. He did.

4. Throughout *Experience*, and thus presumably in life, Martin Amis refers to his father as Kingsley. What a load of nouveau bohemian rubbish. My dad is called Dad. It is his correct title.

self-taught, and not a flower whose growth has been inhibited by Dad's formidable shadow). Blonde, trim and reliably glamorous without ever looking cheap, she is a volcano of impetuous emotion compared to Dad, and there's your yin and yang. She pronounces broccoli as 'broccolai' and cereals as 'surreals' and I don't know why it's only foodstuffs.

Melissa is now in her very early thirties, and a proud mother of three with husband Graham,[5] but to me she will always be between about five and twelve, pre-boys, pre-vanity. The only sister of two older brothers, she used to annoy us gently as if it were her calling, though we rarely actually got annoyed (it was mostly sticking her head round the door with the cartoon greeting 'Cha!, when we had mates there).[6] Melissa was cute, supremely aware of her own ability to amuse and she seems to have forgiven Simon and me for telling her there was a Dr Who monster living in her cupboard.

Honorary *Telly Addict*:

Simon was quite simply my best mate until puberty (mine) drove its inevitable wedge between us. We can still turn on the best-mates tap whenever we meet, and have latterly enjoyed a sporadic email correspondence, but his uniformed careers have generally kept us physically distant, especially the army, which stationed him in such godforsaken places as Hanover in Germany and Colchester in Essex.[7] An unbroken succession of hat-wearing jobs – army, prison service, police – have eroded Simon's hairline, but he always wore it short anyway so it's not such a tragic loss. From where I'm sitting,

---

5. Good, solid sort, likes a pint, Man City fan, plays football at the weekends.

6. I think Melissa had a nascent crush on my friend Paul Garner (he was around the house most often in the early Eighties), but not one that she would have recognised or that me or Paul would have admitted to. 'Cha was an abbreviation for 'Wotcha!' or 'Hotcha!', very common salutations round Northampton way at the time.

7. I attended a Regimental Day parade there in 1985 and tried in vain to embarrass Simon with my Oxfam mac and stupid hair. There is a classic family snapshot of this momentous day in which the pair of us are posing together, he in regimental blazer, slacks and tie, me in untucked striped shirt, Oxfam mac with sleeves pushed up and wild, dyed Eighties hairdo. But you can tell we are mad about each other: there's no animosity anywhere. I am holding a finger between my nose and top lip in approximation of Simon's moustache. Most of his platoon grew moustaches when they realised they were allowed to, in order to distinguish themselves from each other.

he seems to be a model father to his two daughters with wife Lesley,[8] and I admire him now as much as I always secretly have done from my unbroken succession of poofy jobs.

The grandparent generation:

Dad's dad was William John Collins, or Pap Collins as we knew him (in Northampton, it's 'pap' for grandpa or granddad). Pap Collins, a rotund, entertaining housepainter, war veteran and teller of tall tales, was married to Nan Collins, Winnie (née Corby).

Nan Collins was a sweet, non-suffering woman – always, always laughing – who worked wonders with a bit of braising steak and some pastry, and put up with Pap's stubborn idiosyncrasies (like refusing to countenance the advice of doctors), because she loved 'her Billy'. He died first.[9]

Mum's dad was Reginald Percy Ward, or Pap Reg, an upstanding toolmaker turned shop steward who stayed in Northampton during the war (to make tools) and thus lacked the embellished romance of Pap Collins – at least as far as my militarily obsessed brother and I were concerned. The older and more left wing I got, the more I appreciated Pap Reg, pillar of the Amalgamated Engineering Union, and, post-retirement, tribunal man and Pensioner's Voice activist. He became a belated inspiration to me,[10] and was my last grandparent to die, aged 85. I cried at his funeral, as I had cried at all three others.

Pap Reg was married to Nan Mabel (née Noble). She was the dominant figure in our family – to Dad's occasional chagrin – though she was also small of stature, like my mum. Thursday was her day. She would come round our house without fail. A mass of

---

8. Simon met Lesley in 1987 on a training exercise (she was in the Territorial Army at the time) and they were married within a matter of months at a church in her native Taunton. I was Simon's best man and fetched him Creme Eggs for breakfast on the day (his request). So much for anyone who said it wouldn't last.

9. It was one of those marriages where you imagined that one partner simply couldn't live without the other, and yet Nan enjoyed a whole year on her own (before quietly succumbing to pneumonia), seemingly in indomitable spirits and good health, during which she saw the birth and christening of her first grandchild, Simon and Lesley's daughter Charmaine.

10. I was proud to dedicate my only other book, a biography of Billy Bragg (*Still Suitable for Miners*), to Reginald Ward 'for political inspiration' in 1998. I'm glad he saw that.

anxieties who would 'whittle'[11] for weeks before going on holiday. Yet she managed to be funny and controversial along with it, and will forever remain, to me, the quintessential 'Old Northampton' matriarch. I was, I am embarrassed to say, always her favourite, which made it all the more difficult for me when she appeared not to recognise me (and I say *appeared*) after her stroke. Nan Mabel was still in there, but far beneath the broken surface. I never really knew the extent of Nan's inner troubles while I was growing up, and given that I've only learned about them since, it seems inappropriate to introduce them into my story now. She was Nan Mabel, who whittled unnecessarily.

I have three sets of blood uncles and aunties, two on Mum's side, one on Dad's, and various honorary uncles and aunties – in other words friends of Mum and Dad. I will introduce these people as we go along, otherwise we may drown in names (there's a Janis and a Janice, and an Alan and an Allen).

Mum met Dad on an office outing organised by the Atlas Assurance company in Northampton. They got married in 1962 and had me in 1965. Simon was born in 1967; Melissa in 1971, after which Dad had the operation. All three of us are now married and Simon and Melissa five children between them.[12] I lived at home until 1984 when I was 19 and then moved to the capital and stayed there. (It is a rare member of my family that leaves town without eventually coming back, although it should be noted, for fear of stereotyping us as genetically unadventurous, that Pap Reg's brother emigrated to Australia after the war, as did one of Nan Mabel's sisters, to Canada, and they never came back.)

This book will end when I leave home, because after that it's all college and the media, and Northampton fades.

My story is essentially the story of Northampton's 1970s, or if you prefer, any provincial English town's 1970s. It is also the story

---

11. *The Cassell Dictionary of Slang*: '**Whittle** v. to talk emptily, aimlessly, to chatter.' That's as maybe, but in our house it means to fret, to worry, to agonise out loud (esp. before going on holiday to Minehead). *Cassell* also notes that the original sixteenth-century definition is to 'confess on the gallows'. There's something of Nan Mabel in that.
12. Simon and Lesley's: Charmaine and Natasha. Melissa and Graham's: Ben, Jack and William. Not a bad apple among them, yet.

of a field – *the field*, where I learned to ride a bike without stabilisers, kissed Anita Barker and smoked my first cigarette, although not in the same year. It is the story of wellies, sticks, stickers, stitches, comics, cartoons, hamsters, the Alpine lorry and travel sickness tablets.

The big question, and the one I intend to answer is: where did it all go right?

preface

Down the Welfare

We have nothing to lose but our aitches.
George Orwell, *The Road to Wigan Pier* (1937)

I can still taste welfare orange. It has to be at least 33 years since I last drank any, but there it is, in some intuitive corner of my memory. I must have tasted a hundred different kinds of orange juice in my lifetime, and yet I can evoke the powerful intensity of welfare orange as if it were only yesterday.

Contrary to the name, welfare orange wasn't actually free, but it was state-subsidised in order to ensure that young mothers could afford a fix of vitamin C for their children. My mum used to walk 'down the welfare' every Monday with Auntie Sue[1] to pick up orange for me and powdered milk for Simon, then my baby brother. The pair of them would just have enough housekeeping to buy a small, medicine-sized bottle of orange each, although the drink was sufficiently concentrated to last a week when diluted. When we moved house in 1968, from Duston to Abington Vale – on the developing side of Northampton – Mum stopped getting it (the new house in Winsford Way was no longer within pram-pushing distance of the local welfare centre). I missed the vivid, sticky stuff.

---

1. Auntie Sue (Ashby) is as close as you can get to an honorary auntie. Married to Uncle Roger, she remains one of Mum's oldest friends and until recently they lived up the road. A lovely, well-spoken woman, she has the world's most recognisable and elegant hand-writing, all swoops and flourishes. You can see Auntie Sue's Christmas card arriving from 100 yards. Sue and Roger's daughter Melanie was my first friend. There was a girl character in my earliest comic with blonde hair and I called her 'Melanie' in tribute.

Welfare orange is pivotal to my memory of childhood in two ways. First, the very thought of it gives me a Proustian rush. I love those. Secondly, the fact that it was tantamount to a state benefit paints a picture of something I hadn't really given much thought to: the hand-to-mouth financial circumstance of my parents in the early years of their marriage, which certainly makes me feel more vital and real as I sit here in the pampered environs of my adult life. I generally consider myself the product of a middle-class upbringing – things certainly looked that way when I finally left home in 1984 – but you see I was really a child of family allowance, a distant benefactor of Beveridge. Simon and I were suckled on welfare milk, our teeth set on the road to ruin by welfare orange (with a superfluous spoonful of sugar in it, I'm told). We had it hard, we lived on the breadline, we couldn't even afford full-price squash.

Except, of course, life wasn't so bad. In fact it wasn't bad at all. There was little social stigma attached to being 'on welfare' in Duston, because everybody was. We had an indoor toilet, a Ford Anglia and a garage to put it in. There's cine film of me chasing Pap Collins with a water pistol into the garage at Duston, and it doesn't look much like *Angela's Ashes*. (Well, somebody had a cine camera, for a start.) And because my dad worked for an insurance company he was eligible for a competitive mortgage, which is how come we moved when I was about three to the new house – as in newly built – in a new suburb. Not quite *Brideshead Revisited*, I know, but we hardly lived in a box.

This is why I have often wondered about my upbringing over the years. Was it too comfortable? By which I mean was it too comfortable ever to make a decent book? Who boasts of attending the School of No Knocks? My mum's own modest working-class childhood was far away from the breadline (indeed, the family on her father's side were considered 'upper crust' round Northampton's no-nonsense Jimmy's End because their income came from an *office* job within London Midland and Scottish Railway), and yet she loves reading about those who had it hard: Catherine Cookson and the like. It is a vicarious pleasure, just like watching the super-rich suffer on *Dynasty* or *Dallas* used to be, superceded these days by criticising the wallpaper of some Spanish princess in *Hello!* or footballers' wives in *OK!* magazine. If for convenience we categorise the middle classes at the time of my childhood as the semi-detached, then my parents were middle class, but that's an incomplete picture. Talk of upper- and lower-middle class smacks of moving up and down the football league tables, but you might say that by the time I left home, my parents were closer to upper-middle than lower-middle. Indeed, the home I left in 1984 was *fully* detached, with all the implications of that word.

I think I'm right in generalising here and saying that only the middle classes truly romanticise poverty and hardship. There was little of either in my early life, and yet like any family of five with only one breadwinner and a mortgage, we did not have money coming out of our ears. We did not holiday abroad, we never ate out – although that has as much to do with the unenlightened times as with Dad's take-home pay after tax – we enjoyed neither private education nor private healthcare, and my brother and I shared a bedroom. Our Action Men rode in a second-hand armoured car.[2] It was a bread and butter upbringing, with most mod cons, and nobody had consumption.

But while the extremes of abject poverty and aristocratic riches make better fiction, a cosy, middle-class equilibrium can be just as effectively shattered by tragedy. You read about it in the papers every day. It was only when the Yorkshire Ripper stopped attacking prostitutes and killed a 'respectable' girl[3] in 1979 that the general public really sat up and took notice. 'Respectable', semi-detached homes are ideally appointed, dramatically speaking, for a knock on the door bringing terrible news, or institutionalised abuse veiled by net curtains.

So where was mine? I want my money back.

The veneer of my 'respectable', semi-detached home in Winsford Way did not mask a cesspit of secrets and lies. Behind that

---

2. What's more, Nan Collins knitted clothes for them, including some woolly blue trousers which we talked ourselves into using as Arctic wear.

3. Josephine Anne Whitaker became Peter Sutcliffe's eleventh victim on 4 April 1979 in Halifax. She was a building society clerk, and the switchboards were suddenly jammed with information from the public, 'as if a giant, slumbering conscience had at last been prodded awake' (*The Yorkshire Ripper* by Roger Cross).

metaphorical picket fence – actually, we had an unlovely, standard-issue wire mesh fence – lurked a family of five who largely ate together, played together and stayed together. No wicked uncle ever sat me on his knee in the tool shed, and the only deaths I had to cope with while growing up were of a succession of hamsters called Barnaby, who officially belonged to my sister Melissa anyway. (One of them died while we were on holiday, in the care of Jean and Geoff from next door. They considerately replaced it with one identical, which bit Melissa's finger when she gaily took it out of its cage on our return – understandably, not having ever set eyes on her before. Though bleeding, she was too innocent to twig the deception.) Death was brushed under the carpet.

I refuse to believe that I am not emotionally scarred in some way. What a swiz it would be if I'd turned out a well-balanced adult as a result of good parenting, a happy home life and a fairly uneventful passage through the education system. Something damaging must have happened to me in those first 16 or so years of my life; some rejection, crisis or disappointment that left its mark on me deep inside, the sort that stalks your adult life until you dredge it up, face it and achieve what the Americans irritatingly call 'closure'.

* * *

I guess I was pretty mortified by Anita Barker and the stabiliser incident. I'm estimating that my age was about seven. Ever opportunistic, I rode my new bike up to the top of our street to the empty car park of the Road to Morocco pub,[4] with the sole intention of

---

4. It will tell you something about my home life that Dad rarely, if ever, drank in the Road to Morocco – a pub *at the top of our street*. (Who said crap pub names were a new phenomenon? Bafflingly christened after the 1942 Hope and Crosby caper, it had been opened by either a live camel or a live llama, and like so many purpose-built redbrick pubs, was never much of a 'local'.) I went in there once, when Simon and I had befriended the slightly volatile son of the couple who ran it: Sean Mobley. My first pub, albeit outside of opening hours, and a garish, vinyl-covered place it was too. They had a luminous skeleton at the bottom of the stairs leading down to the cellar, as if to suggest a Moroccan jail perhaps (that was pretty cool). In later years, when I was in my mid-teens, we would go to the 'off-sales' door and buy crisps. I'm not saying my dad didn't drink, just that he didn't disappear up the pub come Sunday lunchtimes or to draw a line under arguments. Many a Party Seven was cracked open at the famous Winsford Way soirees though, oh yes.

'bumping into' the freckly Anita from Bideford Close, whom I knew to be sitting on the wall up there. It was my street she was in, my manor, my radar, my Way, and so surely she would respect my patrol, and admire my bike. Unfortunately, as I rounded the corner into the car park, her first words were ...

'Oh, do you still use stabilisers?'

Ouch. I did still use stabilisers, but unselfconsciously. I was even on the cusp of casting them aside like a cripple's crutches at Knock, but until that moment I hadn't regarded them as the mark of a cycling leper. Unfortunately, my memory of this incident does not include any kind of sharp riposte from myself. (What do you say to an unkind sneer like that?) I think I just continued riding in a circle and disappeared in the direction from which I had confidently come, something of a broken reed. If I was at stabiliser age I can't possibly have been interested in girls *per se*, so it was as much the crushing blow of not impressing a schoolfriend from the next street along as anything more subconsciously sexual.

Oh, do you still use stabilisers?

I feel a tinge of that humiliation coming back when I recall it. I needed stabilising on the way home, I can tell you. But did this incident affect me in later life? Did I secretly vow there and then never to rely on 'stabilisers' again? Did it teach me always to do some background research before walking into a potentially beneficial social exchange? Does it explain why I didn't grow into the sort of boy racer who feels his car is an extension of his manhood? (I toddled around in my mum's Mini Metro at 17.)

Do me a favour. The sad fact is, I don't think the Anita Barker episode had any profound effect on me at all, other than on the day, of course. Freckly women don't reduce me to emasculated jelly. Anita was one of the first girls I ever put my arm around, some years later, so I can only assume she didn't hold the stabiliser *faux pas* against me. No, it was just something that happened to a kid in Winsford Way, Northampton in the early Seventies. A lot of things happened to me there. But, like my mum and dad, they didn't fuck me up.

Mind you, no child of mine is ever going to drink welfare orange!

one

Jack Hawkins Knew My Father

If you were in it, you knew all about it.
Lt. Cmdr Ericson, *The Cruel Sea* (1953)

How far back can I remember? If I'm going to discover what it is that screwed me up without my even noticing – or even getting screwed up – I must dig deep. So where does my memory of me begin?

Nothing in the womb, for a start. I don't believe anybody really remembers bobbing around in a sac of amniotic fluid pre-birth – they just think they do because when you're grown up it still feels natural and nice to adopt a foetal position under the quilt. Pull yourselves together.

The first marker flag of memory is often planted by pain or misery. My wife Julie stepped on a nail aged four. Yowch! Run VT!

My own first reel begins aged two-and-a-bit. Nan and Pap Collins took me to Weymouth, and my only mental picture of this jolly holiday is being stood up and washed in the sink against my will and screaming the place down. That's gratitude for you. Nan and Pap kindly take me off my parents' hands for a few days and grant me a formative taste of sea air and plastic spades and all I can remember is playing up like a bastard at a simple act of hygiene.

There are Kodak-moments of me grinning at tin-topped pub tables in the south coast sun wearing a sailor's hat, and I'm told my catch-phrase for the trip was 'Lovely on the wa-ter!' (after a man advertising boat trips), but I don't really remember any of that. Just the soapy tantrum. I don't know if it was the soap, the embarrassment or the unfamiliarity that upset me – can it have been as dark in our holiday apartment as I remember it? – but at least this flashpoint of distress acted as a spark plug in my memory engine. I start remembering bits and pieces after Weymouth.

I have only the dimmest mental picture of our first house at Duston, a village unprettily boxed in by new estates on the western rim of Northampton. (By the way, it's pronounced *Duss'on* should you ever wish to go undercover in the area.) More darkness. Perhaps it was the drab Sixties decor. I recall, through the fug of 30 years, Auntie Wendy[1] once coming to stay (without Uncle Pete); me characteristically hiding from a visitor (no more details available); and being house-called, prone on the settee, by the doctor. I know we lived in Ashcroft Close – a cul-de-sac if you please – and that we self-effacingly called it Ashbox Close (although perhaps that was after we moved). I've even been back there on a nostalgia cruise with Mum and Dad: down the main road past the post office, pub and little shops, right into Eastfield Road, left into Northfield Road, left into Grange Avenue and right. Like L.P. Hartley's past, it was a foreign country.

But I was there. For three years. I've got the tapes to prove it.

My parents were the proud owners of one of those bulky reel-to-reel tape recorders which weighed a ton and grew hot to the touch if you left it on too long, and they had the foresight to record me talking into it as a toddler. For posterity. (They've always been good on posterity, Mum and Dad – school exercise books, letters, swimming certificates, comics, photos, toys, their

---

1. Uncle Pete and Auntie Wendy (Jones), honorary relations, and godparents to Simon. He was a bank manager for the Midland and as a result they kept moving about the country, Leicester, East Goscote, Ashby-de-la-Zouch, Calver (nr. Bakewell), Wisbech, Stowmarket, Bury St Edmunds. Honestly, they were like Orson Welles and Rita Hayworth darting across Europe in the late Forties: Rome, Florence, Venice, Naples, Capri. In keeping with most couples who have no kids of their own, Pete and Wendy seemed to treat us as little grown-ups, rather than idiots (I like to think Julie and I do this now), and I always loved visiting them. Pete also used to give me *Giles* annuals and had a huge old Meccano set.

loft is like a well-insulated Smithsonian Institute. This curator's instinct is one they've passed on to me.)

I've listened to these reel-to-reel tapes as a grown-up, and there I am, at Dad's prompt and in a broad Northampton burr, delivering a two-year-old's approximation of 'Yabba-dabba-doooo!' into the microphone and gamely parroting the theme tunes to *The Monkees*, *Z Cars* and *Dee Time*. What an adorable and already media-centric little poppet I am: [phonetically] 'Hey-hey Murnkiz. Peepuw say murnkee rouuuund.' I even had adorable blond hair then, and adorable red nylon dungarees.

But scratch the surface of the adorable Murnkiz me and you'll find the abominable Weymouth me – and not that far beneath either. Legend has it, I was a walking pain in the arse, and before that a crawling pain in the arse, although archaeologists will never guess it when they unearth the grinning, bright-eyed, red-nylon-dungarees photographs from the rubble and play back those reel-to-reel tapes. (Was I turning it on for the media at that young age, or do all kids make sure you get their best side?)

At least I gave my mum advance warning that I was going to inflict pain in her lower half: I was by all accounts – in fact, by her on-the-spot account – murderously difficult to give birth to. Then I started crying and complaining the moment I was wrapped in swaddling clothes and didn't stop until I was handed over to Mrs Carter at Abington Vale Primary School five cacophonous years later. Mum and Dad reckon the trip to Weymouth galvanised me into a 'little sod'. *Lovely on the wa-ter!*

Nor would I breastfeed, something I now lament, because a squirt of mother's milk might have prevented me developing asthma in adult life.

I even formulated my own disturbing party trick as the Rosemary's Baby of Duss'on. When I was in my cot I would literally bang my head on the wooden bars and gradually move it around the lino by cranial force and sheer bloody-mindedness. Little me. All in all, it really is a wonder my mum ever went through with a second and third baby, but mums are programmed to forget, aren't they? Dad used to have to stand in the doorway of my bedroom until I stopped headbanging and dozed back to sleep.

Then he would silently inch away and I would start again. This was the dance. Welcome to parenthood.

Because Simon came only two-and-a-bit years after me – a wise spot of family planning, I think, although Mum was probably just looking forward to a couple of days in hospital away from me – I didn't have much time to appreciate being an only child. Perhaps I was obliquely demanding a brother as I rode that cot like a steer round the house.

I can't really remember not having a brother. I certainly don't remember Mum coming home with him in the ambulance.[2] They tell me I raced down the path to greet them. But to me, it feels like Simon was always there and what's more he arrived at ready-to-play-with age, a prepackaged little companion for me.

Mum dressed us up in matching clobber as soon as he was on two legs. Strangers would come up to her and ask, 'Ooh, are they twins?' as if to pander to her insane but not uncommon little fantasy. Going back through the family slides (Dad has them carefully catalogued), the thing that strikes you most, apart from how young and glamorous my mum looks, is how many identical outfits Simon and I were dressed in. This grand illusion of twinhood goes on for years: the same tops, trousers, trainers – even *ties* for Christmas Day and professional portraiture. There we are in matching red Ferrari anoraks, matching blue M&S tracksuits, twin Paisley shirts. Nan Mabel knitted us two identical, nautical brown-and-white jumpers – legendarily itchy ones to boot – and there we are, grinning and bearing them in photos taken at Brixham, I believe. By the harbour – do you see? We're wearing twin sailors' caps too. (Why didn't she just sign us up for the Navy and be done with it?) Andrew and Simon. Simon and Andrew. You could say it either way round: we were not twins. You should see us today. We are not twins.

So I will forever be 'number one son' (something my parents call me, with suitable Charlie Chan irony, now and again), but I can assure those of you further down the age-chain that the privileges of being the eldest by two-and-a-bit years are far outweighed

---

2. I'm told all new mums got an ambulance in those days. These days you're lucky if they say goodbye to you.

by the injustices, especially when puberty comes a-knocking and the gap between you and your 'little companion' opens up like the crack in the dam in *Earthquake*. If I may sneak forward and steal an example from when I was 18 ...

I was playing drums in a 'local rock band' in 1983, and 16-year-old Simon was officially sanctioned by Mum and Dad despite being under age to come and see us play a gig at the Black Lion pub in deepest town. Twins once again! The catch was, I had to 'look after him'. Not only did I have to stand by as my little brother ratcheted up two whole years of my teenage life in the blink of an eye, I actually had to physically *stand by*. On the night of the gig I took my resentment out on the drum kit and ignored Simon and his school-chum Kevin while they made themselves pig-sick on beer. But guess whose fault *that* was, come next morning's debriefing? Being the eldest child is like being a minesweeper.

But I fast-forward. I suppose I'm looking to see if I was spoiled at all for being the first-born and worst-born, and I wasn't. At least, not by my fair-minded mum and dad, who did everything in their power to even us out. We'll come to Nan Mabel and Pap Reg later.

* * *

A 1998 study by the Institute of Child Health at Bristol University found that children who bathe every day and wash their hands more than five times are 25 per cent more likely to develop asthma than their dirty peers. It's a simple enough equation: dirt equals infection; infection when young builds a hardy immune system. It's sensible medical advice – rolling around in the muck is good for you.

No-one ever actually gave me or my parents this advice, but I followed it anyway, as I believe all normal kids instinctively do. Dirt, as nineteenth-century Harvard professor John Chipman Gray noted, is only 'matter out of place'. Most of my childhood seems to have been spent covered in matter, up trees, in water, or just 'down the field', snatching whatever bit of earthy nature I could among the suburban seepage of Northampton. ('The field' was just that: a sizeable patch of green left by the planners at the bottom of Winsford Way with a stream running through it, a modest spinney, allotments adjoining and, latterly, a hint of playground, where the plastic seats of the see-saw would routinely be melted away by bigger boys with matches.) I was always on hand to help dig either of my paps' allotments, sneaking an unwashed strawberry or two into my mouth, and when Simon and I were granted our first penknives – on the same day, naturally – our inaugural Big Project was to dig an enormous hole in the side of the riverbank, like armed gophers.

The first dozen years of my life threw more than enough stagnant mud, stickleback water and dog's muck at my trainee immune system. Now, as a health-conscious adult and firm believer in holistic medicine, I thank my parents for letting me roam in this way and for not over-washing me.

I still developed asthma. Since the age of 31 I've been a two-doses-of-Beclomethasone-a-day man, with the option of a quick pull on the Salbutamol inhaler if the wheezing starts. So much for those white-coated timewasters at Bristol University.

* * *

Though they tucked me up, my mum and dad, I was never cosseted, never wrapped in cotton wool or kept in a glass case, even though urban paranoia was really beginning to catch on in the Seventies. All those terrifying public information films warning you not to take sweets from strangers or play near electricity pylons, and never to cross the road without Joe Brown or Alvin Stardust ('E don't need any 'elp, does 'e?). If my mum and dad lived in constant fear of our abduction or accidental death they didn't show it.

Twice I remember them losing their cool.

One evening, after The Magic Roundabout or Noah and Nelly or whatever five-minute buffer signalled the end of children's television, Simon and I had been allowed 'down the field', and at that time fishing was the big thing. Armed with empty jam jars and 'bandy nets' we intrepid hunter-gatherers would trawl the stream for even the tiniest finned entities, take them home as trophies and subsequently leave them in the garage to die. (A 'bandy net' was a cheap, coloured plastic net mounted on a wire hoop stuck into the end of a bamboo pole, the sort of rig often purchased at the seaside. I've never seen the name listed in any slang dictionary, although 'bandy' is an old nineteenth-century colloquialism for a silver sixpence, so perhaps that's how much they used to cost in the time of Oliver Twist.)

This particular fishing expedition fell on one of those September evenings when the night rolls in without warning, and in all the excitement of midget freshwater angling neither Simon and I nor any of our mates had registered that it was pitch black. Suddenly, from out of the darkness Dad appeared to drag us angrily back home, unimpressed by the fact that we'd just caught a 'jopper' (i.e. a big fish, name derivative no doubt of 'giant' and 'whopper' but again not legitimised by any dictionary). I don't suppose it was *that* late, but you don't want your boys out after dark, do you? We were sent to bed with our tails between our legs (and the jopper's tail in its killing jar out in the garage). Why? Because Mum had been 'worried about us'.

The other vivid instance of Mum being worried about us in our absence occurred in broad daylight. Simon and I had arranged to go and meet Pap Collins at his allotment on Billing Road,[3] easy cycling distance from our house, just the other side of the field. We used to love it when Pap appeared on his little moped[4] in that trademark piss-pot helmet – not that we called it that then – and we relished helping him dig up carrots in return for a piece of chocolate in his tiny, smaller-than-a-man shed. However, on this occasion, Pap never appeared.

We waited and waited at the entrance to the allotments, but no Pap. Not that we were worried about *him* – our young imaginations extended as far as blowing up the guns of Navarone, but not to an elderly man having a moped accident. In the event, Pap had simply changed his mind about going down the allotment, and had phoned Mum to let us know. But we'd already left the house.

---

3. Both paps had allotments, and what a fine post-war tradition that is. Pap Collins's was in Billing Road; Pap Reg's in Bants Lane, on the other side of town where he and Nan lived. I'm happy to report that both allotments are still open.
4. Pap Collins never learned to drive; a moped was as far as he got. My other grandparents – younger, that bit more dynamic, flush from Pap Reg's union gig – both drove, he well into his seventies. Nan passed her driving test first time in her late fifties but was then too anxious to ever use the car. At least did it. When I was learning in 1982, Dad used to spur me on, saying, 'If Nan Mabel can pass her test, anyone can.'

Oh well, we thought, let's call on Johnny Green – his house is right next door to the allotments and he's got Mouse Trap and a pond and everything. Ace! (To use the vernacular of the time.) Johnny was home, and the three of us wiled away most of the afternoon there, playing hide and seek in his oversized, tree-filled back garden – quite a luxury, as our little back garden offered the choice of precisely two hiding places: behind the coal bunker and inside the coal bunker. Meanwhile, back at home, ever since Pap's phone call Mum had been beside herself: why hadn't we come straight back? Where were we? Had a stranger offered us sweets? Had we flown a kite too near an electricity pylon?

When we gaily strolled back up Winsford Way (it wasn't late or anything), Dad was out looking for us while Mum sat at home fretting and waiting for a call from Mountain Rescue. Dad shouted at us, Mum cried, we cried, and it was a right old scene. We'd only been in Johnny's back garden!

We learned something that day, as Kyle says on *South Park*: you can go anywhere and do anything as long as Mum doesn't know where you are or what you're doing.

It's funny how insightful I must have been at that young age, because deep down I knew Dad wasn't as worried as Mum (she was always the worrier), and I knew they only shouted at us out of relief at our well-being.

What measure of idyllic childhood was this? I was essentially free to do whatever I wanted, providing I returned before sundown and didn't do one thing when I was supposed to be doing another. I got told off all the time, and had the backs of my legs slapped on more than one occasion, but Mum and Dad managed to care about our welfare without keeping us on a string. Perhaps that's why we didn't rebel – at least not to the point of having to be picked up from the police station or scraped up off the road.

I smoked my first cigarette down the field with a ruddy-faced boy called Pete Thompson in the last year at middle school, when I was 13. When I say *smoked*, I wet the end of it and made the other end glow. It was a vague thrill, but did nothing for me, and I'm grateful for that now.

As a kid you tend to do exactly what you're told not to, and maybe if my parents had constantly warned me not to smoke and threatened me with cancer and damnation I would have tried a bit harder with Pete's Embassy Number Ones. As it is, I know that Mum – an ex-smoker – would have disapproved loudly if I'd taken smoking up as a covert habit, but it was never cast as the original sin.

Getting water inside our wellies carried a sterner punishment. And we risked that all the time.

Let's get this clear: Mum and Dad weren't hippies. They were very much the rock'n'roll generation; married before peace and love, Mum was pregnant with me when President Johnson launched Operation Rolling Thunder in Vietnam. In fact the *laissez-faire* attitude they maintained while Simon and I grew up was quite an achievement for two straights. (Hippies make terrible parents anyway: liberals are just as oppressive as fascists. Mum and Dad were just grateful the world hadn't ended during the Cuban Missile Crisis in 1962.)

My dad's a laid-back sort of bloke. So am I. It must be in the genes then, because Pap Collins was not the worrying kind either. In fact, Pap took it to the extreme, and allowed old-fashioned stoicism to prevent him from ever seeing a doctor until it was too late.[5] He managed to turn 'not worrying' into a self-destructive act. At least my dad speaks up if he has an ache or pain. Whenever I talk myself out of visiting my doctor, I can hear the stubborn, scared voice of my Pap, who claimed he took his own teeth out by tying a piece of string to a doorknob and ended his days in hospital with one leg less than he'd started out with.

My dad worries only out of loyalty to my mum, who worries as a form of catharsis. It's a way of life for her. I think she enjoys a little fret. Yet she managed to hold back throughout my formative years, an act of long-sighted reason for which I am eternally indebted. She lost it completely when I was 17 and she decided I was gay, but then maybe the Cuban Missile Crisis consumed so much of her worry, it

---

5. He had diabetes, undiagnosed for who knows how long. I admire his fighting spirit, and his distrust of doctors (I'm not a fan myself), but there comes a time when you have to give in, ideally when you can still get out of bed.

took her 20 years to get back into her stride. It's a thought. Even my laid-back dad was a bit anxious when those Soviet merchant vessels approached the US blockade on 27 October 1962.

* * *

Were it not for Khrushchev, I could have been born in the London Borough of Sutton (which would have been poetic because that's close to where Julie's mum lives now). Rather adventurously, Dad had lived in a rented flat in London for almost a year when he married Mum. He shared with his best mate and later best man, Jim[6] and I'll bet they had a swinging time. I know they sometimes drank in the same pub as the great British screen actor Jack Hawkins. They never spoke to him, but perhaps they should have. A couple of years after they'd quit London, he lost his voice following a throat cancer operation.[7]

He carried on making films, usually dubbed, until his death in 1973. Jack Hawkins meant something to me only in retrospect – it's likely I never even saw *The Bridge on the River Kwai* or *Zulu* until after he'd departed – but my dad had gone to the pictures to see him in Charles Frend's *The Cruel Sea* back in the Fifties and he'd left an indelible mark on the boy; just as Brigitte Bardot would later do for entirely different reasons. Legend has it that Dad and Jim went to see one Bardot film three times, because you glimpsed her bare back in it. A swinging time.

By the time my mum decided that I was gay in the early Eighties, homosexuality was out in the open and on *Top of the Pops*. But in the early Sixties, when Dad's landlords decided that he and Jim were gay, it was a truly underground lifestyle choice, the stuff of codes and slang and nods and winks. But Dad and Jim, innocent

---

6. Uncle Jim to us. He and Auntie Christine are the other vital non-blood relatives in my life. We had so much *fun* when we visited them and their daughters Lorraine and Sandy in Coventry. They're an awfully tall family, the Brittons. Jim was in computers at the time (he used to give us printout paper with holes down each side to draw on), and Christine was a teacher.

7. In 1967, when I was two, Hawkins appeared on Simon Dee's TV chat show *Dee Time* and won the nation's hearts all over again, gulping for air and hoarse-whispering with valiant good humour.

provincial boys who'd barely unpacked their suitcases, read nothing into the fact that their landlords were *two men* who *lived together* downstairs. Furthermore, he and Jim fancied Brigitte Bardot, which allowed them to share a tiny flat – and a double bed – with impunity. So when London's gayest landlords invited them downstairs for 'a drink' one night, a thick fug of Northampton naiveté prevented them from reading the runes. Dad and Jim swung, but not in that direction. When the penny dropped it must have sounded like a cathedral bell falling to the ground. It was high time they got married to two nice girls from back home.

Two nice girls both called Christine, coincidentally. Dad and Jim married their respective Christines in 1962 and dragged them both down to London where all the swinging was. They stuck it out for less than a year.

Suburban Sutton, let me tell you, is a long way from Carnaby Street, and I don't just meant culturally. Considering it's south of London, Sutton's not even that handy for South London. It's more like Northampton than London in fact (especially today, now that everywhere looks like everywhere else). My future parents had jobs that were situated as far apart from each other as, say, Harpole and Ecton in Northampton.[8] He worked in Kingston, she in Croydon, which meant that every morning the radiant young newly-weds would stand at bus stops on opposite sides of the same road in Sutton and head off in opposite directions. To compound the situation, Jim and Christine – their only real London friends – fell for a baby early and decided to bail out.

So, at the end of that nail-biting year of 1962, with a cosy Christmas spent back in Northampton to remind them of home, the bushy-tailed young couple swallowed their pride and, like the Russian ships, turned back. Back to the bosom of the family.

Even when I'd successfully relocated to the capital in my twenties, I never judged Mum and Dad harshly for not being up to London life. I had three years of college to lower me gently into the moronic inferno; they spent most of their days on opposing poles of public transport, looking forward to a supper of 'batter bits'

---

8. Harpole and Ecton are about as far apart as you can get in Northampton.

from the chip shop and for all they knew the end of the world. In their shoes, I think I might have gone back to Northampton to die.

* * *

How can I ever know what it must have been like? I can't. All this – Guantanamo, Sutton – happened before I was born. Here's what I know for a fact about the world into which I was painfully and noisily delivered around 9 p.m. on 4 March 1965: it was snowing. Sir Winston Churchill had not long been buried in a churchyard near Blenheim Palace after lying in state at Westminster for three days. T.S. Eliot had died that January, and Stan Laurel in February.[9] A statesman, a poet and a comedian died in the first months of 1965 so that, karmically, I might live. I almost wish I believed in reincarnation.

In those first two pre-Andrew months of 1965 the war in Vietnam escalated and Sir Stanley Matthews retired. I arrived in a world where LBJ ran America and Harold Wilson ran Britain. 'I'll Never Find Another You' by The Seekers was at Number One in what was still called the hit parade (monumentally insignificant to me, that one). Laws in this country were emerging from the Dark Ages: the death penalty was abolished in the year of my birth, and within three years it would be okay to get a divorce, be homosexual (a red letter day for Dad and Jim's feather-boa-wearing landlords), take the pill and, if you forgot, have an abortion.

I wish I could tell you that I remember Neil Armstrong walking on the moon in 1969 but I don't. I sort of recall Concorde's maiden flight the same year but only because Nan and Pap bought me a cool little commemorative model with a movable nose. Kent State and Watergate, naturally enough, passed me by. What little I knew of British politics was taught me by Professor Yarwood.

As an insulated modern child in the East Midlands of England,

---

9. Though it would be a full 16 years before I appreciated Eliot, I got into Laurel's work a lot sooner. Interestingly, Laurel and Hardy visited Northampton in October 1953, to play the New Theatre, their first time on stage since returning from Hollywood. Their visit coincided with Car Safety Week and the pair agreed to pose with a 1902 Wolseley to publicise it. Priceless photos were taken by the local paper and can be seen in the second volume of *Northampton: Welcome to the Past* published by W.D. Wharton.

the events of the world had to work pretty hard to impact upon my life. Power cuts were an invasion by greater forces into domestic sanctity but I accepted them, as we all did – Fetch the candles, Dad! – they had no wider implications than not being able to watch *Love Thy Neighbour* on telly. There was oil out there and power, and these things could run short or run out, causing minor inconvenience. What else was there to know? I knew there were 'starving children in Africa', because Mum would threaten to send them my dinner if I didn't eat it. (Not much of a threat when you think about it.) I knew there was an oil shortage in 1973, when I was eight, because the school closed for two days. You note things like that in your diary.

Ah, diaries. I started keeping one in 1972, aged six going on seven. It was a habit – encouraged, to begin with, by my posterity-minded parents – that stayed with me right through my childhood, past the college years into my early twenties. I kept my last diary in 1993, a secret journal – this time tapped into my Mac Classic – which petered out when the relationship that turned into my marriage became more important than writing about it, and there were no more secrets.

My first, an orange Letts Disneyland diary, contained no secrets.

I had a beefberger for dinner. I saw *Deputy Dawg* and *Crackerjack* on TV.

Yes, yes, beef*berger*, but I was six. The entries for 1972 are brief and revolve around comics and TV, and Sunday 27 February has been mysteriously written in by my dad:

Melissa came home from hospital. We are all glad. She looks a lot better. I have promised to be a good boy.[10]

I guess I was not a good boy on that day and either refused to write my diary or got sent to bed early. Fascinating to wonder, isn't it?

---

10. Melissa was hospitalised with bronchitis when she was just ten months old and it was a bit dicey for a while there.

Much better than to know. It's like archaeology, except without Tony Robinson.

Thanks to my twenty-year love affair with the diary, I know pretty much what I did *every day* from age six onwards. Friends' names – Paul Milner, Tina Woods, Jeremy Skoyles, Jonathan Bailey, Melanie Ashby, Carl Merrick, Richard Angerson, Paul Cockle, Paul Givelin – help to flesh out the supporting cast of my youth, and TV programmes help to paint a broader cultural picture of Britain in the Seventies. I'm so glad I kept these diaries. (And *kept* them.)

There is a direct, hereditary link between my own attention to book-keeping and my parents' overflowing loft. Never mind Mum's wedding dress, they still have every single love letter they wrote to each other while courting up there, neatly boxed and labelled, not to mention the life story of each of their kids told in exercise books, *Beano* annuals and badges.

Mum and Dad are not unique in storing junk in the attic, I know, but this need of theirs to hang on to stuff lies at the heart of my own desire to get everything down, to retain that ticket stub, to maintain constant links between the past, present and future. That's what I'm doing by symbolically hanging that naff, framed picture of a kitten in the office where I write; it used to belong to Melissa when she was very young. Nan Mabel and Pap Reg bought it for her, but within days Dad was ordered to take it down because she said it scared her at night. It comforts me to have it up.

I'm sure I don't need to keep all my bank statements and electricity bills from 1987 in a box file, but you never know.

Maybe I do know. Maybe I knew all along that my diaries would one day prove invaluable with their dates and their names and their funny little drawings. Was I writing them out of a sense of fun, or duty, or investment for the future?

The irony of all this genuflection to posterity is that reading these boyhood diaries today won't tell you what I felt, or even what I thought. That will take some serious rebirthing. It can't have been orange Disneyland all the way. Can it?

1972

Selected Extracts From My Diary

The orange Disneyland – my very first – with Mickey and pals on the cover. Inside is a section called HOW TO USE YOUR DIARY, *which offers this advice:* 'Every day you meet new people. Become observant and learn new things. Write them all in your diary when they happen, because writing helps you to become more observant.' *Yeah, don't patronise me, Mickey.*

In the PERSONAL NOTES *at the front of the book I reveal that I am three feet eight inches tall and weigh three stone.*

Incidentally, the entries in this diary dry up after 21 March. No staying power.

Tuesday, 1 January

The Double Deckers came back on TV. We all saw *Play Away* on Nanny's colour television.[1] Melissa can say 'Ba-ba-ba.'

---

1. Quite why Nan and Pap got a colour television before us is a mystery to me. Were they perhaps working for the KGB? Either way, it was at Nan's that I saw my favourite cartoon *Top Cat* in colour for the very first time and thrilled to the revelation that Choo Choo was pink (pink!), Benny was blue, Spook was green etc. It was my version of the Queen's Coronation and I assume it occurred in 1971.

Thursday, 13 January

Today Paul Milner[2] brought his 'Ernie' record to school. And we all heard it. And we liked it.

Monday, 24 January

Today I saw *Bright's Boffins*[3] on television. Mummy and I saw how many words we could get out of Constantinople.

Wednesday, 26 January

Tonight I am going to start to make a Tom and Jerry book and it is called *Party Night For Puss*.

Saturday, 29 January

Today I heard some records on the tape recorder and it was a bit of when I was a baby.[4]

Wednesday, 2 February

Today I saw *The Frog Prince* and *Sir Prancelot* and *Soper At Large* and *Jackanory* and *Play School* on TV.

---

2. Paul Milner lived two streets away in Exmoor Close. A chunky fellow with hair so blond it was white, he turned out to be a real soulmate as we entered our teens: great at drawing and with an identical sense of humour to my own. His dad – who in my memory's eye is Prince Andrew in naval uniform – worked for Geest as the captain of a banana boat and was thus always away. (I'm sure Paul told a horror story about his dad finding a tarantula in a crate of bananas.) I remember overhearing phone calls at their house to Mr Milner when he was shipboard – they had to say 'over' at the end of sentences. That seemed pretty exciting. Over.
3. *Bright's Boffins* is one of those programmes that will never make it on to an *I Love Nostalgia* show: because nobody except me remembers it. Thankfully, Mark Lewisohn's redoubtable *Radio Times Guide to TV Comedy* put me out of my lifelong misery when it was published in 1998: in this children's sitcom (which ran to an astonishing three series on ITV between 1970 and 1972), Alexander Doré played 'a bumbling, old-fashioned (and, quite frankly, mad) scientist-inventor, leader of a team of similarly minded boffins working for an under-funded and irrelevant Whitehall ministry'. Yes, and they worked out of an old railway station. I distinctly remember the character Dogsears, played by that great British clown Gordon Rawlings, he of the hangdog expression – formerly Charlie Moffit on *Coronation Street* in the mid-Sixties, latterly Arkwright in the John Smith's Bitter ads. His finest – or most widely seen – hour came in 1980 when he cameoed as a surprised angler in *Superman II* (34th in the cast) and then 'Man in Cap' in *Superman III* (14th). When I saw him in *II*, I just thought 'Dogsears' silently but happily to myself. He died in 1985.
4. See Chapter 1.

Tuesday, 15 February

Today me and all my school pals and chums all had a visit to the fire station and it was Pancake Day.

Friday, 18 February

Today we had a power cut and I had to write my diary by candle light and it was fun.

Wednesday, 8 March

Today I saw *Star Trek* on television and I went to Jeremy Skoyles's[5] birthday but there wasn't any prizes.

Sunday, 12 March

Today it was Mothers Day and we bought Mum some walnut whips and she liked them.

Thursday, 16 March

Today *Top Cat* came back on television and it was about Top Cat falling in love with a nurse.

Tuesday, 21 March

Today the Budget was on TV so we had to scc children's television on BBC2.

---

5. Jeremy Skoyles, or Jes. Long-term pal, if something of a softy – unless we were just extrapolating from his name. I think perhaps he wore his gloves on a string inside the sleeves of his coat.

two

Cobblers

A love affair with Northampton is a journey into space.
Rod Thompson, 'Energy In Northampton' (1980)

We were allowed to park in the Equity & Law car park on Saturdays. They were clients of my dad's. Our family shopping trips to town involved him getting out of the car and unlocking the padlock of our own private car park, a gravelly yard tucked away round the back of Abington Street, retail's main drag. It wasn't like we had the keys to the town, but it certainly felt like a civic privilege, avoiding the bottleneck (and the payment) at the multi-storey. There was even a cramped Pay and Display directly opposite the Equity & Law, which always had a queue of cars attached even first thing on a Saturday, the occupants of which would gaze at us in jealous awe as we drove past them down the Ridings and entered our own *special* car park.

Thus began the Saturday morning shopping ritual. It took the advent in 1976 of Noel Edmonds's *Multi-Coloured Swap Shop* to disrupt it, after which Mum and Dad allowed Simon and me to stay at home alone (you'd probably get arrested for that nowadays). But in the days before Chegwin and Posh Paws, trips into town went like this. Dad would drive, even though Mum *could*, and, having taken advantage of our *special* car park, we'd set off on the same tried and tested path every week: up through the Co-Op arcade, across Abington Street to Marks & Sparks for fancy food (chunky chicken, cakes) and a chat with Nan Mabel if she was working Saturdays. Functional food (cupboard ingredients, packet stuff) came from Sainsbury's. Then – once it was fully functioning – into the strip-lit gloom of the Grosvenor Centre, Northampton's showcase antiseptic shopping mall boasting 300,000 square feet of retail opportunity. (Sainsbury's later relocated there from Abington Street, but by then we were I think getting the packet food from British Home Stores in the days before 'bhs' rebranding, after which they stopped doing food anyway.)

The Grosvenor was – and is – a dark, stale-aired time tunnel linking the 'old town' Abington Street and the 'even older town' Market Square. Therein, we would dutifully trudge round Beatties department store, where Mum would look at clothes or buy some cotton for the sewing machine or a birthday card. If we were lucky we'd loiter with Dad at the tiny toy department while Mum went to the loo. (She always seemed to need the loo at this point, and Beatties had one.) If we needed felt-tips or a compass for school we'd get them in WH Smith's, and here I would graze, every week handling the Pythonesque *Rutland Dirty Weekend Book* and knowing I would never get it as it had a 'rude lady' on the cover. I could but dream.

Like any child, Saturday shopping was a chore leavened only by the possibility of getting a toy or a comic or a sweet. Simon was paid off with a detour to Millets to check out the crampons and jumpers, I was kept quiet with a spin round Universal Stationers to look at pads and paint-by-number sets. This was a trade-off for the times we had to go and try on shoes, or worse, clothes.

Once we had all that we needed from Abington Street, the centre and the market it was back to the Equity & Law and off to Mum's favoured 'local' shops, which were out of town but nowhere near where we lived: Highgrade the greengrocer's and Masson's the high street butcher. We stayed in the car while Mum and Dad did this bit. It seems quaint now that Mum used to shop around so much for her food, but that's progress. The town centre itself has long since been pedestrianised and castrated; they've got HMV and Gap and McDonald's and beggars and everything now. What used to be the Mounts Swimming Baths up by the fire station is now the Mounts Health Suite.

But that's not my town. My Northampton is Seventies Northampton. You knew where you were then.

* * *

My proud birthplace. A place right out of histor-ee. Best known for being junction 15 off the M1 (and 15a and 16 actually, but I generally come at it from the south), Northampton is everytown and anytown. The sort of place you tear past at high speed. 'Northampton? Yeah I think I drove through there once,' say outsiders, as if once was enough, and it is.

There's no outward mythology to the place. Nothing to remember it by or plan a return visit for. Unless you live somewhere that hasn't got a Comet and a bowling alley in the same car park. With the notable exception of the graphic novel *Big Numbers*, written by Northamptonian Alan Moore (in which the town is fictionalised as 'Hampton'[1]) and Bridget Jones's parents (who live in rural Northants), books, films and culture pass it by. It's just one of those towns.

In his 1979 book *A History of Northamptonshire*, local historian R.L. Greenall describes the county as 'unknown England' and is perceptive in doing so. In the marvellous old volume *Northamptonshire* (first published in 1945 and part of the King's England series[2]) Arthur Mee concurs:

> This thousand square miles in the middle of England is as completely representative of our green and pleasant land as Shakespeare's Warwickshire; but it is all too little known.

Never fares well in comparisons, Northampton. It could've been oh-so-different if Shakespeare had been born 40 miles to the east but he wasn't. His granddaughter Elizabeth Nash died in

---

1. Published in serial form in 1990 by Mad Love, a local publisher who acknowledge the assistance of Northampton Borough Council, Northampton Transit and the Northamptonshire Police at the back of issue #1. Although drawn by American artist Bill Sienkeiwicz, he's clearly worked from photographs of Northampton locations such as the railway station and what could be the Black Lion pub where our band played so often. It's a stunning piece of work by the way.
2. Given to my dad as a prize by Northampton Grammar School in 1953.

Northampton, and that just about sums it up. See Northampton and die. I mean, where is Northamptonshire? Is it in the East Midlands? The South Midlands? The Eastern Counties? It was part of Mercia in Saxon times. Since 1964, it's been in the ITV region of Anglia. Meanwhile our old pal R.L. Greenall notes that 'developments in national communications have drawn it inexorably southwards'.

Certainly Northampton's biggest selling point during the development years of the Seventies and Eighties was that it was '60 miles by road or rail' from London. That was indeed the refrain on a curious little promo single released by the Development Corporation in 1980 – 'Energy In Northampton', sung by Linda Jardim and written and arranged by Rod Thompson.[3] The uplifting little number's lyrical conceit is that aliens in a flying saucer need somewhere to relocate. They choose Northampton, as well they might, with its ample spaceship parking.

The old town was a beneficiary of the pioneering New Towns Act of 1965. By 1968 the ink was dry and its fate was sealed: it would expand to help reduce pressure on the spiralling population of London and the south-east (and outer space, if Rod was to be believed). We let in 70,000 Cockney refugees, basically, except they were prosaically referred to as 'overspill'. Expansion quickly became Northampton's middle name. See a field, build a house,

---

3. Given to me in the form of a seven-inch single as a light-hearted gift by Danny Kelly, my former mentor and editor (he frequents car boot sales). From the back sleeve, a eulogy worth printing in full:

'Northampton has had many love affairs. After all, it is like a human being, having evolved, matured and developed its character with passing years. Succeeding generations of lovers established its importance, traditions, employment, social, recreational and cultural amenities and a strong sense of community. Experience has proved how necessary these qualities of life are.

'But, of course, these qualities take generations to mature. In Northampton we are fortunate. We are able to harness all the advantages of an historic and well-established town of regional importance, with those of an expanding town and major growth point, providing new opportunities for a total population of 180,000 by 1990.

'Add to this – Northampton's location, little more than 60 miles from London, on the M1 motorway with 50% of Britain's industry and 57% of its population within a 100 mile radius; the immediate availability of factories, offices or sites; a workforce of some 87,000; a wide choice of homes to rent or buy – and it's easy to see how love affairs begin ...'

I know what you're thinking: where do I sign?

fill it with spivs. Better yet, in the spirit of suburban sprawl, build a Close or a Drive or a Way. As you know, we lived in one such freshly built Way in Abington Vale, *and* we got in before all those southern chancers with their fancy London ways.

While 19,952 designated acres of green were ploughed up and planted with new houses, my beloved Northampton town centre was also enthusiastically redeveloped. I watched it evolve as I grew up. The twin focal points of the great civic facelift were the Grosvenor Centre and Greyfriars Bus Station – a cathedral-like terminus with the look of two giant upturned skips. The shops and the bus station were joined and served by a brand new multi-storey car park, where we would never need to park, but where I would later work. As a Sainsbury's Saturday boy I had to brave carbon monoxide poisoning and collect trolleys from all levels of the car park, wearing brown flares and a clip-on brown tie for protection against looking good.

The Great Expansion served up other new landmarks: Barclaycard House, one of the then-largest office blocks to be built outside London (230,000 square feet), the Carlsberg Brewery, which has nestled on the banks of the piddling River Nene since 1974 (imagine having your town characterised by probably the worst lager in the world[4]), and a tissue box-shaped hotel called the Saxon Inn, opened in 1973 and since renamed the Moat House.[5]

The developers of the Seventies left the old cobbled Market Square alone, which was thoughtful of them. As Robert Cook writes in *A Century of Northampton* (I've got all the books, you know), the

---

4. HRH Princess Benedikte of Denmark flew in to open the Carlsberg brewery. There was a civic ceremony on a devilishly windy day: when she pulled the string on the plaque, it continued to be obscured by a flapping curtain as the dignitaries applauded and a marching band tramped up and down the concrete. For royal glamour it ranks only behind the day our own dear Queen Elizabeth attended the official opening of the Express Lifts testing tower in 1982. (Yes, the one Terry Wogan nicknamed the Northampton Lighthouse with typical irony on his Radio 2 show.)

5. It seemed glamorous at the time, 'the Saxon' – I think they held dinner-and-dance things there, and I'm certain my hedonistic Uncle Allen and Auntie Janice frequented it. It was always tainted somewhat by its convenience for the local red-light district. Alright, less of a district, actually just the car park and a notorious pub called the Criterion, which was spoken about in hushed tones at school: 'The Cri'. When I hear the word 'criterion' spoken to this day I still think of the oldest profession.

Development Corporation 'uncovered much of antiquity' when they tore up the town, 'and unhappily removed much of it'.

* * *

Not that I gave a flying fig about the history of my town then. As long as there were shops I could buy felt-tips from and somewhere to ride my bike, I was the same as any other kid in any other town: no civic pride, no sense of place, and no interest in the decline of the boot and shoe trade.

Northampton used to be emblemised not by lager but leather. Shoe leather. Hence Northampton Town Football Club's nickname, the Cobblers. It's a shoemaking thing, like pots in Stoke and fish in Hull.

Here's a surprise – even the Industrial Revolution saw fit to pass Northamptonshire by. They used to make a bit of cotton and worsted and lace round here, but it was essentially a market, not a manufacturing town – with ample cart parking no doubt. However, the one thing we did make was shoes. Plenty of cows nearby, see – plus, labour was cheaper than in London (Northampton put women and children to work long before it was the done thing). And, just as British Aerospace cry crocodile tears whenever there's chance of an air war today, so Northampton benefited from the glut of armed and booted conflict in the seventeenth century. Northants stabbed and stitched and cut and tooled most of the French boots in the Franco-Prussian War. Made in Northampton, worn in Sedan (not that it helped).

By 1850, there were reckoned to be about 13,000 shoemakers in the county. Now that really is a load of cobblers. Nowadays, they all work in call centres or River Island.

So the town *is* known for something, albeit something long downsized. And the Cobblers themselves entered the annals of football history in the Sixties by climbing from the fourth division to the first and then dropping right back down to the fourth again in consecutive seasons.[6] Joe Mercer, then manager of Manchester

---

6. Actually, they spent two seasons in Division Three on the way up between 1961 and 1963, but let's not spoil the ultimately humiliating story.

City, said, 'The miracle of 1966 was not England winning the World Cup but Northampton reaching Division One.'

Another proud story about my home team: in 1970, having miraculously reached the fifth round of the FA Cup, they let eight goals in against Manchester United, six of them from the boot (not made in Northampton) of George Best.

It would be disingenuous to say I couldn't wait to leave. After all, I waited 19 years to leave. Most of my sixth-form mates left town a year before I did to go to their exotic universities in Hatfield and the north. To tell you the truth, I had no idea how humdrum and monocultural Northampton was until I got to London in 1984. And even then it took time to sink in – I was dreadfully homesick during my first term at college. I went home at weekends far more than I actually stayed in London.

But was it Northampton that I missed? Or just 19 years of familiarity? Northampton was, after all, the back of my hand. Like Woody Allen's Manhattan, it was my town ... and it always would be.

So how did it shape me? Am I a product of Northampton? A victim of geography? Yes, in the sense that I felt neither northern nor southern when I arrived in the capital; neither posh nor poor. I was always glad not to be hidebound by all that geographical pride shit. I know grown men now who seem to think that coming from either Yorkshire or Lancashire makes a difference. Because I never supported the Cobblers[7] I don't even have that kneejerk, residual local allegiance that ties you to a place each Saturday teatime by the football results. I don't know what league Northampton are in today.

What are Northamptonians like? What are our civic traits? Are we bluff like Yorkshiremen? Do we have an innate sense of humour like Liverpudlians? Is the man who narrates the tremendous *Bygone Northampton* video right when he states, 'If there's one thing that has always united the people of Northamptonshire it is the love of a good parade'? Or is he just reading what's on the sheet of paper in front of him? I know we pulled together during the war, and

---

7. I supported Liverpool through most of the Seventies, then Leeds from 1978 onwards. That can't be good, can it?

we've always turned out in respectable numbers when royalty have visited ('Northampton? Yes, I think one was driven through there once'), but again, that's anytown. There was a carnival every year when I was growing up – a town tradition that dated back to the Thirties – and we always went, to throw pennies from the first-floor window of Pap Reg's office into the buckets of bank managers dressed as women below. A marvellous evening was guaranteed and we were, I suppose, united in our love. But is that it?

Being from Northampton is good if you want to start a new life. Like so many artificially expanded new towns, it does a nice line in blank canvasses.

The Northampton accent may be regarded as something of a handicap out there in the sophisticated world, but it doesn't quite carry the stigma of a Birmingham or a West Country. It's nothing like as recognisable for a start. The Northampton accent is – whaddya know! – a sort of cross between half a dozen others: a heavy dose of West Midlands, a dash of Nottingham, Derby and Leicester, and the cretinous-sounding twang of the country. In 1933, an editorial in the local paper complained, 'In Northampton we suffer, largely, from a lazy lower jaw which drops in the pronunciation of vowels and does not rise to clear-cut rendering of consonants.' People in Northampton, especially the older generation, pronounce 'going down town' as *gooing dane tane*, and 'our old car' would come out as *air uld cah*. I would be referred to by my grandparents as *air* Andrew. Yes is *yis* and yet is *yit*, and 'this afternoon' is streamlined to *sartnoon*. They might also call you *m'duck* as a term of endearment. You are their duck.

The first thing I did when I got to London was work on a London accent. I didn't want to be exclaiming *God blarmey!* all my life.

My wife, who was born in London, calls me northern, but when your home town is only 60 miles by road or rail, it hardly feels like dark, satanic mills and black pudding. As far as I'm concerned, Northampton is up the road. And that simple proximity was, I'm sure, a calming influence on my college years as I adjusted to life away from everything I knew. Like being a student with stabilisers.

There's something primal and necessary about leaving your home town, even if only for a spell like my mum and dad. Having said that, I totally respect Melissa for staying put and sending her boys to the very schools we went to. After years in Colchester and Germany with the forces, Simon and his family were drawn back to Northampton too. There's something poetic and circle-of-life about that. I have no contempt for people who choose not to leave. Northampton's development was all about welcoming people in, not driving them back down the M1 to clog the south-east back up again!

Northampton didn't drive me away: it raised me, it shod me in Doc Martens, it took my virginity, and it prepared me for my own journey into space. That's why I'm so keen to record my 19-year love affair with the place and 'put it all in', as Raymond Carver once wrote. As a home town, it was big enough to get lost in and small enough to have a local rock scene. Urban enough to have jobs and rural enough to have country pubs. Conservative enough to have engendered a modest goth community in the Eighties and tolerant enough to let us occupy the bar of the Berni Inn with our big hair. Even the ugly place names stir my bones: Lumbertubs, Lings, Jimmy's End, Moulton Park, Billing, Ecton, Harpole, Weedon, Brackmills.[8] I still love everything about this place.

This happy childhood I keep fretting about – Northampton did that.

And you are my duck.

---

8. I'm being unfair. Northampton's place names aren't all ugly. Round Spinney has a touch of the Beatrix Potters, as do Weston Favell, Wakes Meadow, Briar Hill, Blackthorn, Kingsley Park and Far Cotton. There's even a place to the south called Camp Hill. Wouldn't you just love to have that on your envelopes?

three

Down the Field

There was a time when meadow, grove and stream,
The earth, and every common sight,
To me did seem
Apparelled in celestial light.
William Wordsworth, 'Recollections of Early Childhood' (1807)

The closest we came to sexual interference as kids was in 1977 when a man turned up at the field in a blue van and invited Simon and me to join in some organised ball games with three others kids we didn't know. He even offered us a drink of ready-diluted squash at half-time from a plastic bottle which he kept in the van.

The man came back every week with his boys in his van and it became a kind of date in our diary, every Friday, with other kids from the estates like Soardsy and Taff joining in. One of the games we played, made up I suspect, was a variant on French cricket called 'Puttocks'.[1] One week Mum overheard Simon and me innocently joking about Mr Atkins and his Puttocks, and she misheard, believing he had shown us his buttocks. He hadn't, but panic set in and she started to ask us a lot of uncomfortable questions. We stopped playing with Mr Atkins after that, even though he had in fact only been recruiting for a Christian youth group. (Oh that's alright then!)

---

1. Intriguingly, 'puttock' is listed in the *Dictionary of Slang* as meaning 'an unpleasant person' or prostitute. Hey, we are all prostitutes.

It's almost as if everything of import that happened to me as a child did so down the field. We practically lived there during the school holidays, and spent every evening there or thereabouts in termtime. It was a good place, verdant and varied, where time stood still (I don't remember any of us wearing watches – we just went home when it felt like we ought to, and usually got it spot on too). They talk of 'dog years', well these were 'field hours', amorphous units of time that stretched all summer long some years, whether I was playing French cricket with potential kiddy-fiddlers, smoking with Pete Thompson or catching sticklebacks in bandy nets. I remember learning the word 'wanker' down the field, and, savouring the way it felt in my mouth without having a clue what it meant,[2] I shouted it out at the top of my lungs all afternoon. They must have heard me right across the allotments and halfway up Milverton Crescent.

* * *

The field was a miniature socialist utopia, a place where all economic groups were welcome and the only social stigma was not wanting to join in. Unless I'm romanticising, as long as you joined in the ad hoc games of football or Stony or Tiggy Off Ground you were alright. A straightforward meritocracy held sway when we picked teams. The team captain was bound to favour anyone who by reputation could thwack a tennis ball – likewise, height and age were a consideration – but selection never hinged on whether or not your dad did something indistinct in an office. It simply wasn't an issue.

All the dads in Winsford Way did something indistinct in an office – except Jack at the top of the street, who was something high up in the police (and as such probably spent as much time in an office as any of our dads). At least we knew what Jack up the road did. He was a policeman. We didn't know or give much of a toss what other kids' dads did. Apparently, Geoff Edwards from next door organised the refurbishment of pubs. (I only found that

---

2. It was bigger boy Jeremy Moss who eventually taught me what 'mastipation' was (his word). It involved 'white stuff' and was beyond my ken completely. Another Jeremy – Skoyles – revealed to me in Art once that if you touched a lady's bosoms it made your willy go big. Again, this seemed like some wild fantasy and I busied myself with my papier mâché.

out retrospectively so it doesn't count.) I doubt any of my mates knew or cared that our dad was in insurance. He had a company car: Vauxhall Viva most of the time and a Cavalier when his circumstances improved, and we parked in the Equity & Law. So? It didn't have any bearing on our elaborate games of combat down the field. The field was a great leveller. The field was neutral. It was no-dads-land.

When I was at Chelsea School of Art many years later, I heard that St Martin's, where all the good-looking, posh girls went, asked what your father did as part of the induction interview. Not being a good-looking, posh girl I was never St Martin's material anyway, so it's all hypothetical, but what a bloody liberty.

Life was so much simpler down the field.

Kids are truly classless little human beings anyway. The education system valiantly endeavours to smooth everyone out, socially and demographically, by dressing them in identical uniforms (I was used to that of course), but even that doesn't quite work, because the shoes are a giveaway – just like large hands are on a male transvestite. And there's a big difference between a brand new school blazer and a worn-in second-hand one. No wonder state communism was doomed.

When I started Abington Vale Middle School, my parents packed me off with my first briefcase – none of your Adidas bags for me. Talk about spot the kid with the white-collar dad! The irony is, it was second-hand; an ancient, falling-apart, hand-me-down, though such thrift did little to disguise those lofty parental aspirations.

When we first moved into Winsford Way it was still under construction and Dad used to take us on early evening building site raids for firewood. I don't want you to think of me as one of those sad middle-class people who finds vicarious romantic thrill in Ken Loach films (in much the same way sad middle-class Ken Loach does), but there *was* something vital and lawless about sneaking inside a house with no doors or windows and nicking offcuts. Simon and I used to love creeping up the echoey, wooden stairs and finding just beams instead of floorboards where 'upstairs' should be. Heady times. And I bet those *Brideshead* boys never half-inched timber.

Coincidentally, when Mum and Dad moved upmarket to Kestrel Close in 'the village' in 1983, much of that was still under construction too. But we no longer needed firewood then.

* * *

It's become a knackered old cliché now – 'It was all fields round here when I was a kid.' But actually, since you ask, it *was* all fields when I was a kid. Go for a nostalgic drive through the old neighbourhood now – Abington Vale, Weston Favell village, out to Little Billing – and it's all houses where the fields used to be. What kind of adventure playground is that for the youth of today? No wonder they're all high on crack and toting a machine gun.

But while the overspill-frantic planners bulldozed the face of central and suburban Northampton, they never touched the field. The field remained as green and pleasant as Shakespeare's Warwickshire and held its ground throughout the Great Expansion, as did Pap's allotments. In fact, the central playing area of my youth was basically unchanged from the late Sixties when we arrived in Abington Vale to the early Eighties when we moved up-village. And it's all still there today. The field is still a field. The climbing frame and swings which were always there are now set into that spongy rubber tarmac – and there's a dogshit bin – but it's essentially as it was, except the trees are taller. A total nostalgia oasis.

It was the outer edges of our childhood world that gradually changed, especially due south, where all the green bits were. It wasn't exactly rolling hills and fragrant meadows apparelled in celestial light as far as the eye could see, but beyond *our* field there were other fields, significant patches of undevelopment between the estates. Long grass to hide in. Sticks to find. Tunnels to venture down. Trees to climb. Streams to wade through, or, if you had a paper round, dump undelivered copies of the *Mercury & Herald* into.[3] I may have had a fundamentally urban childhood, but I

---

3. Not me. I never did have a paper round. I once helped David Hirst (I think) deliver some Spar leaflets door to door, a breezy task made stressful only by barking dogs jumping up at letterboxes. There was no money in it.

spent an awful lot of it communing with nature. I am, of course, grateful for that particular accident of birth.

It will always be the culture of wellies that best evokes my childhood. (Apt really for a footwear town.) Levering our boots off by the heel on the front step and finding our football socks halfway down our ankles; the adrenalin rush of feeling the water pressure on our calves as the stream got deeper beyond Billing Road; getting a leak mended by Dad using a bike puncture repair kit; emptying stones out of them; hiding 'guns' from the Jerries inside them overnight. Try getting that degree of romance out of a Nike trainer, kids today!

Wellies. We were always in wellies, until self-consciousness set in during our early teens and then it was trainers. But that was a sad day – wellies were the best. Wellies were a foot prophylactic; they meant safe wading; communing with water. The stream.

Simon and I knew every inch of the stream that ran through the field. We never physically mapped it but it was all in our heads: where the easiest jumps were, where the current ran fast enough to be called – ha! – 'rapids', where the soil beneath turned to treacherous, slippery clay, where the mythic water rat had been spotted. But by far the most important intelligence was where you could safely wade without water going over the top of your boots.

If it did, this was called a 'soaker': the unforgivable act of misjudging the depth and letting water *inside* your wellies. The very thought of it brings back a knot of dread to me, because if you got a soaker, Mum would *kill* you. That was it. No prisoners. Coming home with wet socks was akin to losing your bike or weeing in your pants. I'm really not sure why such an innocuous and mundane aquatic accident carried such a penalty in our house. As I've said, Mum was no tyrant – but something about a soaker aroused her ire and put the fear of God into us. To Mum I guess it was a signal that we'd literally gone out of our depth; it also meant we had to get out of our wet socks and change into a new pair in the middle of a day, thus creating extra washing for her. If it was a major soaker, the tracksuit bottoms would have to come off too – the stream was, after all, brown. (Dad played no part in this kangaroo court – he was always at work when it happened; this was between Mum and us. I fancy he would have been able to put damp socks into perspective – but then he didn't have to peg them out to dry.)

We were such obedient, fatalistic kids though. If either Si or I got a soaker, what did we do? We trudged straight home! With stream water sloshing about in our wellies! We turned ourselves in! Only once do I remember us doing the sensible thing and staying out until our socks and wellies had dried out in the sun.

But then, apart from the reign of terror that was soaker justice, Si and I had little need to deceive our parents. *They let us get on with it.* We had total right to roam between mealtimes. But we knew our limits. We could – and did – venture as far afield as The Dual Carriageway, which was in fact the A45. It sweeps east from the M1 past Northampton and Wellingborough to Rushden and Higham Ferrers and then fizzles out through sheer lack of interest.

Because once again Mum never sternly warned us to stay away from The Dual Carriageway, we didn't do anything dangerous there, like play in it – or drop stones on passing cars from the bridge. But it did mark the edge of our world. Mainly because there wasn't much the other side of it except Weston Mill and I was a bit fearful of that place. It had a canal and a lock and fast-running water and I'd once seen some older boys diving in there *wearing their jeans* and it put the frighteners on me. I'd also dropped a sandcastle bucket into the lock when the water level was low and the sight of it falling – seemingly for ever – brought home to me just how unyielding that particular waterway was. Streams were one thing, Weston Mill was another.

To the north we never went much further than Northampton's main artery, the Wellingborough Road ('Welly Road' in local parlance). That is, apart from the occasional mooch around Weston Favell Centre – aka 'Supacentre' – an out-of-town shopping and leisure complex opened in 1974 that was clearly way ahead of its time. And crap. Even a committed mooch never took long: the shopping centre itself had a Tesco's, a coffee shop (and we never went 'for a coffee', even as teenagers – *never*), a WH Smith with an alluring downstairs record department, and a novelty shop where, in the summer of 1978, I bought a large *Close Encounters* badge with the change Richard Angerson and I had left after fetching some Tesco's shopping for his mum. (He bought a badge too – can't remember what kind – and his mum had a right go at us for this act of frivolity when we got back. Cuh. Don't get your knickers in a twist, Mrs Angerson, we could have spent it on fags and Top Deck!)

To be fair, the complex did also take in a church and the pocket-sized Lings Cinema, whose poor man's habit of showing new films about six months after the ABC in town would only start to matter to me in my mid-teens; and a leisure centre which was mainly a swimming pool – again, no interest as a hang-out until my mid-teens when we used to go and idly watch people swimming from the 'viewing area' which also sold cans of drink we had no money for.

Due east, it was another big road, the brilliantly named Lumbertubs Way, that hemmed us in, and to the west, 'Abby Park' (Abington Park), opened 1897. So not only did we have access to our own field, there was a sprawling, well-appointed, 126-acre municipal park within easy cycling distance. More grass, more trees, more water, and, let me tell you, untold delights. Never mind the things Roy Batty says he's seen in *Blade Runner* – attack ships on fire off the shoulder of Orion and C-beams glittering in the dark near the Tannhauser gate, yeah, yeah – Abington Park had its own museum (admission: free), a playground, three duck-and swan-filled lakes (one with rowing boats on it), a bandstand, a spinney, a nine-hole miniature golf course, conkers galore in season, tennis courts, a bowling green, a sort of quite-easy maze, an aviary containing peacocks and parakeets, and ice-cream vans all summer long. It was blinkin' Xanadu.

These days kids demand bowling alleys and pizzas and Daytona Racing and multiplexes and things that need batteries. When I was a kid – when it was *all fields* – we were happy as Larry with a bike, some wellies, a gun-shaped stick and the remote, tantalising possibility of a Funny Face lolly. It's not that we were easily pleased – the parameters of pleasure were different. Bits of tree and lollies were all that were available. The advent of Space Invaders at the Westonia chip shop in the early Eighties was too late for me – hormones were starting to make me feel self-conscious about 'playing' by then.

* * *

But there was another side to me. I was also a delicate, lavender-scented creative little flower. I liked drawing from an early age. Adults told me I had a talent for it. I spent a good part of my boyhood sitting up at the living-room table hunched over a pack of felt-tips and a stack of headed notepaper which Dad had snaffled from work. (Much of my childhood artwork has a National Provident Institution logo in the top right-hand corner.) Drawing was, by its very nature, a solitary pursuit – like putting together *Wacky Races* jigsaws or painting soldiers with Humbrol enamel paints, two of my other beloved pastimes away from the field.

It was Simon who would progress from a childhood playing war games with rifle-shaped sticks to patrolling the streets of Armagh with a loaded weapon as a young man, while my career drifted back inside the house and to the felt-tips.

Like many other boys before and since, Simon and I were both in the imaginary army, ranked equal, devouring comics like *Warlord, Valiant* and *Battle,* and films like *The Longest Day* and *Cockleshell Heroes.* We would recreate scenarios from those films with our Action Men, and I guess that penknife burrow in the riverbank was probably a foxhole if it was anything at all. However, only one of us kept up the military theme into and beyond our teens.

I don't know exactly when the desire to create eclipsed my need to wade through streams hoping to catch a glimpse of the non-existent water rat. It's the education system that forces these choices on you: are you an academic achiever or captain of the football team? Are you – in old money – O-level or CSE material? It's streaming that eventually pulls you out of the stream. Simon was less good at passing exams than me, and the armed services offered him a career where other skills are more useful – like killing a goat, folding things neatly and laying down your life to stop *those Russians.* He was going to be allowed to wade through streams for a job. Meanwhile, I had a knack for remembering facts under exam conditions and ended up in the sixth form and higher education.

Before school really starts to mould and shape you – and these days the assessment and unnatural selection begins just the other side of the cradle – you remain a primal being, attracted by the good earth.

I used to cover my hands methodically with the dust off the soles of my shoes at school then lick it off. I mean it. You might need to call Mr Proust again. I had a soot fetish too. (That's *soot* fetish.) In the days before central heating I used to love it when the man came to sweep the chimney. He was fascinating to watch, attaching all those extension poles to his brush and pushing it further and further up the flue while the living room was shrouded in sheets. It was also a major kick to go out the front with him and check that the brush had emerged from the chimney. But the real attraction was the soot. I loved the dry throat you got when the room was full of coal dust, and the feel of that fine powder on your hands. I can't say for sure if I actually ate the stuff, but the desire was there. I never bat an eyelid when pregnant women hunger for coal.

I can feel eyebrows being arched as I confess this. We've already established that getting dirty is normal and I'm just trying to make the point that the 'civilising' influence of age actually goes against primal impulses ... but I sense that I've lost one or two of you.

I didn't go around snacking on filth. I lived in mortal fear of treading in dog's muck – even in those wellies – and my taste for floor-dust and chimney powder was not something I shared with anyone. I knew it wasn't the *done* thing. Spitting into your dusty hands and rubbing them together at school was an under-the-desk activity. But I will say this – when I'm digging the garden now, I like nothing better than to cast aside the spade and use my hands and feel the soil under my nails.

You can take the boy out of the field ...

1973

Selected Extracts From My Diary

A murky green Leeds Permanent Building Society desk diary, spiral-bound and encased in a vinyl dust-jacket. Very smart – Dad clearly got sent it at work. The Leeds Permanent crest on the front bears the motto 'SAFE AND SOUND'. How very apt. It contains information on all the company's branch offices, and tells you that 'no-one may invest more than £10,000 in the Society', which was a lot of money in 1973. This was the first diary I completed the whole way through.

Monday, 1 January
Yesterday I came to Nanny and Pappy's house to sleep. I saw Norman Wisdom on television. Nanny has got a lovely colour television (so have I).

Thursday, 4 January
Today Dean (my cousin)[1] came to our house. And me and my brother watched *Land of the Giants* and *The Flintstones* on our colour television. Nanny Mabel bought me some coloured paints.[2]

Wednesday, 10 January
Today Paul Milner brought his magic set to school and he had me as an assistant.

Thursday, 11 January
Today I went to Catherine Leese's party. Cathy Knight[3] went too and loads more. I won a game but I've forgotten what it was.

Sunday, 14 January

Today me and my brother went to the park with Dad. We put our old kit on and we both played dirt collectors.[4]

Thursday, 25 January

Nearly every day my tooth bleeds and today was one of those days so it means that soon my tooth will come out. I have had one tooth out on its own and I have had five teeth out at the dentist, that makes six altogether.

Monday, 5 February

Today Anita Barker came to watch the television. Mine is a colour telly and Anita hasn't got one. We saw *Pardon My Genie* on it.

---

1. Dean Cave, only child of Auntie Janice (Mum's sister) and Uncle Allen, and our perfect cousin ('He's his family's pride and joy/His mother's little golden boy'). Dean – exactly one year between Simon and me – was our 'significant other' growing up. Though he lived in a different part of town and went to entirely different schools, Simon and I had Dean at the holidays, which seemed to come around so rapidly then, and we got on like a house on fire. (Actually, Dean's house did go on fire once; the kitchen was gutted.) Because of his only-childness Dean accumulated an enormous stash of *stuff*: bigger and better Action Man gear than we ever got, more and varied Dinky toy cars, a radio-controlled car, a ventriloquist's dummy. But Simon and I had each other, and anyway, Dean's penance was to live under iron rule: Janice, with the best intentions in the world, made Dean tidy all his toys away the second they weren't being used, and he kept them, à la Stinky Pete in *Toy Story 2*, in the original boxes. This used to infuriate us, because Dean would treat his *stuff* with too much reverence, a direct result of this oppressive regime. His Action Man, for instance, always kept his hat on, no matter what humiliation and torture our elaborate narratives put him through. Dean's unintentional catch-phrase was, 'I've still got me hat on.' We loved him though. Dean grew up to look just like his dad (who looks just like his) and brought divorce to the family, which was such a scandal – I'd been long-ensconced in London by then – Mum didn't even tell me about it!
2. What Nanny Mabel actually bought me was some coloured *pants*. My first patterned undergarments in a short lifetime of plain ones: decorated with orange and brown shapes, and M&S without a doubt (Nan worked there). I dutifully recorded the gift in my diary and then became instantly embarrassed, like Adam and Eve, and my fig leaf was the added 'i'. Genius when you think about it. On the subject of Stalinist revision, the day before (3 January) I have written that Simon was 'very very naughty today at Nanny's' and then reconsidered, crossing out one of the verys.
3. Knights with an 's'.
4. Not a clue. 'Dirt collectors'? We'll chalk this one up to the childhood imagination and endeavour to protect it from modern innuendo.

Saturday, 10 February

Today I bought myself a *Buzz* comic. It's a new comic and it is very good. I got it instead of *Cor!!*

Monday, 12 February

Today my tooth started wobbling. It will come out tomorrow because I'm taking some toffees to school for lunch.

Tuesday, 13 February

My tooth didn't come out but it is much looser now.

Saturday, 17 February

Today I had a horrible cold but that wasn't the only horrible thing, I had a horrible Lemsip.

Saturday, 24 February

Today I went to Kelvin Lay's[5] party. I had a smashing tea, it was the best tea I've ever had.

Thursday, 1 March

Today my dad bought a new car, it was a white Viva. Our old one was a browny yellowy colour and it was a Viva as well. I haven't rode in it yet but Simon has.

Thursday, 8 March

Today I went to Jeremy's party and we had a super tea. My tooth fell out. It didn't really fall out, somebody knocked it out at school. And Pappy gave me a magazine and it had a poster of The Sweet inside.[6]

Friday, 9 March

Today Andrew Sharp[7] brought some strawberry bon-bons to school and he let me have four or five of them and they were very nice. And this afternoon David Edwards let me have a gobstopper and that was the first one I ever had.

Saturday, 10 March

Today Dad and me went to town and I spent my birthday money on a Slade poster and it's smashing.

Sunday, 18 March

Today Dad let me stop up to play my new game I had for my birthday. It is called Mastermind it is really for grown-ups but we know how to play.

Thursday, 12 April

Today when I was playing on our tractor[8] I fell off and I scraped on the ground. My leg is burnt and it is all blacky brown.

Thursday, 26 April

Today I swapped one of my Top Teams, Kenny Dagleish, for Pat Jennings and Rodney Marsh and Milner gave me Emlyn Hughes free and Richard Griffin[9] gave me David Hay and Paul Madley free.

---

5. Kelvin was the eldest, Harvey the youngest – their parents were Tony and Pat Lay. (Mum and 'Auntie' Pat actually went to school together.) They had a cat called Suki which once bit Kelvin on the knee and made him cry. He's a policeman now, just like his dad. I think Kelvin and an unnamed mate once pulled me down the grass bank at middle school by my legs for a cruel jape, and I pretended to have asthma to make them feel guilty. How ironic. (It didn't work.)

6. *Weekend* magazine, a lively precursor of things like *Chat* and *Bella* which held an allure for me on two counts: it had pop posters in it (at a time when pop was entering my life), and a weekly feature wherein true-life tales of human peril were illustrated with a dramatic photo-reconstruction, something I would morbidly pore over ('My legs were trapped and the train was coming', that type of thing). An early hint at my subsequent masochistic fascination with disaster. Even at this age I was learning to control my fear.

7. Or 'Sharpy' as we knew him. Round-faced boy who lived in Chelfham Close.

8. A toy tractor, naturally.

9. Richard Griffin, also known as Griff. Someone who occupied the 'best friend' slot for a while. He – along with David Edwards (Eddy) – was unfortunate enough to be one of the first kids in class to be fitted with glasses. He had I think slightly older, starchier parents than the rest of us, but was nonetheless the only kid I knew who had a Shaker Maker and, boy, was I jealous of that. (A heavily TV-advertised 'craft' toy: you filled plastic moulds with some noxious pink agent and shook it vigorously as if mixing a cocktail. The gunk set hard in the shape of Donald Duck or similar and when it had shrivelled dry you painted it. That was it. The USP was the shaking. Immortalised in name by Oasis in 1994.)

Tuesday, 1 May

Today when I was walking home from school Jeremy Moss came rushing up and he said he had just seen David Boulter run over by a motorcycle and his leg is broken and it is quite flat.

Friday, 4 May

Today I saw *The Grumbleweeds* on telly and it is great. There are jokes, impressions and two special guests every week and there is Maurice, Albert, Robin, Graham and Carl. Carl is my favourite.

Monday, 7 May

Today I stopped for school dinners for the very first time but I took sandwiches and you sit on a special table if you have sandwiches. If there's no room you sit on another table.

Friday, 18 May

Today a new series of *It's a Knockout*. It was Woodstock v Bicester, I wanted Bicester to win. They did. The score was B 14 and W 8. They had some crazy games.

Sunday, 27 May

Today it was a very sunny day and me and Simon went over Maria and Justine's[10] and we all played in the paddling pool and Simon fell off the slide and his head was bleeding.

Monday, 4 June *Holiday*

In the afternoon we went to the Model Village at Yarmouth then we went to the Aquarium and in the evening we went to

---

10. Maria and Justine Edwards, daughters of Geoff and Jean, our next-door neighbours (we holidayed together in Yarmouth that summer). Because most of the houses in our estate had low, wire-mesh fences as standard issue, an awful lot of handing over of kids by parents occurred (they were too high for us to scale without assistance). All rather convenient and sociable. The Prouts, whose garden backed on to ours, erected a high wooden fence for privacy, as was their right, but we would simply peer through the slats as if they had something to hide. We put up a high wooden fence between us and the Edwards eventually – just a few boards, not the whole length of the garden, and nothing to do with the family feud I have since learned about.

the Joyland fair with Maria. I went on the snail ride, a round-about, some bumper cars, penny slot machines and we all went on a novelty Noah's Ark, there was a little monkey, a hall of mirrors, little model scenes and the boat swayed about.

Thursday, 7 June

Today in the evening me, Dad and Simon were going to the waxworks but it was closed so we went to the Joyland fair and when we came back to the car Dad bought us an ice cream and they were a foot high counting the cornet and it had a flake in it.

Monday, July 9

Dad bought us a cricket bat. We got our school reports, I got grade A in English, grade B in reading and grade A in maths and they are about the best grades you can get.

Thursday, 12 July

I went to Jonathan Green's party and Richard Woodhall went mad on the swing and it fell on top of him and he cut his head open and Mrs Green had to ring up his mum and she took him to hospital.[11]

Thursday, 2 August

This week at the park the fair is on. I had a candy floss again. I won a biro and a Dracula's vampire bat and I scared Nanny with it.

Tuesday, 14 August

We went to Auntie Mary's[12] new house. It is very old and it's going to be all painted up. There is a pigs field next to it.

---

11. We all had swings. It was as if they were issued along with the coal bunker and the wire fence. Wooden seat, chains, steel-tube frame held in the ground with metal hooks, but Richard Woodall was really going at it, and they must have worked loose. The Edwards had a slide.

12. Mary Gardener. Not a blood auntie, a friend of Mum's from back in the Duss'on welfare days. She and her husband had bought this barn in a field in Roade and intended to convert it, 25 years before there were entire theme evenings on BBC2 showing you how to do this. Their kids, who must have been about the same age as us, had an Evel Kneivel toy, the kind that did stunts in the TV advert but not in real life.

Thursday, 23 August

My cousin Dean came for dinner. I had a Lord Toffingham lolly, so did Simon. Melissa had a Lemonade Sparkle and Dean had a Kinky.

Saturday, 1 September

Dad bought me a Liverpool football kit. I went down the field to fly Carl's[13] kite with him and it got stuck in the tree but a big boy got it down.

Monday, 24 September

We stayed for sandwiches and in the evening we saw *Sykes* and *Star Trek*. *Sykes* was good but *Star Trek* was a repeat.

Wednesday, 3 October

Mum bought me a 'Monster Mash' record. It costs 45p.[14]

Friday, 5 October

We watched *Dave Allen* on telly, it was on at 8.15 and finished a whole three-quarters of an hour later at 9.00.

Wednesday, 10 October

We went to Paul Cockle's farm at school. It was a pig farm so it was very smelly. I fell off the haystack while I was climbing.[15]

Thursday, 18 October

Cockle brought a pig's ear, a pig's windpipe, two pig's eyes and a piece of pig's skin. I had a haircut over the road at Carol's.[16]

Tuesday, 13 November

Today I became famous because I am so good at drawing. Mrs Crutchley told me to do a picture of cartoons. I drew some clowns and some spooks.

Wednesday, 14 November

We had a day off school because it was Princess Anne's wedding. She married Captain Mark Phillips and we watched it on telly. We went to Nan's house for dinner and tea and she bought me a disguise outfit.

Friday, 16 November
Today it was art and we are making puppets out of papier mâché. I am making Jimmy Savile but I haven't put his hair on yet!

Wednesday, 19 December
The school was open and we had a cartoon film show before play, and a party after. Santa Claus came to the infants but not the juniors (HUH!).

Tuesday, 25 December
I got Subbuteo, Meccano set 3, Cluedo, tracksuit, a hamster, Sorry (a game), *Cor!!* annual, football annual, *Shiver and Shake* annual, a calendar, a Disneyland diary, another team for Subbuteo and some more balls, some coloured pencils and two drawing pads, two pencils, origami and loads more.

---

13. Carl Merrick, an only child who lived on the intersection of Winsford Way and the slightly posher Milverton Crescent (the Merricks had a car porch, a canoe and a beautiful Samoyed dog). I think he was a year older than me – he certainly carried the aura of a kid who *knows more*. I liked Carl a lot; he would frequently just *give* me things, like a figurine of Charlie George, or his old Surf Flyer skateboard. When he swapped his Haunted House board game with me the deal was so obviously weighted in my favour: he only got a John Bull printing set in return. But Carl cared not – he was fed up with his game, and coveted the little rubber alphabet, so to hell with the size or price differential. (Definitely older.) The Merricks must have moved away as he disappears from my life after 1977 without any fond farewell.
14. I may have known the value of nothing, but I knew the price of everything.
15. I also took fright on a tour of the pigsties. It was hot, loud and dank in this cavernous barn and one of the pigs jumped up and put its head over the side of its pen. Filled with fear – of what? pig attack? – I went back out the way I'd come in and waited outside on my own for it all to be over, like a softy. Didn't write that down in my diary, did I?
16. Carol Cater, home-hairdresser and wife of sales rep Chris. A childless and overtly sexy couple, he was in those days very much a prototype for Paul on the sitcom *Ever Decreasing Circles* (played sublimely by Peter Egan) and she had jet-black hair and the come-hither look of a young Dorien (Lesley Joseph) off another future sitcom, *Birds of a Feather*. I had my hair done by Carol for years; she cut my first 'spike' in 1980, supplied me with my first henna in 1981, and latterly endured a string of impossible pop star pictures torn from *Smash Hits* to copy: Sting (when he was cool), Nick Heyward, Bono ('That looks like a root perm,' she explained, scaring me away for good).

four

St Francis, I Gave You the Best Years of My Life

'Boys,' sa headmaster GRIMES, smiling horibly,
'st. custard's hav come to the end of another term.'
Can there be a note of relief in his craked voice?
There can be no doubt of the feelings of the little pupils.
CHEERS! HURRAH! WHIZZ-O!
CHARGE! TA-RAN-TA-RA!
The little chaps raise the roof of big skool, which do not
take much doing as most of it is coming off already.

Nigel Molesworth, *Whizz for Atomms* (1956)

I loved, and I mean *loved*, the Molesworth books, written by ex-prep schoolmaster Geoffrey Willans and visualised by the spidery nib of Ronald Searle, whose work I knew from the title sequences of the St Trinian's films and *Those Magnificent Men in Their Flying Machines*. We had a book club at middle school called Scoop (the one at primary school was Chip) and through it I ordered the frankly inappropriate and scurrilous Molesworth volume *Down with Skool!*, purely on the strength of the Searle cartoon on the cover. I would not be disappointed.[1]

Down with Skool! was one of four Molesworth books, first published back in the Fifties, collected from *Punch* magazine, not that I was aware of their vintage or their genesis. (The other volumes were *Whizz for Atomms, How to be Topp* and *Back in the Jug Agane.*) If they hadn't been illustrated with cartoons I doubt I'd have read them, but once sucked in, I became duly obsessed with St Custard's school; with Molesworth, Grabber, Grimes and Fotherington-Thomas, and the creative spelling and lack of grammar in the trademark prose. Molesworth spoke of 'swots, bulies, cissies, milksops, greedy guts and oiks with whom i am forced to mingle hem-hem' and introduced the term 'chiz' into my vocabulary ('a chiz is a swiz or swindle as any fule kno'). Molesworth appreciation in adulthood is like belonging to a secret sect. The phrase 'as any fule kno' is like a code. You either get it – and form a wry smile at the very memory – or exist forever in concentric circles of unyielding darkness. Try it at your next dinner party.

What's interesting to me now about Molesworth is that St Custard's was a boarding school. As in fee-paying. Live-in. For poshos. Mention of 'new bugs', 'mater and pater' and 'writing home on Sunda' should have alerted me to the fact that this was a scholastic universe far away from my own. But I never twigged. Skool was skool. And down with it chiz chiz.

* * *

1. While we're on the subject of ordering things sight unseen from these la-di-da book clubs, I also remember purchasing *Carrie's War* by Nina Bawden. This was the source novel of the 1974 kids TV series about Second World War evacuees, and I only wanted it because of the telly programme. A familiar tale: love the TV show; buy the book; *never read the book.* I optimistically bought Alex Haley's black-experience doorstop *Roots* some years later, for the same reasons (it was my favourite TV show of the time) – now there's a volume whose spine has remained resolutely intact ever since. *Ice Cold in Alex* by Christopher Landon – I wonder why Scoop got money off me for that? I liked the cover though, and what parent would discourage their kids from building up a library? Particularly one that stayed in such mint condition too.

To be fair, I did try to read *Carrie's War* on the long drive home from Wales one year but it made me car-sick (reading generally did). I'll never forget the TV series though: Druid's Bottom! Mr Johnny the mental bloke! Dropping the skull down the well! I was glad I didn't have to be evacuated and get spooked down the lane by Mr Johnny. (We'll come to my childhood fear of the handicapped later.)

Abington Vale Primary School – which achieved the impossible and *took me out of the field*, at least during the week – was a first-rate place. Brand new, red-brick, like so much of late Sixties Abington Vale, and built to serve the local estates. All the kids who went there, aged between five and ten, lived nearby. Quite villagey, in a way, but without the silage and flaming torches.

It sat within comfortable walking distance of Winsford Way and in the infants (that is, the first and second year) 'home time' meant a benign picket line of expectant, chattering, bouffanted mums at the school gates, most with prams, waiting to troop us all back to our semi-detached plots in streets like Milverton Crescent, Lynmouth Avenue and Crediton Close. Why they were all named after towns in Devon and Somerset I don't know. Perhaps one of the planners holidayed in the West Country.

However, all this healthy walking didn't last long. To help ensure that OPEC could hold the rest of the world to ransom for the rest of the decade, we 'tinies' soon fell into a rota of being driven to school with other kids from the estates. Quite unnecessary. What *were* we, crippled? Perhaps the paranoia-inducing public information films has started to bite, but I doubt that somehow, judging by the freedom we enjoyed the rest of the time. I put it down to the simple fact of *having cars*.[2]

When it was Dad's turn to drive us in, he would make us laugh by playing the game of 'kangaroo petrol', which involved him 'bouncing' the car up Abington Park Crescent using the accelerator. 'We've got kangaroo petrol!' Good old Dad. I don't remember Mr Needham or Mrs Stenson providing in-car vaudeville entertainment.

The playground at Abington Vale Primary School was 76.75 metres long. I know this to be the case because on 15 June 1973, page 81 in my maths text book required me to measure the playground with one of those wheels you push along which clicks to register every metre. It clicked 76 times. This, as you will have noted, is the kind of evocative information you get from my diaries. In truth, entries for the primary school years are rarely that

---

2. It's like something my college friend Jane Chipchase once said, partly in jest: 'Oh look there's an ashtray – I'd better start smoking.'

helpful. For instance, when I moved up to Class 6 in September I merely noted, 'We have got the same teacher as the last class.' Cheers, Samuel Pepys.

The unnamed teacher was, in fact, Mrs Munro; a raven-haired woman of even temperament – one of the 'young' teachers, by which I mean she didn't look like someone's nan – and she had a mentally and physically handicapped son called Steven whom she occasionally brought into school just to scare the life out of me. As I say, we'll come to my childhood fear of the handicapped later ...

I digress. Before we get to the relative safety of Mrs Munro, we must first pass through hell.

Now, looking back, I can see that I enjoyed primary school by and large. I had no reason not to. It was a bright, clean, well-stocked little one-storey establishment whose 76.75-metre playground came replete with hopscotch grid and climbing frame, and it had its own sports field up the back. There was the aforementioned Chip club, I made loads of friends and only shat my pants once.[3] Simon's children have since passed through the very same school and Melissa's eldest boys are there as I write (Simon even moved house to ensure his girls were in the catchment area). But I'm telling you now and I'm telling you this: Mum literally had to drag me through the gates when I first started, kicking and screaming. I didn't know much at the age of five, but I knew I did not want to go to Abington Vale Primary School, or any other.

Mum had tried acclimatising me – *like other kids* – by putting me into a day nursery, or play school, but I wasn't falling for that. It was obvious to me that whichever way you sliced it, school was a big place full of people I didn't know with the huge disadvantage of not being home. Never mind that all you did there was paint pictures and listen to stories, you might as well have been packing me off to Treblinka.

We know that I was a little sod, pre-school. So imagine how

---

3. Nothing too explosive – indeed I impressed *myself*, so grown-up and measured was my response to the mishap. I had simply misjudged the length of time it would take to run from the playground to the toilet in Mrs Crutchley's classroom. Luckily I was wearing those 'coloured paints' Nan bought me.

anxious my poor mother must have been to offload me elsewhere for a few blessed hours a week after five years of my headbanging and mithering. I know I did spend some time at nursery school but these are dim memories of a dark, cavernous place with the whiff of carbolic soap about it. I think they had a slide there but I was probably too introspective and homesick to go down it. I discover now that my ill-visited play school was held in the hall of Victoria Road Congregational Church. I was suspicious of organised religion even then.

My first day of proper school, 1970, involved much wailing and gnashing of milk teeth, though I remember the surrender more vividly than the skirmish, when Mum finally handed me over to Mrs Carter and helper Mrs Sutton and I was truly off her hands. (I know I'm not unique in kicking up at this most stressful of times – Julie has since told me that she was so difficult to prise from her mother's legs she clawed great holes in her tights.) I'm told that I gave it the full Tasmanian Devil on subsequent school mornings, but I must have settled down within a week or two. I remember the very first thing I did on that very first morning. Mrs Carter (one of the someone's-nan teachers – she wore a mysterious support bandage under her tights the whole time) asked me what I wanted to do. I had the choice of anything – apart from going home – and, through my snivelling, I managed to convey to her that I wanted to draw a picture. So I was furnished with copious thumb-like wax crayons and a sheet of that cheap, shiny off-white school paper and I drew a picture. Of a man.

Playtime was a trauma all of its own. (Perhaps we're getting somewhere.) We were *forced* to go outside and *play* in the playground. I know – it's a good thing the European Court of Human Rights hadn't been established. Not having any friends – can this be true? – I stood as close to the outside door of my classroom as physically possible without actually clinging pathetically to the handle, and I guess the scent of my victimhood was strong. A bigger boy (he must have been seven – practically shaving age) came up to me and methodically twisted both my ears and squeezed my nose, then walked nonchalantly away. Not a word was spoken. I was so shocked I didn't even cry. Not quite being roasted over an open fire, Tom

Brown style, but it taught me the rules of playground engagement.

Benevolent Mrs Carter let me forgo the next couple of play-times (I sat in class on my own), but I was pretty soon out there again where all the *play* took place. In short, and to the disappointment of all psychologists looking in, I adapted to school and its rituals in no time – stacking the chairs up on our desks at the end of the afternoon (for the cleaners); recognising our coat hooks by the little pictures above them; sucking school milk through a red plastic straw and hating the last few drops, which were full of 'bits' due to the crate being left out in the warm; washing out the plastic paint palettes in the sink after art; recruiting for playground games by starting a 'chain' with other boys and marching up and down the quad with our arms round each other's shoulders shouting 'All in for Army!' or 'All in for Bulldogs!' until the requisite quorum was acquired; dreading Welsh headmaster Mr Rees filling in for an absent teacher in class and jumping to it whenever he uttered his catch-phrase 'Sharply!'; and standing still like statues when teacher blew the whistle for the end of playtime and *waiting* to be instructed indoors.

My first term went off without further incident. Though I wasn't very impressed when Angela Leslie touched the back of my neck with a dried starfish from the nature table, but she did let me feel her hair, which was cool because she was the only black kid in our class.[4]

* * *

A year later I was in Mrs Cox's class (another nan), followed by Mrs Munro – who remained our class teacher for two years as if perhaps she was being held back a year – and finally Mrs Crutchley (nan), who eventually waved us off as fully formed ten-year-olds into the wider world. She even taught us some rudimentary French.[5] The key

---

4. I wish Northampton had thrown a more varied ethnic mix at me but that's just the way it was then: one black girl in our class, and two Asian. The Leslie family lived over the back from us in Huntsham Close, next door to the Prouts, and I don't recall any careless talk of house prices falling. Despite the whiteness of our estate, little comment was ever made about skin colour – I'm retroactively proud to say. See Chapter 13.

difference between this and middle school was that we stayed in one classroom for the whole day at primary: your class teacher taught you everything, including PE and 'arts and crafts' (with a few floating teachers in reserve like Miss Rowan and Mr Belford, no doubt fresh out of teacher training college at Loughborough or somesuch).

There were Peter and Jane books to read, featuring Pat the dog who had a ball and the ball was red, and then you moved up to a colour-coded series of pirate books: red, yellow, green and blue (but not necessarily in that order). We worked our way through reading books and maths books at our own steam and moved on when we were ready. This strikes me as a very even-handed system. Don't you have to do exams the moment you're through the door these days, and if one child fails to meet Ofsted targets for five-year-olds the entire school is closed down and sold to the private sector?

We recited the Lord's Prayer[6] at the end of each afternoon by our stacked chairs, and we sang hymns at assembly, but the school wasn't heavy on the religion. We were taught Bible stories as if they were historical fact, which some might see as indoctrination, but neither fire nor brimstone were involved. I wasn't scared of God. He seemed alright – he gave us our daily bread, after all. Some of the bigger boys (aged ten, eligible to vote) devised a subversive accompaniment to the hymn 'O Jesus I Have Promised' in which they would 'count' the three beats between the first and second line with a slap on the thigh, a clap of the hands and a slap on the cheek with the mouth in an 'O' shape (which is enormous fun – I suggest you try it at the next boring wedding or church service you attend) and we all thought that was very cool, like singing that the shepherds washed their socks by night.

O Jesus I have promised ... slap, clap, slap ... to serve thee to the end ...

---

5. How confusing that was. We were 'given' French names, and mine was Simon (*See-mon*). Someone else got André. *C'est ridicule!*

6. Off the top of my head then: Our Father, who art in Heaven, hallowed be thy name, thy kingdom come, thy will be done, on Earth as it is in Heaven, give us this day our daily bread, and forgive us our trespasses, as we forgive those who trespass against us, [*and lead us not into temptation but deliver us from evil – oops*], for thine is the kingdom, the power and the glory, for ever and ever, Amen. (Get 'em while they're young, you see.)

It wasn't a particularly naughty school. If Abington Vale had an equivalent of *Grange Hill*'s Gripper Stebson it was a boy called Nelly. His real name was Neil Harwood and he was obviously at the back of the queue when they handed out hard nicknames. But Nelly wasn't a bully, just a respected bigger boy who had what you might call an attitude problem (it was he who led the slap-clap-slap chorus). There was no trouble here, nothing to see. If my diaries for 1971–74 are anything to go by, Abington Vale Primary was some kind of utopia: all I did was put on plays for the rest of the class, draw pictures of 'spooks' and hippos, clamber on the PE 'apparatus' (bars, ropes and ladders stored around the edges of the school hall) and make a twat of myself at sport. On this last point, we have these excerpts:

> Today we went up the field to play rounders with Class 6. I only scored half a rounder but some scored six ... [*make the most of that semi-rounder glory, Collins*] ... We played rounders at school. Our team lost but Johnny got loads of people out because he is good at catching and I stood near him so that if he missed the ball I would try and catch it ... [*note judicious use of the word 'try'*] ... Today we played rounders and we won with a great score of seven and a half rounders. I didn't get a rounder but Matthew did and so did Mr Belford ... [*we're getting the picture now*] ... We played soccer at school and I was in defence. I got filthy and we lost 1–5 ... We played football. I was in rotten old defence again and we lost 3–2 ... I did country dancing instead of football. We did the Flying Scotsman, Virginia Reel (my favourite), Ocean Wave and Red River Valley.[7]

Not a future captain of the team then. No matter that I was King of the Field and Lord High Admiral of the Stream at home and spent more time up trees than on the ground, I was simply not cut

---

7. I'd love to be able to tell you more about these dances, or indeed why the Virginia Reel was my favourite, but the steps have gone from my memory. I know that a do-si-do involves going round your partner in a circle. That'll never leave me.

out for the hand/foot/eye coordination of organised sport. (And never would be, notwithstanding a brief and unexplained flirtation with boys' hockey at middle school.) Put me in a PE kit and I go to pieces. In the event of war I'm a fielder.

I was smaller than average for my age (1 metre 21 centimetres at eight according to the height chart circa Mrs Munro), but let's be honest, it was never a major problem because less cachet was attached to sporting prowess at primary school. If you could do (my favourite) the Virginia Reel you were alright. There was no such thing as a poof then. I'll bet there is today.

Unlike St Custard's, this was a co-educational school. Country dancing meant holding girls' hands. Cathy Knights's hands in my case. She was a buck-toothed girl with long brown hair whose parents must have been well off – they lived in one of the big houses on Abington Park Crescent, which was a bit like overlooking Central Park in New York. I liked her, though I refuse to countenance the notion that there was any frisson in this hand-holding.

There was no talk of girlfriends or 'going out with' just yet. A brief craze for kiss-chase, certainly, but this was hardly loaded with confused self-discovery – you ran *away* from your fate after all. Could it be that it was all so simple then? No battle of the sexes. No male shame in choosing the do-si-do over the offside trap. No undercurrent of sexual tension to hand-holding or even, in the name of playground sport, kissing. A certain amount of whispering occurred in Class 6 when a girl called Caroline came in wearing a my-first-bra – and that's a cross-your-heart to bear we boys will never fully appreciate – but again, it was the sheer novelty of the garment rather than any rum clues of physical development that aroused comment.

These were good years. Clearly not the best years of my life – they're happening now, obviously – but nothing to write home about on 'Sunda'.

* * *

In September 1975, to use Molesworthspeak, I became a new bug – at Abington Vale Middle School. Too young and shallow for sentimental farewells when I left Abington Vale Primary in July, the changeover was fairly blasé (there's no mention of leaving in my diary – I came fourth in the sack race on Friday and went on holiday to Wales on Saturday, never to return to my alma mater). 'I went back to school only it is a new middle school,' shrugs the diary entry for 1 September.

Still, educational jet lag was reduced by two things:

1) It was called Abington Vale Middle School. Where else were the pupils of Abington Vale Primary School going to go?

2) It was physically even closer to our house than primary school. Even *having a car* was no excuse to drive there.

* * *

So off we all went to 'big skool'. Because it was a good deal larger (two storeys, two blocks, mobile classrooms, science labs, tennis nets, a library and a gym), pupils came from much further afield than just Abington Vale and as a result most of my primary school crew were randomly scattered throughout different classes, now called forms. Of the old gang, only Angus (Bristol-born Richard Angerson) was in mine – so for the sake of convenience we became instant best mates, and stayed that way for the entire four years. My nickname was 'Collie'. We were Collie and Angus. Inseparable, except when forced apart by the myriad groups-within-groups that characterised middle school life.

The changes didn't appear to affect me adversely. Yet despite my own commendably laid-back attitude, middle school was a culture shock and it made me grow up a bit. For a kick-off, the place used to be a St Trinian's-style girls' school – we were only the second mixed year to be inducted, which meant that the top two years were all girls. Bear in mind these were girls aged 12 and 13, in the throes of puberty, and you'll understand how intimidating the set-up was. We kept well out of their way. They really did have hockey sticks.

But it wasn't just bigger girls replacing the bigger boys (and the fact that we now had a witch-like head*mistress*, Miss Malins), there were institutional changes too. No more sitting around in one classroom all day, idling through pirate books and breaking out the poster paints – at middle school it was timetables, periods, double periods, years, options, groups, prefects, a bell going off at regular intervals and 'break' instead of playtime (chiz). And there were so many teachers now, we had to deal with surname clashes. There was plain old Mrs Jones, the initialised Mrs D Jones and Mr Jones. However, only one Mr Leleux.

Even though it was a modern comprehensive, ghosts of the past stalked the corridors. I think they even had a head girl when we arrived, but that was phased out when someone noticed that rationing had also ended. Nevertheless, all pupils were shuffled by surname into five colour-coded 'houses', named after saints – St Francis, St Stephen, St Michael, St Luke, St Matthew. Welcome to Hogwarts! Angus and I were in St Francis and we all wore a green badge to identify ourselves. There were green sashes for prefects too, but no marching season I'm happy to report. The musty idea was to instil in us some spurious sense of artificial rivalry. St Francis could have St Stephen any time, that sort of thing. We had saints' days where you went home early, and house assemblies at the end of each term where 'credits' were added up.

I don't know if the arcane credits system is common, so here's how it worked: you were awarded credits for doing creditable things, like scoring a goal for the school team (amazingly, I was never to earn one this way), making a good puppet in art, or – the milksop academic route – by accumulating three 'goods' for written work. You secured a 'good' in your exercise book for doing a good thing like getting all the answers right in a test, while a 'very good' was the fast-track route to two goods. Because no stigma was attached to academic excellence at middle school (that would come later), I gaily ratcheted up goods, very goods and credits over the next four years, but I never came out with the highest score at the end of term. That was always some Homo Superior who was clever *and* on the school team.

My first form teacher was the bearded Mr Walman (who, amazingly, teaches at the school to this day, albeit now unbearded). 'He is very nice,' I told my diary. And although my diary masks any deep anxiety or antipathy by always looking on the bright side and saying everybody new is 'nice', Mr Walman was nice. Mr Leleux, though, was a bastard. Pronounced Lur-luur (take the piss at your peril), he was the school librarian; once a week we had a lesson with him in the library, during which we learned all about the Dewey classification system, which was about all you *could* learn in a library lesson apart from how to be quiet, and at the end we got to pick a couple of dog-eared old books which he would sign out and stamp (you could tell he loved stamping). Leleux was a fat old relic from another time who rode a black ARP warden's bike to prove it: he used to shout at us every week without fail and hit the table with a ruler and it was enough to put you off libraries and reading for ever. No sense of the wonder of books, Leleux – more interested in barking at kids like a sea cow.[8]

Like any school, the staff could be divided down the middle. There were nice teachers – Miss Parsons (PE), Mrs Hulland (maths), Mrs Hooton (cookery), Mr Edley (games; lunchtime table tennis club, which Angus and I keenly joined in term one), Miss Scott (needlework), and Mrs Dennison (English). And there were bastards who got a perverse kick out of shouting – Mr Brice (woodwork, although to be fair he only shouted if someone did something stupid with a chisel), Miss Malins (assemblies; corridors), Mr Leleux (library) and Miss Borton (also cookery: too much make-up and long fingernails). Then you had Mrs Peck (needlework) who could go either way.

Yes, needlework and cookery. Abington Vale Middle was the height of modernity. Because of its former life it boasted excellent facilities in the lady sciences: home economics and sewing. So a double period of art could mean baking a pineapple upside-down cake or running up a patchwork draught excluder on a sewing machine. Again I look back on this experience as a character-building one. It was a triumph for women's lib: girls did woodwork, while the boys learned how to thread a bobbin and flour a rolling pin.

---

8. More book disappointment: fascinated as I was by black and white horror movies, I was thrilled one week to find *Notre Dame de Paris* by Victor Hugo among the library's ancient stock – no doubt the original 1831 translation – and duly borrowed it. What a damp squib. It was really long and had no pictures of Lon Chaney in it.

In December 1976, Angus, Soardsy (Martin Soards) and I were asked by Mrs Hooton if we would like to recarpet 'the flat' in our lunch hours. The flat was a facsimile living quarters located off the cookery room, where, presumably, pupils could play mummies and daddies although it seemed chiefly to be used by the designery teachers as a mini-staff room. This was a major project which we accepted gladly (staying indoors in winter *and* there were credits in it). We pulled up the old carpet and laid brand new carpet tiles in a fancy interlocking pattern over a series of weeks – the sort of practical experience you can't buy. It was a great success and a credit windfall, except for one *faux pas*: when half the tiles were in place, we had to lay paper notices down requesting visitors not to walk on the carpet yet. In our enthusiasm, we covered these warnings with swastikas – for a joke! They upset one of the Jewish teachers and we were ticked off by Mrs Hooton. A valuable life lesson there in the first year of punk situationism and the reclaiming of symbols.

I also note from my 1976–77 diaries that Jes, Angus and I were very pleased with 'a sequence' we'd worked out in PE under the auspices of Miss Sabin (nice). We're talking about gymnastics of a distinctly homoerotic stripe here, the sort which would culminate in a *Triumph of the Will* style 'gym display' in front of the rest of the school and sometimes the parents. All told, isn't it amazing how unselfconscious we all were at this age? I was even in the choir. On 17 November 1977 – the year of the Sex Pistols' 'God Save The Queen' – I'm proud to announce in my diary that the teddy I'd made in needlework, Arthur, 'came second in the teddy contest – HOORAY!'. Far closer to Fotherington-Thomas ('hullo clouds hullo sky') than Molesworth, and yet without dishonour or a good pasting.

Middle school was a paradox, but a happy one: it had many of the traditional trappings of a St Custard's – hall monitors, form captains, homework, chess club, cross-country runs, school sausages, French, algebra, detention, rugby with Mr Bates (I was usually hooker, due to my mini size) – but none of the awkwardness, pressure and inner conflict that comes with the mid-teens, hormones and O-levels. Never mind the patina of protest in some of 1977's diary entries ('we were let out of Colditz ten minutes early'), this was play school.

During my three-year tenure, my circle of friends expanded. The old core of Griff, Eddy, Johnny Green, Paul Milner, Kim Gupta, Jes and Angus were joined by Doyan (John Lewis), Dobs (Stephen Tite), Watto (Dave Watson) and Nigel Wilson.[9] My repertoire of skills expanded too. We're moving ahead a bit here, but when I left middle school in the summer of '78, I could cook, sew, weave, saw, carpet-tile, breast-stroke, climb a rope, play table tennis, pass a rugby ball, *parlez un peu de français* and construct a *Kon-Tiki* raft out of drinking straws.[10] A renaissance child, no?

I had a fairly natural academic affinity, one which was allowed to blossom at middle school. They gave us exams at the end of each year (a quantum leap from the odd spelling test at primary school) but these did not faze me. At the end of year one, 1976, I came top of the class, with marks like 81 out of 100 for English, 85 for RE and 92 for geography. I fell to second place in 1977, but I came top again in 1978. Star pupil. Combination choirboy-cum-carpeting-genius. Credits to spare. I even put my arm around Anita Barker on the last day of term because she was crying.[11] I was king of the world! St Francis would have been so proud of me – had he not been so busy saying hullo birds hullo woodland creatures in thirteenth-century Assisi.

Sadly, life would be less simple when I was back in the jug agane. But don't skip forward to upper school just yet – there was more to life than skool. There was home time.

---

9. Nigel Wilson was a lovely chap who lived at the top of our street on Bridgewater Drive. He became briefly notorious at middle school for saying to someone in class, 'Look, I can move my trousers.' I'll leave the method to your imagination. My friend Paul Bush would always thereafter faithfully refer to him as Nigel 'I can move my trousers' Wilson.
10. A Miss Lindsay craft project. Consult the *Cambridge Biographical Dictionary*: '**Heyerdahl, Thor** (1914–2002) Anthropologist, born in Latvik, Norway. In 1947 he proved, by sailing a balsa raft (the *Kon-Tiki*) from Peru to Tuamotu I in the South Pacific, that the Peruvian Indians could have settled in Polynesia.' No mention of drinking straws.
11. And as Anita has since reminded me (thanks once again to Friends Reunited), 'I probably did cry buckets the last day of school, but that's understandable as I was moving away.' To Luton, indeed.

1974

Selected Extracts From My Diary

Another orange Disneyland diary, same model as the inaugural one. It's been cunningly designed to fit any year (you fill in the days of the week yourself). Interestingly, while 1973 was written in more sophisticated but ugly joined-up writing, I regress here to non-joined-up writing. Why? No idea. Equally, why does this diary grind to a halt after 28 June? No idea. Too busy 'country dancing' perhaps?

In the Personal Notes *at the front of the book I reveal that I am now four feet one inch tall and weigh four stone. Porker.*

Friday, 4 January
I played with Carl all day. We played pulling each other about in Carl's sleeping bag.

Saturday, 5 January
We went shopping in the morning, Simon bought a beret[1] and I bought a Subbuteo team.

Tuesday, 8 January
Dad went to London. We saw Abbott and Costello and Mum had a Young Wives meeting.[2]

Friday, 11 January
Me, Griffin and Boults all did a Basil Brush show. I was Basil Brush, Boults was Mr Roy and Griffin was the special guest.

Monday, 14 January

We stayed for sandwiches. I had two cheese sandwiches, a packet of crisps, an Ice Breaker, a wafer and some Ribena.

Sunday, 20 January

Nanny and Pappy came and I made a gondola, two penguins and a frog out of origami.[3]

Thursday, 24 January

I went to John Portwood's party.[4] He was nine. I bought him a pad, two Pop-A-Points and a rubber.

---

1. Simon, though only seven, is already taking his commitment to the armed services very seriously. He has discovered 'army surplus'. Though the pair of us were equally gung ho for Action Man, Airfix soldiers, war games, war films and military comics, there was a point at which Simon's interest outstripped mine. Pap Collins, the old soldier, sensing a kindred spirit, gave Simon his medals and two cap badges – Royal Artillery and Lancashire Fusiliers – which my brother treasured even then (and treats as holy sacraments now that Pap, like the majority of those who fought, is gone). The beret bought on this particular occasion from the old Army & Navy on the Market Square was a green one similar to the Royal Marine beret or Intelligence Corps, Simon now informs me. In 1984, by which time he was doing his basic training, I accompanied Si on a mission to London – some months before I moved there, so it was still a foreign field – to acquire *another* beret from Silverman's in Mile End. Why? Simon takes up the story: 'At the time Kangol (now a designer label I believe) used to supply the army's berets and they were cloth-banded and had too much material to them and were not as easy to shape as the leather-banded type previously supplied by Compton Webb. We weren't allowed to wear leather-banded berets in training but would be when we joined our units. So we all started buying them and getting them shaped up ready for when we passed out. Silverman's were the only surplus company who still sold the old ones.'
2. Abington Vale Young Wives was a secular social group founded by like-minded youthful female spouses in and around the estate who had no church to unite them. They met once a month to chat, drink coffee and support one another. No bra-burning took place but I expect the man-free atmosphere was heady. These were Mum's sacred evenings. When the venue was our house (they rotated), Dad would be banished upstairs with Simon and I, where male bonding would occur, in direct answer to the girl power brewing beneath us. (Young Wives was later renamed, with some dignity I thought, Wives.)
3. I had a real yen for the ancient Japanese art of paper-folding. I think Robert Harbin was 'the man' in this regard, he wrote all the instructional books, which I devoured. Got pretty good at it. I can to this day make a 'flapping bird' from memory.
4. John Portwood's entry from Friends Reunited: 'Hi everyone. I am now working as an IT Project Manager at Thorntons and eating too many chocolates each day! I am married and living near Nottingham.' Good on him. Not one of my major friends but it's always nice to know that people are alive and well.

Monday, 28 January
We stayed for sandwiches and I had two cheese sandwiches and a chunk of cheese, a packet of crisps, a Fondant Fancy, a wafer and some Ribena.

Friday, 1 February
Me, Griffin, Kim[5] and Cockle did a play called *Abbott and Costello Meet The Horror* and I saw *Perils Of Pendragon* on telly.

Monday, 11 February
At three o'clock me, Griffin, Cockle and Kim did our Abbot and Costello play to Class 3, my brother's class.

Tuesday, 12 February
We saw *Question of Sport* on telly and Henry Cooper's team won.

Monday, 25 February
In the evening Nanny had drama group and I stayed up till 9 o'clock and played cards with Pappy.

Saturday, 1 March
I made a new comic called *Crunch* and I made my own free gifts.

Monday, 3 March *Day before my birthday*
I got a glow in the dark monster, the Hunchback of Notre Dame, from Paul Cockle.

Tuesday 4 March *My birthday*
I got another late present from Cathy Knight.[6] It was a *Stop the Pigeon* puzzle book.

---

5. Another enduring pal, Kim Gupta (I'm now assuming his first name had been anglicised from something more authentically Asian). The son of a doctor, Kim's ethnic mix was otherwise irrelevant to us. The fact that he lived in a massive house on Weston Way was more important. A clever lad, it was always him or Anita Barker I jostled with for top marks at middle school.
6. Still haven't got this Knight/Knights thing sorted out, have I? She's called Williams these days. The Reverend Catherine Williams actually.

Wednesday, 5 March

Jonathan Bailey[7] bought me a late present, Dr Jekyll glow in the dark model and a tube of glue, so I made the Hunchback.

Friday, 7 March

I had a cold and a cough and I had an aspirin and now I feel better.

Monday, 10 March

On Saturday night we had a thief who stole Dad's golf clubs and now we've found out he stole Dad's chequebook and building society book.[8]

Wednesday, 12 March

We practised for the country dancing festival. My partner is Cathy Knight.

Thursday, 13 March

I got a *Phantom Of The Opera* glow model and a late present from Dad, Mouse Trap.

Monday, 17 March

Simon and I played outside on bikes till 7 o'clock because it's light at nights now. We got filthy.

Tuesday, 18 March

Griffin was away and we moved desks around and we Vimmed them.

---

7. Can't tell you a huge amount about Jonathan Bailey other than he was – we later discovered – epileptic. He surely deserves to be remembered for more than a medical condition but there you are. He had freckles.

8. Our grandparent generation lamented the loss of the days when you could leave your back door open and 'people were in and out of each other's houses'. As well they might. Dad nostalgically left the garage door up one night (and by extension the car inside it unlocked) and an interloper saw his chance. Years later I spent the summer with a girl whose family lived in Jersey, and they left the doors unlocked all the time. Now that's island mentality.

Saturday, 22 March
Me and Simon played Subbuteo but Simon was silly so he had to go to bed and I had a game with Dad.

Wednesday, 3 April
We did a dress rehearsal for our country dancing festival. My partner is Cathy Knight.

Thursday, 4 April
We played soccer and we lost. We saw *Are You Being Served* and Simon was naughty.

Friday, 5 April
We broke up from school. I played with Carl and Dad bought me a Liverpool lampshade.

Thursday, 11 April
Dean came up for the day and he bought the Chihuahua Bambi[9] up as well.

Friday, 12 April
I played with Carl nearly all day and we got our new suite because we've sold our old one.

Monday, 22 April
We started back to school and in the evening I gave the Phantom Of The Opera another coat of paint.

Wednesday, 24 April
We rehearsed the country dancing festival today. My partner is Cathy Knight.

---

9. What was it about the Ward family and these miniature Mexican dogs? Janice had one – Bambi (who were they trying to kid with this allusion to Disney cuteness?) – and Mum's brother Brian and his wife Janis (note distinct spelling) had a *set*: Pip and Perry. At least those two were of the hairy school; the bald Bambi was often disparagingly referred to as 'the rat' (especially by Nan Mabel). There really is a sense of the Chihuahua not being a *proper* dog. Aren't they called toys in competition?

Sunday, 28 April

Dad found his old *Dr No* book and I have started reading it and it is ever so good.

Tuesday, 30 April

In the evening Dad made Simon real orange juice and me banana flip.[10]

Wednesday, 1 May

We did our May Day festival and Mum came to watch and I was in two dances and my partner was Cathy.

Thursday, 2 May

We played rounders because the football season is over and we don't play football any more.

Sunday, 5 May

Tonight Mum let us see the last part of *The Brothers*[11] and we wished we had seen the other episodes.

Tuesday, 14 May

Davvy[12] brought his Frankenstein glow model to school and it looks brilliant.

Wednesday, 15 May

Miss Rowan took us for art and me and Griffin are doing a sawdust mosaic of a log camp. And me and Griffin joined the choir.

---

10. They must have invested in an electric blender by this stage, hip young trendsetters that they were, as I believe a 'banana flip' was milk jooshed up with a banana.
11. Grown-up BBC melodrama about Midlands-based haulage firm Hammond Transport Services, it ran from 1972 to 1976, so we were coming in late here. No idea what appealed to me, aged nine, about *The Brothers*.
12. Paul Daverson. I have a feeling he resurfaced years later as a bona fide town-centre punk.

Wednesday, 22 May

We went to choir and learned a new song, 'Maytime' and we like it very much.

Wednesday, 5 June

I did another three pages in my maths book. I am now on page 50 and it is simple.

Monday, 10 June

Paul Cockle gave me Dracula glow in the dark model free. It was painted and made.

Tuesday, 11 June

I painted over Dracula in better colours and it looks much better now.

Saturday, 15 June

It was lovely and hot and I went down Carl's and we put our trunks on and played with the hose.

Monday, 17 June

I stayed for sandwiches. I had tomato sandwiches, a can of Coke, a packet of crisps and a piece of ginger cake.

Tuesday, 18 June

Today it was the area school sports where five different schools take part and I was the reserve in the sack race.

Wednesday, 26 June

At school at 6.30 we all had a Womble Disco.[13] They sold drinks, ice creams and crisps. I went with Carl.

---

13. The same as a regular disco except there were pictures of Wombles on the wall. This was not, however, my first disco. That was Christmas 1973, again at school, and even though I illiterately describe it in my diary as a 'discotec', it seems we played musical bumps – all sit down when the music stops – which I think would have pushed the boundaries at Studio 54. Or maybe not.

1975

Selected Extracts From My Diary

A rather nice National Employers' Life desk diary: red, padded and with the logo and year picked out in 'gold'. The front is filled with more guff about the firm who sent the thing out – with compliments – to my dad ('NEL provides a comprehensive life assurance service to meet all present-day needs' *etc.). What's odd is that Dad seems to have used it, putting in the odd appointment and important date: incomprehensible code like 'G. Gross – re SERP' and 'DJ Rawlings B61'. Presumably he decided not to use it and gave it to me some way into the year. I must have copied the early entries out of another diary. What dedication.*

Key change in style: I now write in capitals, as per the speech bubbles in comics, and many of the entries are illustrated with little cartoons of me and my pals.

I have also drawn a pretty good flick book of a stick man losing his head and getting a new one in the bottom corner of the diary.

Thursday, 2 January
Simon and I played Action Man and we played that my Action Man was stuck on an island (Simon's bed) and Simon's Action Man had to rescue me in his helicopter.

Saturday, 11 January
Dad bought me a scrapbook and I have made it into a horror scrapbook and I am having a page for each monster. I saw *Carry On Laughing*.

Wednesday, 15 January

We had art at school with Miss Rowan, the subject was blue and cold so me and Griffin drew and painted a picture of an igloo with two Eskimos by it.

Sunday, 26 January

Me and Simon stopped up till 8.15 to watch *Colditz*. It was brilliant because two men have escaped but me and Simon think the Germans will catch them.

Wednesday, 29 January

Nanny Mabel baby-sitted and she slept in my bed so I had to sleep in Dean's sleeping bag on the lounger by the side of Simon's bed.

Saturday, 1 February

I had *Cracker* (my second issue but really Number 4 but I missed issues 1 and 2) and the free gift was a funny face maker with 40 brilliant funny faces.

Wednesday, 5 February

Me and Simon went with Dad to the dentist and I've got to have two fillings and I've got to have them on my birthday. Dad says it is Mr Wright's present for me!!

Wednesday, 19 February

We practised *Wind In The Willows* yet again.[1] Me and Simon played an Action Man game at the barracks going on leave in the tank for two weeks and it was brill.

Tuesday, 4 March

It was my birthday and I had one filling. My party's on Sunday. I got Mum, Dad, Nan and Pap's presents. A felt tip with three refills, a dictionary, a French dictionary, two packs of felt tips and the Mummy glow in the dark model.

Saturday, 8 March

This afternoon we went shopping with my birthday money and

Griffin came in the end. I bought a brill Lego gravelworks and it has a conveyor belt and a brill crane. I've already built it up.

Sunday, 9 March

It was my party. Griffin, Ed, Johnny and Dean came and I got two drawing books, a pen wobbler, some paints, a charcoal pencil and a packet of pencils.

Thursday, 20 March

We did our play *Wind In The Willows* and I was Toad. I had ever such a lot to say and so did Eddy who was Rat. I liked it when we had the fight with the weasels.

Wednesday, 26 March

Me and Simon stayed up to see a brill film which we didn't know the name of.

---

1. I don't know what went right here: I played Toad, top billing and a delicious comic turn to boot (Eddy played Rat, David Boulter was perfectly cast as Badger and Catherine Howard was Mole). Though welcome, this was anything but characteristic of my school drama career: *Willows* was the only time I had my name above the title, as it were, despite my predisposal towards minor showing off. I didn't even get a part in the all-year primary school production of *Joseph* in 1973. I made a bid for glory at middle school by joining the drama club 1976–77 – guaranteeing at least a spear-carrying part in school plays. I had to be content with

(a) 'small boy' in *The First Patient*, a one-act comedy set in a dentist's waiting room;
(b) another small boy, that bathetic cripple Tiny Tim in *A Christmas Carol* ('God bless us every one!'); and
(c) with crushing inevitability a spear-carrier in *The Happy Man* (Angus and I played a pair of 'sentinels' who motionlessly flank the depressed king's throne throughout the play – even when Anita Barker tickles us with her feather duster – and then utter one line at the very end: 'Blimey!').

I had tried the actor-manager route, casting myself in consecutive, self-written skits, notably for the annual middle school talent contest, playing Watson in *The Puppy of the Baskervilles* in 1975 and the hapless patient in *The Dentist*, 1976, a violent, Python-influenced two-hander in which Angus donned the white coat and the laying out of my dad's tool kit before we started generated the most laughs. We came third with *Baskervilles*; *The Dentist* came nowhere. My dramatic profile improved at upper school, where I helped write and stage a sixth-form revue in 1982, and was then head-hunted to play the porter in *Macbeth*, February 1983 ('I pray you'll remember the porter').

Saturday, 17 May

Me and Simon watched a film with Eric Morecambe and Ernie Wise called *The Intelligence Men*. After that we watched *Look – Mike Yarwood!* He did Denis Healey and our favourite (Steptoe).

Monday, 26 May

I had German measles. Me and Simon stayed up till 10.00 to watch this brilliant war film called *The Longest Day* starring Richard Burton, Robert Mitchell,[2] John Wayne and Red Buttons.

Tuesday, 27 May

It was hot and me and Carl and Maria played a great game. I was in my room and I tied my Action Man to the open window and I got him wedged in the gutter and Carl threw balls to knock him out.

Thursday, 29 May

It was Simon's birthday and he got lots of presents and as a treat Dad took us to the pictures to see *The Poseidon Adventure* and *Please Sir!* They were both brilliant especially *The Poseidon Adventure*.[3]

Saturday, 31 May

Simon had his birthday party. Simon Coles, Paul Givelin, Jonathan Ashby and Dean all came. I started making a book all about *The Poseidon Adventure*. I have already drawn all the stars and written about them.

Monday, 2 June

Simon had to go to Birmingham with Dad to have an allergy test. As a treat Dad bought him (with his birthday money) a new Action Man with gripping hands[4] and an assault craft and Dad bought me the book of *The Poseidon Adventure*.

Sunday, 15 June

Me and Simon stayed up tonight and watched a horror film till 10.00. It was *The Hunchback of Notre Dame* starring Charles Laughton.[5]

Saturday, 5 July *Holiday*

We got to Anglesey to stay for a week but it was all tatty and horrible so we asked Mrs Roberts, the owner of the farmhouse where we were going in the second week and she let us stay in the bungalow and we have settled in. I have bought two comics and two holiday specials.

Thursday, 24 July

In the morning me and Simon went down to help Pappy Collins in the allotments. We picked some beans, onions, potato, beetroot and some carrots for Sooty.[6] In the afternoon I did my 320-piece jigsaw of Piccadilly Circus.

Thursday, 31 July

I came down Nanny's to sleep till Monday. I made two cars and a garage out of Lego and I played speeding them into the garage and smashing them up and seeing who got broken up completely first.

Saturday, 2 August

I watched telly all morning. After tea (two crisp sandwiches) we

---

2. Mitchum.

3. See Chapter 10.

4. Gripping hands was the second landmark Action Man improvement in our short lifetime (the first had been the unveiling of 'realistic hair', a pleasing fuzz crop that mocked the previous shiny brown noggin). These new hands were made of moulded rubber – perishable in the long term but a significant upgrade from the frozen plastic hands of yore, fixed in a rifle-bearing position, trigger finger permanently cocked. The next depressing evolution from those Palitoy boffins was 'eagle eyes' (depressing only in that no pestered parent could possibly keep up, and the fact that it just created a master race effect, with fixed-hand, fixed-eye, no-fuzz Action Man finding himself relegated to menial jobs and eventually exiled to ghettos).

5. RKO's 1939 classic, directed by William Dieterle and costing an astronomical $2 million. A treat for any boy. Except that this diary entry was written *before* we stayed up to watch what would have been my inaugural black and white horror film. The next day (in different pen), I have added the crestfallen truth: 'Well we were going to but we were scared and we saw *The Wooden Horse* (a brill escape from prison camp film).' I blew it. Chickened out of seeing Laughton in full Quasimodo make-up. Such would be my uneasy relationship with the films I was obsessed by.

6. Guinea pig. Melissa's. You start on hamsters and work your way up.

went to a pub and I had two Cokes and when we came back I watched telly till 9.00 and me and Pap played Rummy till half past.

Thursday, 7 August
Me, Simon and Dean went to the play scheme which is a place near my school and it has a big bus all painted, with a slide, and you do what you like. We went with Griff and we had great fun. We had our faces painted. I looked horrible.

Saturday, 16 August
Mum and Dad went shopping and Griff and Eddy came round and Dad bought Simon two packs of little soldiers[7] so he let me have his English and German big soldiers and Dad bought me some Australians and I have painted them.

Saturday, 23 August
In the morning we went shopping and Nan bought me a packet of Russian soldiers and we got Simon a pack of Japs.

Saturday, 1 September
I went back to school only it is a new middle school. I am in the same class as Angus and our teacher is Mr Walman and he is very nice. I sit next to Angus as well. The headmistress is Miss Malins.

Sunday, 7 September
In the morning I swapped three rubber things that go on the ends of a pencil for the Russians, Afrika Korps and the Field Marshalls in little soldiers and two rubbers with Wilson. I covered my two French books and my hymn book.

Saturday 13 September *Blackpool with Nan and Pap*
In the morning I bought Melissa a book, Mum a flower holder,

---

7. A distinction worth making clear: 'little soldiers' were HO/OO scale, and 'big soldiers' were 1/32 scale. All Airfix, and a long-term Simon-and-Andrew staple. To avoid confusion, Simon collected little soldiers and I collected big (both had their advantages: he got more in a packet, mine were easier to paint).

Simon an Action Man bed and me a Dr Who book and a half-track. We went to the Tower and we saw the animals being fed and we went to see Freddie Starr and it finished at quarter past eleven.

Friday, 19 September

We did art. I was with Miss Scott for sewing. I started sewing Mum some oven gloves and so far they're good. I watched *Dad's Army* and *The Liver Birds* and I had an ice cold Coke.[8]

Sunday, 21 September

In the afternoon Nan and Pap came round and I had a lovely tea: cheese sandwiches, pork pie and crisps and fruit cake for afters. We watched *Celebrity Squares* and *Black Beauty*. We both had an ice cold Coke.

Tuesday, 7 October

I went to the dentist. It was St Francis Day (skills) and St Francis went home 10 minutes early. We all got special badges. We had science and we are making little crystals. Our little group is me, Angus, Kim and Milner. Me and Simon saw *Oil Strike North*.

Friday, 17 October

I stayed for dinners and I actually won some marbles:[9] one off

---

8. As a registered adult junkie for ice-cold drinks, I find it quaint that such a thing was noteworthy then. But it was.

9. Marbles was the sport of kings between 1975 and 1977. I think perhaps the likes of John Lewis, Andy Virgin and Dave Watson, who joined Abington Vale Middle School from somewhere due north like Boothville or Parklands, imported the craze. But the playground at Abington Vale was tailor-made, with a modern drainage system that meant concrete channels all around the perimeter with a furrow the perfect width for marble-rolling. A tiered marble hierarchy held sway: 'gobbies' or 'gobs' were large-size marbles, which had to be struck twice by the regular kind in order to be claimed; 'habitats' or 'habbies' were opaque – also worth two of your standard glassy marble (though if you had a mutant transparent one without its regulation wisp of colour, it was a 'clear' and worth a 'habby' or a 'gobby'). Ball bearings, or 'ball bears', extremely rare, were another matter altogether. Some bright spark, probably Lewis, discovered that there were miniature ball bearings in the end of a certain type of ink cartridge and attempted to play with those, but it was risky as they actually went irretrievably down the drain. Such innocent larks. Honestly, breaktime was like a Victorian etching of boys at play.

Griff and two off Angus and two off Watson and even one off Lewis. We had cooking and we did stuffed egg salad and we cut the tomatoes up all criss-cross. I saw *Invisible Man, Liver Birds* and *PC Penrose.*

Saturday, 1 November

This evening I started making a new army comic called *Army* and I'm making loads of army stories like 'D-Day' and 'Target: Adolf Hitler'.

Tuesday, 4 November

Maths was good because we did geometry. I went to Wilson's house and we played Car Capers. I made two Arab kits for my two gripping Action Men out of two hankies[10] and I did some sums for Dad on his calculator.

Wednesday, 12 November

I gave Dad £2 and he bought me the Goodies LP and it's got 'Wild Thing' and 'Funky Gibbon' and loads more. This afternoon for art we had Mrs Peck about fabrics and it was brill. Tonight after playing the Goodies LP we saw *Carry On Spying* and it was brilliant.

Thursday, 13 November

We had basketball in the afternoon and we had millions of sweating hard races in teams – of course our team won every game. Our team was me, Roobarb, Deeksy, Jez and Marias. We saw Ken Dodd and *Get Some In!* I still like Lilley and Smith but now I like Richardson as well.

Tuesday, 2 December

Science was brilliant because we had a film about planets. Tonight me, Simon and Dad saw *Invisible Man, Are You Being Served* and *The Doll* and if I tried to figure out who murdered who my brains would go potty.

---

10. I told you we were poor. Poor but resourceful.

Wednesday, 10 December

This afternoon instead of art all the second year had a load of education films. One about trains, aeroplanes, silversmiths and, the best one, bread. Tonight we saw a fab war film *Ice Cold in Alex*.

Friday, 19 December

Last day of term. St Francis came first in the credits (skills) and this afternoon was the talent competition. Me, Griff, Angus, Lewis, Johnny and Roman did *Puppy of the Baskervilles*. We came third and got two credits each. Some teachers did a brilliant play starring Mrs Dennison, Mr Hanna, Miss Sabin and Mr Walman and Mrs Bream, it was fab.

Thursday, 25 December

My presents were: a watch, an Action Man Special Missions Pod,[11] a Humbrol paint set, *Beano* annual, microscope set, desk set, a Parker pen, Idi Amin book,[12] stapler, crayons, jigsaw, magic book, geometry set, diary, *Shiver and Shake* annual, Sketch-master, horror book, drawing book, Escape From Colditz game. Tonight we played Cluedo and I had some Cockburns port again.[13]

Friday, 26 December

This morning I played with my microscope set and we looked at some of Dad's blood and spit. This afternoon Dean came and he brought his fab Action Man HQ[14] and his machine gun and French Resistance kit. And we all watched *Disney Time* and part of *Dad's Army*. Tonight all of us played Chase The Ace and Newmarket. I won 17p in all. We went to bed at 10.00.

---

11. A modest black plastic tube containing a yellow inflatable dinghy. I am pleased to report that this item, along with most of our Action Man uniforms, boots, guns and equipment, lives on – in a box at my parents' house, where it continues to grant hours of pleasure to my nephews Ben and Jack.
12. See Chapter 13.
13. I'm not very happy about this. You can't give a baby booze! (We must assume it was no more than a nip.)
14. And there was us with our Special Missions Pod.

five

Spook and Fancy

The British Elvis.
(A 12-year-old David Bowie answers the question
'What do you want to be when you grow up?')

When I was in Mrs Munro's class, aged 7–8, she asked us what we wanted to be when we grew up. We were instructed to draw a picture of it in our jotters. No problem. I had already decided what I wanted to be and it was this: a 'cartoonist'. (I guardedly apply those inverted commas only because I think my idea of what a cartoonist actually *did* for a living was a little – shall we say – two-dimensional.)

I remember the picture I drew that day, so clearly I could reproduce it for you now – if I had a jotter.

In it, the grown-up Andrew is sitting at a table with a big pencil in his fist and a wad of paper before him and he is just *drawing cartoons. Really fast.* Pictures of identifiable figures like Top Cat and members of the Hair Bear Bunch are flying off the table and falling around me like autumn leaves.

A somewhat idealised vision of the cartoonist's lot I grant you: just draw cartoons until it's time to clock off and go home – but draw them *really fast.* Understandably for a 7–8-year-old, I had no concept of who I was drawing the cartoons *for*, or why these people would want me to just draw Hair Bear on a sheet of paper and give it to them (after I'd picked it up off the floor of course); but this was a mere formality, like benefits and share options. As far as my young mind was concerned, cartoonists produced cartoons like bakers baked bread and fishermen fished for fish. I drew cartoons like this at home and I would like to turn that into a career please.

Perhaps I knew that somewhere down the long and industrialised animation process there *were* people who simply churned out preliminary sketches with pencils in their hands, and maybe pieces of paper did fly off their desks. In any case, I wanted to be one of them when I grew up. Have felt tips – will earn a handsome living.

And so it eventually came to pass. Some twelve years after the jotter vision, having graduated from Chelsea School of Art in 1987 with a 2:1 in Graphic Design (Mum and Dad have the certificate up), I spent at least a calendar year living solely off my artistic wits, drawing cartoons for money. That's all I did. It was hairy at times but not once in that first trading year did I go overdrawn at the bank on the day of the month my mortgage payment went out (the 21st – it's etched on my mind). I drew cartoons not of the Hair Bear Bunch, but of reindeers for corporate Christmas cards (including one for Virgin Atlantic), and cartoon cyclists for a Variety Club bike ride poster, and a cartoon sheepdog to help schoolchildren learn to love the benevolent works of ICI (I had uncomplicated morals in 1988), and cartoon owls and wizards and bears to go on the cover of *Puzzled* puzzle books, the kind you buy at stations. And sometimes, yes, I drew roughs with a pencil and the paper flew off my table.

I know, career Nostradamus.

Do other kids of 7–8 know precisely what they're going to be when they grow up? Or do they just pick a random job, draw a picture of it and hope for the best? A lot of kids inevitably want to do what their dad does (or these days of course their stepdad). It's a logical if unimaginative place to start and that's why doctors beget doctors, actors form acting dynasties and circus people never seem to advertise for trainee clowns and acrobats. But my dad did something indistinct in an office! What inspiration was that to a boy who regularly blew up the guns at Navarone?

Dad was, in layman's terms, an 'insurance man', which meant so little to me as a child that I actually pretended he was a policeman once. It was in Mrs Cox's class so I must have been about 6 or 7: we had been asked to write down what job our dads did in our exercise books and draw a picture of it. Well how would *you* draw a man explaining the benefits of taking out full cover with personal liability? Paul Cockle's dad was a pig farmer: easy. Kim Gupta's dad was a doctor: finished! My dad was an insurance man. I couldn't even spell 'insurance'.

So it was that I denied my own father and drew him as a copper. There were mitigating circumstances – it was nearly home time and you had to queue up at Mrs Cox's desk for spellings and the queue was looking long and there was no way I was going to miss *Pixie & Dixie* on telly. So with little or no regard for the dishonesty and bald opportunism of my actions I wrote these words:

'My dad is a policeman.'

And drew a picture of him doing it. Easy. Finished!

My friends were really impressed. Probably thought he was a detective or something as he always wore plain clothes when he drove us to school.

It's no surprise that I didn't want to be an insurance man. It appears I didn't even want my dad to be one. And to his eternal credit, he never *once* suggested it as a desirable career path either. He never put his arm around me, looked out of the window and said, 'Son, people will always want insurance ...'

It was, however, a proud moment for him when he took me to the AA Portakabin on the way to the M1 and signed me up for membership in 1985, sagely advising me to pay the extra for Home Start (which of course I needed more than any other service when I was at Chelsea Art School in Mum's knackered old Metro). He didn't but should've said, 'You're a man now, son. Fully covered. Nothing more I can teach you.'

Dad recently retired, but he was an insurance man for the whole of his working life. Started out as an office boy and ended up a company director. It may seem dull and officey – box files and bulldog clips – but as I grew older and wiser I realised it's actually quite an existential job, insurance. It's an entire industry founded on imponderables and unthinkables; they actually sell you death, pestilence, infirmity, accident and 'acts of God' (as they are still called with a straight face). People *will* always want insurance.

Insurance men are very much like policemen in fact: much

maligned until you *need* one. Never mind Woody Allen's facetious line from *Love and Death* (which raised my hackles on Dad's behalf when I first heard it): 'There are worse things than death. If you've ever spent an evening with an insurance salesman, then you'll know what I'm talking about.'

Yeah, and when your Central Park East apartment goes on fire, who you gonna call, Woody? There's nothing wrong with insurance salesmen, or spending an evening with one, and anyway my dad wasn't a salesman, he was a 'man'.

That said, office life held no allure for me, aged 7–8. I wanted to draw Spook and Fancy off *Top Cat* and I wanted to be paid through the nose for it. Why? Because I could. I had ... a talent for it. I WAS TALENTED.

Talent. I'm uncomfortable with the word, and don't give me Mozart or McCartney. I prefer aptitude, faculty, capacity, bent ... the more prosaic definitions for 'being good at something'. Talent suggests gift, and gift suggests God given and I don't believe in God or his acts so how can I countenance him giving things out?

I could draw though. In fact I could draw like a boy possessed. From an early age if you put a pen in my hand I could make a recognisable shape with it on paper. I quickly graduated to copying – in itself quite a skill, but little more – and pretty soon there wasn't a character in *TV Comic* or *Yogi and His Toy* that I couldn't reproduce by hand: Mighty Moth, Deputy Dawg, Texan Ted ('Big hat, big head'), not just Spook and Fancy but every member of Top Cat and his gang.

Then I moved up to reproducing the casts of *Wacky Races*, *The Hair Bear Bunch*, *Josie and the Pussycats*, the family out of the Giles annuals (which Uncle Pete kept for me) and anyone and everyone from my regular comics: *Beano*, *Buster*, *Knockout*, *Whizzer and Chips*, *Shiver and Shake*, *Beezer*, *Whoopee!*, *Monster Fun*, *Cracker*, *Krazy* and its memorable spin-off *Cheeky Weekly*. Devouring these – and the inimitable style therein of artists like Leo Baxendale, Robert Nixon, Tom Patterson and Frank McDiarmid, whose signatures I would soon be seeking out like favourite brands – I was able to create my own hybrid characters, and eventually my own comic strips and entire comics. My comics were called things like *Bingo!*, *Ace!* and

Smasher'n'Gloop.[1] I sold one of my earliest self-made comics in Class 3 to Jonathan Bailey for 2p and Richard Goodhall told me I could be arrested because I didn't have a licence and I believed him. I'm sure I could've squared it with my dad, the policeman.

Drawing was my middle name. All I ever got for birthday presents were felt-tips and pads and crayons and colouring books and paints and Pop-a-Point pencils. In my early days I drew a lot of clowns because I was scared of them, and later I drew characters from old black and white horror movies because I was scared of them too – as in, too scared to watch the films when they came on TV but not too scared to fill my room with Aurora glow-in-the-dark models of the Hunchback of Notre Dame, Frankenstein's Monster and the Phantom of the Opera. (There I go again, controlling my fear by getting it down.)

Relatives would *ooh* and *aah* at my drawings. 'Isn't he good at drawing?' they would coo. 'I'm going to be a cartoonist when I grow up,' I would say, and they probably thought to themselves, 'Dream on.' So I did.

I only ever sent one letter to *Jim'll Fix It.* It was in 1976. I asked Jim – or Jim'll as we called him – to fix it for me to meet my hero, the aforementioned *Daily Express* cartoonist Giles, so I could show him how good *I* was at cartoons. I even drew some Giles characters on my letter and used coloured pens on the envelope as if no Jim wannabe had ever thought of that before. It was all for naught; I never got a sniff. But then neither did Simon and he'd asked Jim'll to fix it for him to visit the Action Man factory, which ought to

---

1. All these comic still exist. They're howlingly derivative but the effort I put into constantly starting new ones is impressive (even if it's rare I actually completed one). Here is a definitive catalogue of my childhood, home-made comics with a selection of story titles for flavour: *Smash* (Crazy Cars, Stan the Modelling Man, Puffer); *Spook* ('the scariest comic you've seen'); *Horror* (Hunchback, Squelch, Witchy); *Scare*; *Bingo* (earliest incarnation: Dad's Army, Pet Pete, Fred); *Smasher'n'Gloop* (Barmy Army; Griffin's Gang, From Dr Pecker to Mr Slide; Spiddo – 'he loves paper to eat'); *Bingo* (second incarnation: Potty Pop Groups, Scotso, Raver Rabbit and Hippie Potamus, The Tomato Squirter, Apple – 'Hi! I'm as big as a person'); *Bingo* (third version: Superbloke, The Land That Time's Forgotten About, Freak Fever), *Target* (Action Man, Walter Margin, Teef, Bionic Reg), *Ace!* (Evil McWeevil, Closed University, Stupidstars); *The Kidz*; *Ferret's Own*; *Smashed Hits* (more of a parody than a comic).

have been right up the programme's street with their appetite for subliminal advertising. (It might have been just the piece of cross-promotion to save Palitoy from the storm cloud of post-Vietnam pacifism, but alas, no.)

Anyway, you get the picture. I was a child prodigy and it was Jim'll's loss if he couldn't see it from my letter. I took Mum and Dad's arts patronage for granted of course, as kids are wont to do. My parents never tried to stop me drawing. They never discouraged me from thinking of it as a career option – even when school started *talking about* career options, the point at which less empowering parents might have developed cold feet.

One parents' evening at middle school they brought up the subject of my artistic bent and I don't know exactly what was said, but the upshot was, I was allowed to go into Mrs Andrews's art class at lunchtimes to do 'extra art'. A bit like overtime really. (Angus came with me – he was shit at art, but we were buddies and it felt like a privilege to be indoors when you had to go outdoors.)

In 1977, when I was twelve, Mum and Dad entered me for special Saturday morning art classes at Nene College, the local 'tech' which is these days a university because they've got a photocopier *and* a kettle. Sixty kids took the entrance exam, including Angus, which involved drawing 'a load of old junk' (hey! art school!), and doing some painting. I passed. Angus, who was very much along for the ride, did not. Thus, alone, I entered a brave new world of advanced art, taught in echoey old rooms by people who chain-smoked and weren't Mrs Andrews. We did tone and shade and colour exercises and everything.[2]

Why didn't I just put the beret on and be done with it?

I did appreciate the fact that my parents allowed me to explore my inner self through cartoons and colour exercises, but not fully until years later. As I've said, you see, they thought I had talent; a

---

2. The Saturday morning art classes, which were free, ran until March 1980 when they fell victim to education cuts. I made some good friends there, notably Neil Stuart and David Freak (real name, although I think he played up to it with his long, Phil Oakeyesque hair and uncompromising musical tastes), who in turn introduced me to the delights of the film society run up at Northampton College of Further Education (see diary 1980). The mind was forever broadened.

gift handed down to me from God with a big ribbon around it like a packet of Pop-a-Point pencils. And yet – geneticists will be ahead of me here – my dad could also draw a bit. Maybe I got it from him, along with the thick, dark, Italianate hair, inner calm and the over-enthusiastic eyebrows.

My dad could draw as a kid, but he'd never pursued it – too busy prioritising by playing football and cricket and, on the strike of his 16th birthday, *earning a living*. His ability withered away like an unwatered plant. And *here's* where I join the talent lobby: it seems self-evident to me that nurture counts for far more than nature. The genetic *potential* to draw Officer Dibble might be there, but if you ignore it and go and do something less boring instead, it will shrivel on the vine. If I'd been discouraged from making endless comics called *Smasher'n'Gloop*, or starved of all that praise, I might never have progressed any further than copying Beetle Bailey. My immense artistic genius needed cultivating just like Picasso's and Turner's and Giles's.

If you don't believe me, here is a cautionary tale.

After leaving college in 1987 I fell in with a group of medical students through a mutual friend. It was clearly my way of subliminally putting off 'leaving' higher education. Why acclimatise to civilian life, I figured, when you can just attach yourself to someone else's college and carry on drinking subsidised Fosters and going to house parties like nothing has happened? For most of my first year out of Chelsea, the one where I drew cartoons for money, I was a surrogate of St George's Medical School in Tooting. I spent my evenings at a hospital through choice. I even joined an amateur theatre group which rehearsed and staged plays there.[3]

As a general rule, I found that medical students, while admirably up for it (boozing, staying out, eating takeaway food)

---

3. Leading light among whom was Matthew Hall, later the household name Harry Hill. Matt – as I still know him – seemed to write all the productions on his old manual typewriter, and most of the annual revue, but always graciously stepped back from the juiciest parts. Under his auspices, we renamed the group Renaissance Comedy Associates and took a comic play to the Edinburgh Fringe in 1989, *President Kennedy's Big Night Out* (which Matt and I wrote together). *The Times* listed it ('silliness and bizarre logic make for an entertaining spoof') though the *Scotsman* spoke of a 'general malaise'.

were 'of a type'. Mostly sons and daughters of doctors (more hereditary careers), they all seemed to have been to public school, and for all I knew the very same one. Quite unlike the middle-class bohemians I'd mixed with at art school, they displayed a super-human, boorish self-confidence and behaved as if the world owed them a living. The girls seemed like they would throw a tantrum at any moment, and the boys were always minutes away from drinking a pint of their own vomit for a bet. Lots of Jeremys and Fionas.

The theatre group, however, tended to attract the aesthetes. Nigel Tunstall was not a natural-born doctor. He was a film buff, like me, a reader of novels, like me, and a wannabe writer, like me. We clicked instantly. We took over the St George's Film Club and ran Mickey Rourke double bills for our own pleasure; we travelled to Hampstead's Everyman cinema to watch *Slamdance* and *Gardens of Stone* and anything by Peter Greenaway; and when I started my first fanzine, Nigel agonised over a Brian De Palma think-piece for weeks on end, as if he had been commissioned by *Cahiers du Cinema*. We also clicked because he'd not been to public school and his dad wasn't a doctor.

One weekend Nigel and I visited his parents in Bournemouth and it turned out to be a revelatory experience. At one stage during our stay, his dad, who worked for the Post Office, insisted on getting out Nigel's drawings from when he was a kid, for my benefit. I hadn't been aware that Nigel *did* any drawings when he was a kid, but here they were, kept – just like mine – for parental posterity in a suitcase. While Mr Tunstall looked on proudly we sifted through them. They were brilliant; the work of a real child prodigy. Not copied or derivative cartoons like mine but beautiful, detailed sketches, many of them drawn from life (as opposed to *Yogi and His Toy*) or simply from Nigel's young imagination. I was knocked out.

But Mr Tunstall's pride was tinged I felt with sadness. We may as well have been admiring the work of a child who'd died. Nigel's natural ability had been curtailed by his parents. His talent was cut off by the early decision – theirs – for him to go into medicine. He hadn't even been allowed to take art at O-level (well, what's the point, and you need all the sciences). The drawing simply stopped, and Nigel was pushed down the academic route.

Just like my dad and many of that immediate post-war generation, Mr Tunstall had been denied the opportunity to go to university and he regretted it. But it seemed to me that he was taking out
what he wrongly saw as his own failure on his only son by forcing
him to pursue a respectable academic career when he could have
done something creative.

It struck me then how lucky I had been.

You can't blame parents for fucking up their kids. They may not
mean to but they do. Perhaps that's why I'm intent on not having
any. I mean, what if I pushed my son into the arts when he really
wanted to be an insurance man?

* * *

The great Italian filmmaker Bernardo Bertolucci told me that he
used to be shy. He told me this when I interviewed him for the
radio, by the way – he wasn't round my house for a cup of tea and
a natter. Anyway, as a shy young man in Rome, when he went out
on the town with his mates, he would stand with his back to the wall
clutching a glass of Scotch while everyone else danced. Many years
later, his analyst told him that he wasn't shy at all: on the contrary,
by separating himself from the group the young Bertolucci was
drawing attention to himself. He was in fact an exhibitionist!

Well, that's Freud for you. Everything means the opposite. If
you dream about a cat, it represents a dog. But it made me think
about my own shyness as a child. I was a reluctant show-off, better
at blending in than standing out, especially in 'rotten old defence'
at football. But was I secretly attracting attention to myself, or is
Bertolucci's shrink trying it on? Pre-school I used to cry or hide if
anyone I didn't know came to the house – no chance of me taking
sweets off a stranger; I required ID first – and I would never go to
the shops by myself, not even the little newsagent at the top of Nan
Mabel's street. Perhaps I was seeking attention, not avoiding it.

Drawing pictures, especially cartoons, may seem like a quiet,
introverted, solitary thing to do, but you always draw a crowd. I
may not have been a born leader of men at school but I always had
cartoons up my sleeve if I wanted to grab the limelight by illustrating a carol sheet or making a poster. Richard Griffin and I drew

cartoons for 2p each at a primary school fete, surrounded on all sides by a constant stream of admirers – and paying customers (we raised £1.30 for the school according to my diary, which is well over 60 cartoons between us).

At middle school when exams became the only true yardstick of performance, as I've mentioned I found myself top of the class twice, in 1976 and 1978. But the latter was a Pyrrhic victory: it was a fix. One of the exam marks that led to me beating off stiff competition from Anita and Kim was for Classical Studies, a somewhat rarefied subject taught by our form teacher Mrs Dennison. It was Greek mythology, basically, Zeus and Poseidon and all that – a fiction subject, like RE. But because this was only middle school and these were not *proper* exams, you were awarded marks for illustrating the fiction subjects. This was actually very unfair on those to whom drawing did not come naturally, but there it is.

I drew some very fetching pictures for my Classical Studies exam that year. But here's the rub: I also got part of a question about Narcissus *wrong*. And yet my final mark for Classical Studies came back as 100 out of 100. A perfect paper.

I had unwittingly compensated for my lack of knowledge (or basic recall) with decoration, and they'd let me get away with it! What kind of example is that? You blew the Narcissus story but you drew a really funny cartoon of him gazing at his reflection in the water so we'll turn a blind eye.

I knew, and they knew, that it was a miscarriage of justice. But it taught me an important lesson about sleight of hand (and the corruption of the system). This drawing lark could get me places when I grew up, I thought. If not quite on to *Jim'll Fix It*.

six

Has It Got an Aspirin in It?

I got chills, they're multiplyin'
John Travolta, 'You're The One That I Want' (1978)

How I wish I'd been David Bowie. As a teenager he was punched in the eye at school by a kid wearing a large ring, and ended up in the London Eye Hospital. Undergoing a number of tricky operations on the sphincter muscles in his eye, he spent the next eight months laid up. During this period of enforced bed-rest he underwent a Damascene conversion. First of all, he improved his mind, reading American and European literature, and filling his head with music and the arts. But more crucially Bowie made the decision to reinvent himself. 'I felt very, very puny as a human. I thought, "Fuck that, I want to be a Superman."'[1] The injury also made his eye go funny-lookin', a future visual trademark in his career as a pop alien.

What have I got to match that? The occasional chill.

By far the most significant ailment of my childhood was a chill. This meant no swimming at Kingsthorpe on a Saturday or, if I was

---

1. *Rolling Stone* magazine, 12 February 1976. Bowie also said, 'I took a look at my thoughts, my appearance, my expressions, my idiosyncrasies and didn't like them. So I stripped myself down, chucked things out and replaced them with a completely new personality.'

lucky enough to get one in the week, a day off school. Barely enough time to read the Scoop catalogue, let along undergo a Damascene conversion.

I'd love to tell you I was a sickly, asthmatic child like, say, Martin Scorsese, and that it shaped me in later life, as it did him. ('He was so allergic to animals he was taking his life in his hands if he petted a dog,' wrote Peter Biskind of the young Scorcese.) But I was neither sickly nor asthmatic. Malady, bed-rest and hospital charts did not define me like some of my most admired artists – Dennis Potter had psoriasis; Ian Dury, polio; Frank McCourt, tuberculosis; Peter Fonda, a suspected tapeworm; David Bowie, his gammy eye. Christ, even Des O'Connor had rickets. No, I'm afraid my childhood was untroubled by dramatic injury or life-threatening illness. I was fine, thanks.

I don't mean to sound ungrateful. A chill was better than no complaint at all. At least it had something of the exotic about it, like frostbite or trench foot. We were much more likely to get a chill than, say, a common cold. Common? Ha! Not in our house. Mum was obsessed with chills, the getting of them and the dealing with them; chills were her life. If any of us felt the slightest bit 'off' – as she called it – a diagnostic hand would be applied to our foreheads and she would tell us we had a chill. I was never sure if you caught one, or just developed one.

Check out this definitive diary entry for 20 July 1976, while we were on holiday in Wales:

We went to Llanbedrog for the day. I felt a bit off. Mum says I have a chill.

For years afterwards I assumed Mum had made the whole thing up. A bit like her signature diagnosis of a sore arm or leg: 'You probably slept on it funny.' I have never met anyone in my life who ever had a chill, unless from eating ice cream too fast or seeing a ghost. And I doubt John Travolta really had one in *Grease* – I mean, he would never have been allowed to go to that fair would he? Which is why I was so thrilled when I recently found the following definition in no less than the Royal Society of Medicine's *Health Encyclopaedia*:

CHILL A sudden short fever causing shivering (rigor) and a feeling of coldness. This may be caused by any acute infection, not necessarily of the respiratory tract.

I'm in the book. There *is* such a thing as a chill, and it's 'sudden', 'short' and 'acute', which explains why it was only ever worth one day off. Always trust your mum. After all, might it *not* be because you slept on it funny?[2]

Chills had their bad side too, no matter how short and sudden they were. You felt feverish and cold for a start, and there was all that rigor – and worse, you were in for a soluble aspirin, sometimes two. Like all good parents, Mum and Dad had proprietary medicines and creams for all ills stashed away: Junior Disprin, Vicks VapoRub, Betnovate, Savlon, Bonjela, Mu-cron, Dramamine and – eek! – Joy Rides. (More on those evil little pink bastards anon.)

On 28 March 1974, according to my diary,

I had a stuffed up nose and Mum gave me a Karvol capsule and some Vick.

I'm a card-carrying sceptic when it comes to the wonders of conventional medicine today, but I have a devout belief in the placebo effect and mind over matter, so if the very act of Mum administering (or threatening) potions and pills made us feel better, all power to her. Here's a diary entry, also from 1974, which makes a good case for psychosomatic treatment:

I had a cold and a cough and I had an aspirin and now I feel better.

I bet. I was probably fooling myself so I wouldn't have to take any more aspirins. The very thought of one, bitterly fizzing in the bottom of a glass, makes me nauseous even now.

Mum and Dad would secretly dissolve one in a hot drink of

---

2. During my immediate post-college years I did indeed once wake up with a 'dead arm'. It took the best part of a day to return to normal. I had slept on it funny.

squash and tell us it was just a hot drink of squash. While you had to admire their optimism, they had overlooked the two giveaway signals that it was *not just squash*. One, they would stand over us while we drank it, which they never did with a non-medicinal drink. And two, it tasted of soluble aspirin.

'There you go, a nice hot drink of orange. It'll make you feel better.'

'Has it got an aspirin in it?'

'No.'

Takes sip. Gags. 'It tastes of aspirin.'

'Don't be silly. Now drink it all up.'

'It's got an aspirin in it.'

'Of course it hasn't.'

Takes second sip. Gags again. 'I've had enough now.'

'You have to drink it all, Andrew.'

'But there's bits in the bottom.'

'They're bits of orange. Come on. It'll do you good.'

'But if it's just an aspirin-free hot drink of squash, why will it do me good? Squash is full of sugar, additives and artificial colourings that will make me hyperactive and turn my skin yellow, especially in the Seventies, and hot water is no better for me *per se* than cold water. I detect subterfuge. If it's just orange, I challenge *you* to drink it!' (I never said that, of course – too busy gagging.)

They tried undercover aspirin, otherwise known as Lemsip, but that was no better, despite the so-called *lem*.

* * *

Don't imagine we were poorly all the time, by the way. Ours was a pretty healthy household, despite all the chips and fizzy drink we kids consumed (*and* all the stagnant water we played in). I was hardy, full of energy and seemingly unbreakable. Never snapped a bone or knocked myself out, spent not a single night in hospital. I simply had a chill every now and again but this *was* the Seventies, the decade when oil kept running out. It was chilly.

I was, as they say, a slave to mouth ulcers. Had them so often they became the norm. A lot to do with the fact that I chewed my tongue as a kid – and ate all that sweet, acidic food – and not especially newsworthy (although Dr Randall did once tell me I had 'a devil of an ulcer').

I picked up all the once-only viral diseases on cue: measles, mumps, rubella (aka German measles) – although my body cruelly saved up chickenpox until I was 19 and really terribly vain. It was like collecting football stickers round our way: 'Mumps – got it; measles – got it; rubella – haven't ...' You could swap them as well. 'I'll give you swollen neck glands if you give me spots and a fever.'

I don't recall being laid low or even inconvenienced by illness. It was just a fact of life: miss a bit of school, get better, go back to school, pick up where you left off. On Monday 26 May 1975, my diary reads, matter-of-factly:

> I had German measles. Me and Simon stayed up till 10.00 to watch this brilliant war film called *The Longest Day*.

I didn't even go to bed early. The day before I'd been gambolling around Salcey Forest and by Wednesday I was playing croquet in Carl Merrick's back garden. Encephalitis? Bring it on.

Simon worked a bit harder. He managed to generate extra-curricular medical concern on two fronts. One, by being allergic to dogs, which took a battery of tests involving multiple needles in far-off Birmingham to establish; and two, by getting nosebleeds all the time. I don't just mean getting one when accidentally hit in the face with a football; he could virtually bleed from the nose at will, like a haemoglobin stopcock. If he so much as stubbed his toe or got excited, blood would start pouring from his nostrils. All my life I've known the correct way to get bloodstains out of white hankies – there was always one soaking in cold water in the sink in our house, turning the water red the way Coco Pops turn the milk brown. Such gore was commonplace. He was always being 'nipped down to casualty' to have his nose bunged up.

Eventually it got so bad Simon had to go into hospital overnight to have his nose sewn up. Cauterised, they called it, which I thought meant cutting it up into quarters, although there was no evidence of that when we went to fetch him home from Northampton General and give him whatever big Action Man present his incapacity had earned him. Simon was now officially a man; walking wounded.

I couldn't match that, although I did end up with stitches twice. The first time, when I was about three, I tripped over my toys – you couldn't see the floor of the living room for scattered plastic bricks, train track and bendy Topo Gigios. Thinking on my feet, or off them, I broke my own fall using my forehead on the corner of a wall. I don't remember it hurting much, but I do remember the colour draining out of Mum's face like a Tom & Jerry cartoon when I went into the kitchen and asked, 'Is it bleeding?' Put it this way, she didn't bother checking to see if I had a chill.

A bath towel was quickly applied to my split head – which *was* bleeding – and, it being a weekday, Geoff Edwards from next door drove me to casualty.[3] (What was Geoff doing at home in the middle of the day? Weren't there pubs that needed refurbishing?) Two stitches; it was all over very quickly and I wasn't old enough to be vain about – or proud of – the scar caused by the NHS needlework. You can still see it. Just there, above my right eyebrow. You have to look closely. I'm pretty certain I received a toy when I had the stitches out – as if a surfeit of toys hadn't been my downfall. No irony in the Seventies.

A few years later I was messing about in the living room with Simon, wearing paper party hats, and mine slipped down over my eyes. Temporarily blinded I tripped, fell, bounced off the settee and pretty much popped my cheek on the sharp wooden corner of what was then called a music centre. It only needed one stitch (this time Chris Cater from over the road drove me to casualty) but once it had healed, the hole in my face formed a perfect dimple and, once again, it's still with me. I may not be emotionally

---

3. When the family spoke of it, this day was rather luridly described as the one when I 'cracked my head open'. On another occasion, I was indulging in the frowned-upon habit of tipping on my chair while sat at the dining table, drawing. You, like my parents, can see this coming: I tipped too far and went crashing through the French windows. The miracle of it was, I walked away without a single cut, despite all the broken glass Mum had to pick out of my hair. Little stunt man.

scarred but my face tells eight million stories. Alright, two, and now you've heard both of them.[4]

I feel deprived that I never, say, broke my arm. Eddy did, and Paul Gregor, and countless others at school. What a crowd-puller that is. David Boulter broke his leg; so did Sarah who lived over the road. Someone was always in plaster, getting it signed. Not me. The day after my second stitch, people thought I had chocolate on my cheek and kept helpfully pointing it out. I'm sure the same happened to Action Man when he acquired his trademark cheek scar after – one assumes – hand-to-hand combat with a German.

'You've got chocolate on your face.'

'It's a scar actually. You should see the other guy.'

* * *

Other guys had battle scars; I got a dimple. I often fell off high things – some sacks of pig pellets stacked at Paul Cockle's farm, for instance – and I regularly nicked myself with darts and model knives, but nothing major, no war stories. I am like the outdone Chief Brody in that famous scene below deck in *Jaws*, except his appendix scar beats my dimple hands down. Until I started hanging round with medical students in the late Eighties, I only visited hospitals during visiting hours.

I recently sprained my left knee, aged 36. Don't scoff, it was majorly debilitating: I developed a proper, foot-dragging limp and I was buying Tubigrip and Ibuleve gel and everything – sympathy and admiration at last! However, instead of being able to say it was a foot-balling injury or something sexy I had sustained at the gym, I had in fact pulled my knee shopping. Specifically, while striding purpose-fully to Borders. That's the story of my life: an insult to injury.

So, no rickets, no fractures, no outpatients. If, however, child-hood visits to the dentist were a badge of honour, I was well deco-rated. Records show that I'd had five teeth extracted at the

---

4. Actually, I stuck a dart in my finger in 1976, although it didn't require hospital treat-ment. Having tired of regular games of darts out in the garage we took to pinning pictures on the dartboard – to make it more interesting. I was fixing one up with some spare darts and missed. Went straight in to my finger where nail meets flesh.

dentist's by the tender age of eight. (Is that a lot? It sounds a lot.) I had my first filling on my tenth birthday – Dad joked that it was my present from Mr Wright, our family dentist. How I laughed. Mr Wright, incidentally, had crooked teeth. So, coincidentally, did Mr Eagland, my orthodontist. Physicians, heal thyselves.

Yes, orthodontist. Be impressed. Here's where we get to *my* equivalent of going to Birmingham for allergy tests – I had additional dentist's appointments. Twice as many as the other kids. Not only were there regular check-ups, fillings and extractions with Mr Wright, Dad also took me to a *second* dentist – a specialist – because my teeth were crooked. I never had to stay in overnight obviously, but I did have to put up with extra pain and discomfort and, well, I guess it made a man of me.

Visits to Mr Eagland – whose surgery was actually situated opposite Northampton General Hospital as if to tantalise me – usually involved having impressions taken of my offending teeth (never had *those* at the regular dentist's) and undergoing a whole atrocity exhibition of mouth X-rays. Not quite open-heart surgery but impressive nonetheless (after all, everybody leaves the room while you get X-rayed). Impressions meant having a cold metal U-shaped mould filled with rubber-tasting dental Polyfilla rammed on to my teeth and left there while it hardened like cavity wall insulation foam. Then it was levered off, with Eagland's foot hard against my chest. The biggest threat to my health was from gagging to death: don't swallow, the grinning Eagland would tell me. I wouldn't grin quite so readily if I had teeth as crooked as his. (Actually, I did have teeth as crooked as his.)

The upshot of all these extra-curricular dental visits was a brace. How very American of me. Fortunately it wasn't a brace that was spot-welded to the teeth on the outside like some first-grader at junior high, but one designed to push my wonky incisors out from behind. In other words, you couldn't actually see my brace – all the work went on backstage. Well, you *could* see it, if you caught me rinsing the Golden Wonder residue out of it in the sink at school, but I didn't exactly wave it around. Unlike a plaster cast or a bandage or even an inhaler, a brace was never cool. I'm not sure how I managed it but I once rather humiliatingly got my brace snagged on someone else's school jumper and out it came, attached to this other kid like a pair of hungry false teeth. *He* saw it.

I wore my brace from the age of 11 till just before I turned 16, at which point Mr Eagland felt I was old enough to decide for myself whether or not I wished to continue with my orthodontic treatment. My decision was predictable.

It was like being allowed to vote or see an 'AA' film for the first time: I had made an important, unilateral decision about my own health. No more mouthfill for me. The brace was consigned to some medical incinerator, and my souvenir plaster teeth were stowed in a box of junk in my bedroom, occasionally whipped out to impress girls with. (They were a big hit, as you can imagine.) Perhaps I should have persevered with the brace. My teeth set to work as soon as it was obvious that the wire and plastic contraption would visit them no more – after four years of pressure they were free again to grow in whichever direction they felt like. And they did, like the little Union Jack arrows at the start of *Dad's Army.*

I've always liked the Pam Ayres poem 'Oh, I Wish I'd Looked After Me Teeth' (I was a huge Pam Ayres fan in the mid-Seventies):

I wish I'd been that much more willin'
When I had more tooth there than fillin'
To pass up gobstoppers,
From respect to me choppers
And to buy something else with me shillin'[5]

Pity I didn't appreciate Pam's message at the time. As I write I still have a full head of teeth, but they're not much to look at. (I hated David Bowie and Martin Amis for getting theirs expensively fixed in America – two crooked-toothed role models lost in the space of a couple of years. Traitors.) Perhaps if I'd eaten less Fruit Salads

---

5. My heart is warmed by the fact that Pam Ayres is still going. A complete anthology of her comic verse, *The Works*, reprinted to celebrate her 25 years in showbiz, is available from BBC Books. 'Oh, I Wish I'd Looked After Me Teeth' dates back to 1974.

and more fruit salad, and stuck with Mr Eagland's treatment I'd be a TV presenter by now.

* * *

I had an ingrown toenail in 1979. I know, we're clutching at straws now in the search for some romantic medical trauma, but for a kid who never tasted hospital food this was the closest I came to the electronic board game Operation. Although the chiropodist only used a local anaesthetic and it was all over in a matter of half an hour, having the offending shard of nail cut out of my big toe did involve Dr Costain and his nurse wearing surgical masks and gloves. I was too old for a toy afterwards, but I *was* very brave and I did feel faint back home when the anaesthetic wore off.

Remember how exciting Operation looked in the TV ads? For a start it took batteries, which knocked Cluedo into a cocked hat. Sam the patient's nose flashed red if you touched the sides while removing his 'funny bone' with the metal tweezers – and it buzzed, which I think was supposed to be Sam screaming! And the look of horror on the actress playing Mum's face when she heard one of the child actors say, 'Now it's my turn to operate!'

'Operate?!?'

We never had Operation. Not because we were deprived, it was just the way the numbers fell in the birthday and Christmas present lottery – after all, you couldn't have *everything* in the Kays mail-order catalogue. (Well, you could if you were cousin Dean, but he didn't have any brothers and sisters, as we were constantly reminded.) For the record, of the heavily TV-advertised board games, neither did we have Buck-A-Roo, Ker-Plunk, Game of Life, Battlin' Tops or Crossfire, and by the time I got Haunted House second-hand from Carl Merrick – he was, significantly, bored with it – the cardboard dividers were all bent. We had Mouse Trap, after much parental pestering – indeed, I solemnly *promised* Dad that I would *never* get bored with it. Well, it looked so complex and wondrous in the TV ads. And to be fair to MB Games, I didn't get bored with it for ages. The day I took it out into the back garden at Nan Mabel's and filled the tub into which the diver plunges with *real* water – to make it more exciting – was the day I had officially got bored with Mouse Trap.

I dare say I would've got bored with Operation a lot quicker. Once you'd made it flash and buzz a few times, and successfully removed the tap from Sam's patella (water on the knee), it was all over bar the shouting.

My ingrown toenail was removed skilfully and without anything flashing or buzzing in about the time it would've taken me to tire of the board game. I was given the nail as a souvenir (more medical detritus wrapped up and taken home like cake after a party) and I kept it for a while, but I don't think I ever showed it to anyone to impress them. I had been under the knife, albeit one morning during the school holidays, and it felt a bit like a rite of passage.

I am still a hospital virgin. I have only ever accompanied other people to casualty since my second stitch twenty-odd years ago and I have never weed in a bedpan. The longest I've ever been laid up was in my early thirties when my fatigued body made me have two weeks off work with a mysterious 'flu'. I didn't read any American and European literature but I did make an important decision: work less hard. After all, being ill is rubbish.

I spent all of my formative years running on whatever naturally occurring kiddy fuel keeps you mobile and boundless even when you eat no greens and drink only thick squash.

I admit, I wish I'd looked after me teeth, but I wasn't 'very, very puny' like David Bowie, I *was* a Superman. Alright, a Superman with a chill and a devil of an ulcer.

1976

Selected Extracts From My Diary

A blue diary from the publisher Collins, which I'm sure gave me a huge amount of satisfaction at the time. I have customised it by simply applying a single football sticker to the cover – upside down to prove what a trainee Dadaist I am, aged eleven. The sticker bears the squinting face of JOHN HOLLINS *of Queen's Park Rangers. Another little joke (my dad's name being* JOHN COLLINS*). Hey, we had to make our own entertainment in 1976.*

Very little graffiti on the inside covers, though this diary was a major shift forward, artistically. We move up to two days per page: much more space to fill – or feel guilty for not filling – and a spare half page every week called NOTES*, utilised variously: a plan view of Action Man's fictional barracks (Holston Barracks); a list of my favourite Peanuts characters (from the top, Charlie Brown, Linus, Sally, Lucy, Freda, Schroeder, Snoopy, Woodstock …); a catalogue of my jokes and tricks (snappy gum, mouse matchbox, nail thru' finger, etc.); and marginally improved little cartoons to illustrate the text, such as, 26 April: a big rock falling in the stream and soaking Simon while we were dam-building.*

And it's back to joined-up writing with OCCASIONAL CAPITALS *for emphasis.*

Thursday, 1 January

Dean slept last night and this morning we watched television. This afternoon me and Simon played a fab game of Action Man with four Action Men. Simon's gripping was Captain Carson and his other one was Sergeant Scott (Scotty) and my gripping was Lieutenant Simpson and my non-gripping was Warrant Officer

Nixon.[1] We were in the scout car, tank and turbo copter. And we fought a load of Germans with our bare hands, then we all went down the park. Before tea me and Simon saw *Spiderman*. Tonight me and Simon watched *Carry On Again Doctor* and it was brill. And then *Love Thy Neighbour* and *Two Ronnies*.

Monday, 5 January

This morning Simon and I played a brill game of Action Man about two vandals smashing up our camp. After that I went round Wilson's and he had got Up Periscope for Christmas and Escape From Colditz Castle (it is different to my Colditz). Roobarb was also there so all three of us played Escape From Colditz Castle. This afternoon Auntie Sue came round and Johnny, Simon and I played spies and we were after Melanie and Melissa. Tonight me and Simon started playing Colditz but we had to have a hair wash and then it was *Ask the Family* so we had to pack up. After *Ask the Family* it was *Z Cars*.

Wednesday, 7 January

This morning we had double maths and we did more fractions. This afternoon we had art. Our group was with Mrs Hooton and we did writing about milk because we didn't have the stuff to make milk shakes. We are going to make milk shake next week, with scrambled egg on toast. Mum didn't get me 'King of the Cops' record,[2] but I listened to Wilson's when he came round and I've copied the words out on paper. Tonight Uncle

---

1. Because Simon was that bit more committed to the army than me (i.e. he didn't waste any of his valuable combat time doing jigsaws or making comics), we both accepted that he outranked me in the Action Man platoon: he had two gripping-hands Action Men while one of mine was still a spastic non-gripping. Captain Carson, his newest 'soldier doll' (as trademark-shy *Blue Peter* euphemistically called them) was naturally in charge. My Action Men, Simpson and Nixon, were Carson's bitches.
2. 'King of the Cops' by Billy Howard, a novelty record to the tune of Roger Miller's 'King of the Road' which to my Yarwood-raised delight included impressions of all the main TV cops: Kojak, McCloud, Columbo. It reached Number Six in the charts, although I remember it as a Number One, likewise CW McCall's 'Convoy', which in fact reached Number Two a month after Howard peaked. (Funny how nostalgia idealises even mundane points of commerce like chart positions in its quest to smooth all the corners.)

Brian and Auntie Janis baby-sitted and me and Simon watched *Oh No – It's Selwyn Froggitt!*

Thursday, 8 January

I stayed for dinners and we had chicken pie and for afters sponge with chocolate custard. This afternoon we had games and our group did rugby with Mr Hanna and it was brilliant.[3] I was in the scrum and I got filthy. It's lucky we have showers. I went round Wilson's after school and we played Up Periscope. Tonight me and Simon had an ice cold drink of orangeade and we watched *Top of the Pops* ('King of the Cops' wasn't on it) and after that we saw a new series called *Happy Ever After* starring Terry Scott.

Sunday, 11 January

This morning I started making a new comic called *Crunch*. I have done three pages already. This afternoon we went down Nanny Collins and I got my *Monster Fun*. We all looked at Nan's old photos. We watched *The Prince and the Pauper*[4] and *Holiday '76* and they showed you a holiday in Scotland. After tea me and Simon played Subbuteo and the score was 0–0. Then we watched *World About Us* about insects and we went up to bed and I ordered my Scoop book (*Ice Cold in Alex*) and got my dinner money ready.

Monday, 12 January

This morning our class went swimming for the first time (I've never been to a swimming pool before). I can't swim so I started at the shallow end (3ft). I used arm bands to start with and then

---

3. A special public relations use of the adjective 'brilliant', meaning bloody awful. I hated rugby, it was a brute sport.

4. I was angered recently to hear a link on Channel 4's *Top Ten TV Families* (a strand I once wrote links for myself) stating that *Butterflies* was Nicholas Lyndhurst's debut TV appearance. Bollocks. He played the title role in *The Prince and the Pauper* and we used to watch him every Sunday (not to mention *The Tomorrow People*, *Heidi* and *Going Straight*, in which he played Fletch's 17-year-old son Raymond). Do people who make TV programmes about TV know nothing about TV?

I used just one and I can nearly do the breast stroke. After school Wilson came round and we did our RE and history homework. After my tea (lovely toast) I remembered about my Identi-Kit[5] so Dad got it out of the cupboard and I've made loads of faces up. Tonight I watched *Ask the Family* and *Z Cars*, then while Simon read to Dad downstairs I read my comics.

Wednesday, 21 January

This morning Simon got his Action Man book delivered. This afternoon we did cookery and we made lovely cheese and potato pie. Wilson didn't come to school but I went round his and I let him borrow my *Dr No* book to read and he let me borrow his *Live and Let Die* and *Man with the Golden Gun*. I ate some of my cheese and potato pie for tea. Tonight we saw *This Is Your Life* (Patrick Mower), *Mother Makes Five* and brilliant *Morecambe & Wise*.

Saturday, 31 January

This morning when Mum and Dad went shopping Kim came round and we played chess (I lost). Dad got me some library books: *Whales, Dolphins and Man*, a book about Britain and meat-eaters.[6] This afternoon we played a load of records like 'Make A Daft Noise For Christmas', 'In Dulce Jubilo' and 'El Bimbo'.[7] We watched *Play Away* and *The Mouse Factory*, *Tom & Jerry*, *Dr Who* and *New Faces*. Nanny came to baby-sit and we watched the big film.

---

5. Hours of fun with this simple toy, a benign version of the pre-computer police identikit, with assorted eyes, ears and mouthparts to place on a selection of head shapes. No batteries required.

6. 'Libraries gave us power' – opening line from the song 'A Design for Life' and family motto of the band who wrote it, Manic Street Preachers. My childhood was punctuated by regular trips to the town library, where I would crick my neck over the varnish-smelling shelves, coughs echoing round the place. I can't say I read Marx and Engels at Northampton Library, but I did fill my head with natural history, drawing and the cinema. And the complete works of cartoonist Norman Thelwell. It's power of a sort.

7. 'Make A Daft Noise For Christmas' by The Goodies (probably my then-favourite band; Number 20, December 1975), 'In Dulce Jubilo' by Mike Oldfield (one of Mum's, twinned with the softly spoken 'On Horseback'; Number Four, December 1975), and 'El Bimbo' by Bimbo Jet, a French 'male/female vocal/instrumental group' according to the *Guinness*, though neither record nor artist mean a damned thing to me now (Number 12, July 1975).

Tuesday, 10 February

Me and Milner let Kim join O.O.A.M.[8] and Daniel Harrison ('DD') is our ally undercover third year agent. Kim's code name is 'Y'. After school I had my hair cut over the road. After tea I played chess with Simon twice then we had a hair wash and came down. I put some Bonjela on my horrible ulcer. We watched Winter Olympics, *Ellery Queen* and *Pro–Celebrity Golf.*

Thursday, 12 February

I stayed for dinners and I got belly ache. It was very wet so we couldn't have games so we had brilliant[9] cross-country running. We had two laps of the park, one warm-up and another race (I didn't get puffed out or get stitch). Then we had science and we tested our home-made bricks. Tonight Mum sewed some of my squares for my patchwork draught excluder. Melissa came down so she could watch *Top of the Pops.* Then we watched *Happy Ever After.*

Monday, 1 March

We had swimming this morning and I stayed for dinners. Ulp! Mr Walman discovered O.O.A.M. He thought it was funny (sweat). Tonight we and Milner made up the Teachers Anti-Mob Association (T.A.M.A.) – Mr Walman, Mr Hanna, Mrs Bream and Mrs Hulland. We've done loads to it and Milner says that when he moves[10] he will let me have the O.O.A.M. file.

---

8. The Organisation of Anti-Mob (the 'Mob' being the staff of Abington Vale Middle School), a Molesworth-influenced 'secret society' conceived by myself and Milner at breaktime to amuse ourselves. We turned our paranoid fantasy into a file, a loose collection of cartoons based on the idea that we were on to their game and with various gadgets and cunning would expose the Mob as sadistic torturers of innocent pupils. I was agent 'X'. Milner was 'Z' (I think). It was hugely creative fun.

9. See note 3. Who was I trying to convince?

10. Milner moved to Dorset that year, my first experience of losing a friend, although we kept in touch (my first pen pal) and I even visited him on the south coast. He started the Poole branch of O.O.A.M. He's one of the only schoolfriends I have actually met in adult life; he now lives in Tunbridge Wells with wife and two daughters. His dad returned to shore from the banana boats and became harbourmaster at Poole.

Tuesday, 2 March

Wilson and I showed Mr Walman *FAB!*[11] and he showed it to Miss Malins who thought it was very good. I got my Scoop book, *Whizz for Atomms* (it is great). Milner came round after school. The telly went wrong and all smoke came out of it and tonight when Uncle Brian and Auntie Janis baby-sitted we had to watch the golf on my little portable telly.[12]

Thursday, 4 March *MY BIRTHDAY*

From Nanny Mabel and Pap Reg two drawing books, a box of paper (memo tank)[13] and a brill pack of felt tips. From Dad and Mum I got some drawing inks, a pen and different nibs, a drawing book and *The Goodies File* book. From Nan and Pap Collins I got £2.00 and £1.50 from Auntie Margaret. From Auntie Janice's money Dad bought me another new Liverpool mug and two Subbuteo goals. And I've still got five presents from my party to come. I got Wilson's present, some paints.[14]

Thursday, 1 April

I got a letter from Milner (it's funny! and it's five pages). This morning I went to Mr Eagland the orthondontic (got it right)[15] surgeon. This afternoon we had a four-lap cross-country round the school. When we went down the field tonight Angus said he was coming but he didn't. AHA! I've just remembered I must

---

11. Yet another home-made comic, this time in conjunction with Nigel Wilson. He was very much the passenger, artistically.

12. I rather ungratefully fail to mention the black and white portable telly in my otherwise exhaustive Christmas present list for 1975 – perhaps because it was a 'joint' present, 'for all of us'. If you ask me, I think Mum and Dad were way too generous in giving us this luxury item, especially as it was kept in our bedroom. Simon and I knew that it was more than our lives were worth to watch it after lights-out, although we did later develop a method for doing so: with the sound turned completely down and with a squash racket poised to turn it off without getting out of bed if we heard footsteps (you pushed the knob in). I know.

13. White plastic cube filled with multicoloured square notelets which became the O.O.A.M. File. Funky in those days, now given away by insurance companies and car dealerships with their logo on the side.

14. These actually were paints.

15. Got it wrong.

cover my hymn book, must rush ... BYEEE! Oops! Forgot to tell you! Got a new car (yellow Cavalier).

Tuesday, 6 April

Usual lessons. Only we missed ALL of French because after assembly Mr Jones had a talk with the boys about someone who went to the loo *on the loo floor*! After tea Simon went to Cubs[16] and I went down the field with Lewis, played boats, on the see-saw etc. Then came back and played darts (Lewis won both games). With 60p of the £1 Dad owed me he bought me *The Making of the Movie Jaws*.[17] I'm going to read it.

Wednesday, 7 April

Usual lessons at school. As there is a water shortage Mrs Pearson put out a box for 'water saving suggestions'.[18] Now she is giving out a sheet to everyone. She asked me to draw two illustrations for it. Now all the school will see my drawings. (FANS ... AUTOGRAPHS LATER!)

Tuesday, 13 April *EASTER HOLS*

This morning I got a dart in my finger. It hurts a bit. And I painted Salem Witch and I've put little strands of glue all around it and it looks like spider webs. WHAT A GENIUS I AM!!

Friday, 16 April

This morning Simon and I cleared the cupboard out. Then we went shopping (Simon bought a *Look-In* and there is a competition

---

16. As close as he could get to a green uniform at this early stage. Si was in the Cubs from age nine, then automatically became a Scout at 11 and waited until he was old enough to join the Royal Anglian Regiment Army Cadet Force (Salamanca Platoon) at 13.

17. Actually *The Jaws Log*, published in 1975 and written by Carl Gottlieb. 'It's an easy read, energizing and with some of the zest of the movie' – Pauline Kael. Not that I would know, as I didn't see the movie until March 1977.

18. The famous long hot summer of '76 led to nationwide water shortages and a deluge of cracked-reservoir footage on the news – although I'm surprised to see measures in place as early as April. The only appearance of Northampton in the mighty *Chronicle of the 20th Century* comes on p. 1107: a photo of Pitsford Reservoir and its 'parched, cracked surface'. Fame at last.

in it – you can win a Six Million Dollar Man). This afternoon I painted Godzilla (it looks great!!) and I went down the field and I played with Lewis and Kim (they got soaked). They showed me a brill place for jumping but the bank is giving way. Dad has started putting the paving slabs down for our patio. I've just had a drink of cold fizzy pop. I'm just about to start reading *Kizzy* to Simon.

Sunday, 18 April

This morning Simon and I went down the field and Pap was at his allotment so we went up and he has got a bird's nest with a baby bird in. Simon got soaked when he fell in the stream so he is banned from the field. This afternoon I played with Carl with a load of old sheets. We had great fun. I had a lovely home-made milk shake. Dad has finished our new patio.

Thursday, 22 April

Dean came. We went down the field in the morning and found a great den and we got loads of sticks for guns. Trouble is ... between 2.30 and 6.00 somebody (we think) raided our den and all guns (except two) were gone. So we found a load more and we've hidden them better. And we found a load of Mini-Warlord guns (they are special). We've hidden them in our wellies ready for tomorrow. I had a postcard from Milner.

Wednesday, 5 May

Last night Liverpool clinched the League Championship by beating Wolves 3–1. Toshack, Kennedy and Keegan scored. YAHOOOO. Cobblers are in the third division next season. DITTO!!!! We had Mrs Peck this afternoon and OOOH! The Queen Mother landed in a helicopter in Abington Park. All our school went. It was a great helicopter. I got Melissa a Paddington book and Simon got a pad and three felt tips and I'm going to make a card now.

Thursday, 3 June

Dean stayed all morning and till 3.00. We played down the field all the time in our new tree den. Simon and I made up Warlord Badges.[19] You can get them if you do a good thing.

Tuesday, 8 June

14/20 in the French test. In history a girl, we think, pressed the fire alarm and everyone went out but it was a false alarm. After tea I went down the field with Gibby[20] (Simon went to Cubs) and we found a brill tree/bush which we made into a den with one secret entrance.

Saturday, 26 June

It was boiling and I got all sunburnt. We played with Jonathan and Peter[21] most of the day. We had the paddling pool out. We went down Pap's allotment and picked some strawbs. I wrote my letter to Milner. I got some brill flip-flops.

Tuesday, 29 June

There was no choir today. At dinner time the ice cream man gave away free broken lollies. I got one. A lemon one. 94/100 in French (joint first with Julie Sharp). Dad got me a folder for my *MFCs*.[22] Kev,[23] Gibbs and Kev Jnr came to play. Watched *Angels*.

Wednesday, 30 June

Maths 138/200 ... cr ... hmmm ... blush ... oh well, I got 92/100

---

19. All this talk of Warlords (guns, badges) derives from a comic called *Warlord*.
20. Nickname of Paul Givelin, lithe younger brother of barrel-chested Andrew Givelin, sometimes referred to as Taff, as they were ... Welsh. Dad was a bank manager.
21. Boys next door, opposite side to the Edwards, the Hannas. Their dad John was an amateur photography enthusiast and once lent me a grown-up SLR camera.
22. *Monster Fun Comic*, published by Fleetway. It ran for a total of just 72 issues from June 1975 to October 1976 when it was merged with *Buster* (subsumed being a more accurate word). Probably my favourite childhood comic, its stars were Kid Kong, Creature Teacher and Gums, the sublime *Jaws* spoof. Frankie Stein was 'Editor-in-chief', a refugee from the recently nixed *Shiver & Shake*, my second favourite comic.
23. Kev Pilbrow, whose surname I have just this minute recalled by sheer force of memory, as he is logged simply as 'Kevin' when he joins our school mid-term in April '76. His nickname was Nivek (geddit?). Within two weeks of his arrival Nivek was ferociously sick in maths 'all over his book, desk, floor, briefcase and blazer – it was *red*'.

for geog. though. Hooray!! No cooking BOO HISS YAH BOO. We did (don't read this next word) *theory*. It was hot, too hot for cooking. The trip to Whipsnade tomorrow. Wahay!! My partner's Angus.

Thursday, 1 July *TRIP TO WHIPSNADE ZOO*

My partner was Jes after all. I was in Mrs D Jones' group. She brought her two children. The hippos had their backs to us. BOO! We had a questionnaire. My packed lunch was with an ice cold drink, chicken sams, an apple pie, two yogurts and some crisps. We went on the playground. We went in the dolphinarium.

Wednesday, 7 July

Jes, Angus and I made up F.A.G.I.C. (we call it Fagit), the Field, Adventure, Good-fun and Interest Club. We made fresh fruit salad with Mrs Hooton. We went to Nan Collins' after tea, we got a £ for our holidays. Nan got me a *Monster Fun* hol special.

Saturday, 10 July *OFF ON OUR HOLS!!!*

We arrived at Llithfaen near Pwllheli. We are staying at Mr and Mrs Williams' farmhouse. There is a big farm. We arrived at 9–10 o'clock. We had a fish and chip takeaway dinner (I had chips and beans). We went on Pwllheli beach. I got my trousers wet when a big wave splashed up. We had a lovely tea. We walked round the fields. There is a dog, cow and calf (we have only just seen them). It wasn't particularly hot but it was not really cold.

Monday, 12 July

We went to Pwllheli for the day. Dad got the book *Rommel? Gunner Who?* and I got a postcard for Form 2-1, a *Frankie Stein* hol special and an Asterix paperback. I played in the sea. We discovered a little shrew over the road from our farmhouse. We named him 'Vernon the Short'. We went for a ride in Mr Williams' hay cart with two other men. We went to a pub, past Nefyn. Just now, Simon, Dad and I saw a frog in the front garden.

Tuesday, 10 August

Dean came to Nan's. We played Action Man in the sink. They got soaked. I came home from Nan's. Simon's got friendly with Suttle.[24] Melissa's got a new hairstyle. Simon and I are gonna play Bugsy[25] now.

Tuesday, 31 August

I made a Lego house for my Devlins[26] tonight. Dad took Simon and I to Wellingborough Golf Club. We did nine holes. It didn't rain. Simon and I couldn't hit many balls really. Then we went in the bar in the clubhouse. We had a Coke on draught. We watched TV.

Sunday, 5 September

Simon and I played with Mossy and Suttle on bikes down the field. Mossy and I can climb a great new tree. We played Herbies[27] on bikes. When Mossy's glider went over the stream, Mossy and I went over and on the way back I put my foot right in the stream. I changed then. We had a HAIR WASH.

Monday, 13 September

We had art – woodwork. B for my pencil box. Kev and Jes came round and we were bored for a bit. Angus, Jes and I have started

---

24. Simon Suttle. I hope, in adult life, he is not obvious.
25. A variant on the colloquial claim 'bagsy'. This innocent game involved moving methodically through the toy section of 'the club book' (the Kays catalogue, the bible on Mum's side of the family), taking it in turns to choose one item each per page. And that's it. My heart aches in admiration for my younger self here: content merely to fantasise about what toys we might like to own, with no hope of ever getting them, and yet whiling away happy hours in the act of looking at pictures. It's surely what Tiny Tim would have done, had the Cratchitts access to a club book.
26. Plastic 1/32 scale figures that came attached to a series of fancy, collectable chopper bikes, possibly made by Matchbox – we named them Devlins after stunt-rider Ernie Devlin, star of the short-lived Hanna-Barbera cartoon *Devlin*, conceived solely to cash in on the Knievel dollar (and featuring the voice of Mickey Dolenz as Ernie's mechanic brother Todd). I have just watched a QuickTime movie of the opening titles on a website devoted to H-B cartoons, maintained by an unhinged US enthusiast, as are all the best sites.
27. Wheelies, after the famous driverless VW.

A.K.C. (the Anti-Kim Campaign). We hate Kim. Stupid isn't he? We sent him to Coventry.[28]

Tuesday, 14 September

We've stopped calling Kim a loony and all that but we still can't stand the sight of him. Normal lessons. Simon went to Cubs. Kev bought a load of crisps.

Wednesday, 15 September

I trod on a drawing pin this morning. Kim was acting stupid as usual. Soardsy gave me a Corona Fizzical sticker. Kev came and we watched *Carry On Nurse*.

Friday, 17 September

It was brilliant, absolutely fab. It was great. It was the best games lesson I've ever had. We had cross-country. (One lap round the park. I came 28th. Credit. I went with Busho.[29]) Then some of us played rugby with too many people and there weren't many rules. Kev and I got killed.

---

28. What's with the fickle attitude to Kim? One minute he's in O.O.A.M., the next he's in Coventry. I shall have to put it down to the vagaries of pre-teen loyalty, or the fact that Kim was an enormously clever and confident boy – perhaps it rubbed us up the wrong way with our deficiencies (although Jes was, I note, form captain this term). As the Anti-Kim Campaign hots up, drawings appear in my diary with the hapless doctor's son dispatched in inventive ways: bodily encased in cement; sliced in two with a cutlass; pinned under an upturned bed of nails with myself, Angus, Jes and Nivek standing atop. Nothing worse than ignoring him actually took place in the real world. (Irrational this may have been, but I can assure you it had nothing to do with the colour of Kim's skin. See Chapter 13 for more candid details on that score.)

29. Paul Bush, the one with the cruel name for Nigel Wilson. Became a huge pal of mine this year and stayed that way beyond the end of middle school, even though we went to different upper schools. The years 1976–78 were our salad days, characterised by supreme Pythonesque silliness, sleepovers and daft drawings (such as the off-colour bone-through-nose native he's etched in my 1978 diary, followed by the rudimentary Wookiee). Paul, who sucked his thumb like I chewed my tongue, lived in a village outside Northampton, Earls Barton, but we managed to bridge the physical gap. His family had a summerhouse in their back garden (the kind that revolve, as seen in the climax to the great lost 1969 *Dad's Army* episode 'The Battle of Godfrey's Cottage'), and he later introduced me to the pleasures of Peter Gabriel.

Saturday, 18 September

I got my *War Paper* (a poster of Hitler in it). In the afternoon Angus, Jes and I played on bikes all the time. We lost Jes up Weston Way. We changed the poster board. We've got the Dr Who, Hitler,[30] Keep Mum She's Not So Dumb and Tommy Gun posters up. We can't watch *Two Ronnies*. BOOOO!

Friday, 1 October

Homework from maths and science. 18/20 for French test. Rugby in games. Showers. Kev came and we played over Billing Road by the stream in the sinking mud.

Sunday, 3 October

To Nan Collins' for the day. I made a boat/gun-emplacement for my Action Man. Lovely dinner. Lovely tea. Simon gave me a brill James Bond gun with a bullet. WOW! But I've given it back. I don't want it.

Monday, 4 October

I've finished my rattle in woodwork. Kev didn't come. We started copper foil pictures. Kim was acting loony as usual. Kim is a twit. The world would be a better place without the big pouff. He escaped from some loony bin.

Wednesday, 6 October

Jes, Kev, Angus and I have started the Ultimate Gang. Only us four are in it. Nothing happened at the doctor's – it was about my enlarged tonsils. Hockey. Kim was being a pouff as usual. *Carry On Regardless* and *Benny Hill*. Melissa is still off school.

---

30. Look I'm sorry. The *War Papers* were complete, loving reprints of newspapers from the Second World War, they came out weekly and no doubt stopped coming out after about two months, as is the way of all things that build up week by week into a collection you will treasure. The early editions gave away free repro posters, and the Hitler one, a famous portrait, went on our poster board. We pinned him up with the very finest historical intentions.

Thursday, 7 October

Did more to our copper pictures in woodwork. That was our last lesson of woodwork. French test: 12/12 = credit. Kim was being loonyish as usual. Kev came. We went to the sinking sand kingdom and over and under the bridge. Shower. I got an ulcer.

Sunday, 10 October

Did drawing in the morning. Simon went to church parade. In the afternoon Wyn,[31] Robert and I went to Wilson's party. We went to the Brayfield Stock Car Racing. Two overturned and one smashed into the post next to us. His wheel got caught on the fence. We had a hot dog. Tea: chips, beans, fish fingers and a rum'n'raisin chocolate ice cream thing. We played cards and Frustration. Auntie Gladys, Pap and Nan Collins came all afternoon while I was at Wilson's. I watched *Fawlty Towers*.

Tuesday, 12 October

It's a wonder it's not the 13th today (unlucky) because: Kev's away with rheumatism, Mum couldn't get my *Krazy* comic, I couldn't get it when I went to the shops either and I've just gone and had a bath when I was supposed to have a hands and face. OH WELL! Nan C is baby-sitting. We can go on the climbing frame at school now. Sandwiches. Choir.

Friday, 22 October *HOLS*

We got to Ilfracombe (after six hours driving) but the bungalow was cold and damp. So we came home (12 hours over, in all). Melissa was sick there and back. We didn't have dinner, just tea at a Wimpy. I had two whole Wimpys. Simon had egg'n'chips (so did Melissa). Dad had a Wimpy and so did Mum. We got home about 10.00. We were tired. Nan and Pap were here waiting for us.

Saturday, 23 October

We started our hols in Northampton (it's half term you see). Dad and Mum didn't need to do much shopping in the morn-

---

31. Wyn Murphy; Welsh lad, another thumb-sucker.

ing. In the afternoon we bought – Simon: landing craft, lorry, little truck (for soldiers), Andrew: three jokes and tricks (dummy lit cigs, puff puff cigs, plate lifter), two Tempos, blue and mauve. Got Jasper Carrott record.

Sunday, 24 October

Carl gave me some wonder plastic. In the afternoon I went with Carl to Irchester Park. Just had a Dubonnet and lime. Played Nan's De Luxe Scrabble.

Tuesday, 26 October

Cleared garage out in the morning (Dad, Melissa and I that is). I've got my own special painting bench. We went to the Model Shop, Tesco and Bodley's. Simon got pontoon bridge for titch soldiers and I got desert outpost for 8th Army. I've just painted that, complete with vulture, Grecian urns, bench and ladder. Simon went to Colesey's.

Wednesday, 27 October

We went to Twycross Zoo (for the day). There were orangutans, gorillas, loads of monkeys, lions, tigers, leopards, cheetahs, pets corner, otters, reptile house, camels, llamas, birds, tapirs, crocs, vultures, pigs, elephants, tortoises (giant ones), porcupines, giraffes, more monkeys, snakes, penguins, chimps, baby orang-utans, baby chimp, wallabies, kangaroos and more. NO HIPPOS. Had chip shop chips for tea. I had chicken (and beans). Got a rubber spider from zoo. The baby chimp kept whacking the glass when I leaned against it. I took a photo of a parrot. There was a mynah bird. The lion was roaring and Simon took a photo of it. Melissa got a zebra (called Benjy Friendy Smiley!!). My spider is called Dudley.

Tuesday, 2 November

Got choir badge. Jes got 100 lines for shouting at me in history. We (Angus and I) were mucking about, acting hard and he shouted. Hence: 100 lines. 19/20 in French test. Music test. Mum put blue covers on our beds.

Wednesday, 3 November

Hockey. Jes got all snotty because Angus and I tried to run away from him. Only a joke. But he's got so snotty Angus and I got him out the Ultimate Gang. Had conversation in French with Mademoiselle Olvonkablblblbl (Mademoiselle Olivier or something). *Goldfinger* (on TV).

Wednesday, 24 November

Did indoor games instead of hockey. No homework. Mrs Moxham said that I should go to her on Monday instead of cookery.[32] Just now Simon jumped on my bed and hit my head. I called him a pouff and he kept booting my face and then I hit my head on the radiator. What a loony he is. Pam Ayres on *This Is Your Life*.

Wednesday, 1 December

It got a bit frosty this morning, hence: skiddy playground. Soardsy, Angus and I went to Mrs Hooton at din-dins to do more to the carpeting.[33] Had to move all the stuff. Mrs Dennison is still away, had Miss Sabin instead. Did Xmas card for Mum's squash coach. Si did cookery (milk shake and Angel Delight). Parents could come again (Mum didn't). Kev Keegan bashed up his back in the bike race in *Superstars*.

Thursday, 2 December

Had Miss Lindsay for art. Homework. Mr Walman wants me to do a poster for the end-of-term film, *The Shakiest Gun in the West*. I've done it. Mr Hanna's science lesson carried on till 25 past 12 and I was late! Angus and I moved the old carpet from the flat.

---

32. Two things about Mrs Moxham. One, she took me out of class regularly at this time in order to do 'tests' on me (no electrodes, just patterns and numbers in books) as part of a paper she was doing on 'gifted children'. Fans! Autographs later etc. I was just happy to get out of lessons. Two, after Jonathan Bailey had an 'epo' (an epileptic fit) while we were on the school trip to France in 1978, a rumour went round that Mrs Moxham slept in the vacant bed in the boys' dormitory after we had all gone back to sleep, and a boy called Keith claimed he had seen her undressing. Yeah, right.
33. See Chapter 4.

After assembly Mr Jones gave a talk to the boys about: no spit-ting, no practical jokes, no mud, no wasting paper towels and no pea-shooters.[34]

Wednesday, 8 December

Mrs Dennison still away. Had Miss Sabin. Si got a diary. Had pirates in PE. No homework. Went to Mrs Moxham for another test instead of RE. Emery[35] came off his bike 'cos of a wet track in cycling in *Superstars*.

Saturday, 25 December *CHRISTMAS DAY*

I got: Monopoly, big (giant) drawing book, felt tips, 1977 diary, inks, big soldiers, loads of Britains,[36] paints, stamps, stamp album, Press-Ups (a game), brushes, Tempos, *MFC* annual, *Frankie* annual, *Cor! Book of Gags*, glue, model, darts, £1, Pam Ayres book, slippers and more. Lovely dinner. I got some fab presents. Played Monopoly. Went to bed at 9.10. Also I got: Quality Streets, Roses and a Terry's Chocolate Orange and a selection box.

---

34. Pea-shooters? Where are we, Bash Street School?
35. David *Hemery* actually, British athlete, famous for being one of the few white record-breakers at the 1968 Olympics.
36. Britains made fine quality painted plastic die-cast figures, including a superb range of cowboys and Indians. All our zoo and farm animals were Britains.

seven

Supermousse

*In the 70s, foreign holidays broadened British culinary tastes.
Frozen foods responded by giving families a widening
range of recipes every day of the week without the need
to find the ingredients or special skills to cook them.*
'50 Years of Frozen Foods', the British Frozen Food Federation website

*What do I smell?
I smell home cooking
It's only the river
It's only the river*
Talking Heads, 'Cities' (1979)

They say you are what you eat, and of course they're right. (They also say it's not the end of the world, and you can't always get what you want, and they're right again.) As a kid growing up I was shepherd's pie. Or, to qualify that, I was shepherd's pie on Thursdays, which is when Mum made it and when I ate it. Here's her recipe, handed down, we may assume, from more frugal times than the seventies:

Line the bottom of a lightly greased oven-proof dish with slices of corned beef or 'bully beef' as Pap Collins would call it, recalling the war years, much to our delight. Spread with tomato ketchup or, if preferred, brown sauce. Cover with generous layer of pre-cooked, mashed potato. Drag fork across surface to create ridges, add knob of butter and bake until golden and sauce is bubbling.

Mmm-mmmm, pie! The tomato sauce was the secret ingredient. Likewise, the currants in Nan Mabel's famous treacle tart (again, nowhere to be found in any fancy recipe book – and don't even think about sultanas). It was more of a treacle pie than a tart, in that it had a pastry lid, but what the hell, I'd eat one now if Nan were here to make it.

I mention these two significant home-made dishes of my child-hood – *what do I smell? I smell home cooking* – as a reminder to myself. Because it's tempting to look back and see only packet food and processed crap on the Collins family dinner table of my youth. (With a box of those bright orange 'breadcrumbs' and some hundreds and thousands standing by.)

I cling to the nostalgic conviction that we ate better in our pre-McDonald's world than the kids of today, but it's a close run thing. Given the choice, children of any era will instinctively choose the brightly coloured food with a picture of Mr Tickle on the side of the packet over the home-made organic flapjack in a Tupperware tub. I was alarmed recently to discover that kids today – the urban, Western variety at any rate – don't even know how to open and eat a boiled egg. This ancient art is in danger of dying out, like lace-making or walking, gradually eroded to a stump by progress. Pretty soon, the only place you'll be able to see the dipping of bread soldiers into a runny egg is one of those 'living history' folk villages. A young relative of mine once explained that he likes his eggs 'flat'.

Their pop music's not as good as ours was either.

But hold hard! What if my gastronomic superiority is misplaced? Sure, we had boiled eggs when we were yesterday's kids – having them 'flat' was for special occasions and holidays only – but an egg was still as close as we sailed to healthy eating. A balanced meal for us meant something out of a box, something out of a tin and something out of a sachet. It was all *stuff*: baked beans, spaghetti hoops, luncheon meat, Dairylea, Cheese Singles, beefburgers, fish fingers, Sugar Puffs, Frosties, Golden Syrup, Rise

& Shine,[1] Angel Delight, Instant Whip, Dream Topping, Smash, Supermousse or a Mini-Roll.

During our annual self-catering holiday in North Wales, 1976, I helpfully recorded many of the meals we ate. Nutritionists look away now.

SUNDAY
    Beans on toast, Dimple, cup of tea, Mini-Roll, cheese + biscuits
TUESDAY
    Fish fingers, rolls, fried potatoes, half bun, choc cake, cuppa tea
WEDNESDAY
    Beans, sossies, pineapples, choc cake, cuppa
THURSDAY
    Beans on toast, treacle tart, Melissa's mousse!![2]
SATURDAY
    Chips, fish fingers, sossie, tomato sauce, Mini-Roll, Club, cuppa
TUESDAY
    Beans, bacon, pineapple mousse

A Dimple was a cake, in case it's not ringing any bells. An individual chocolate-coated piece of chocolate sponge filled with chocolate cream (named solely to mock my face). Probably Lyons. Now bear in mind we were on holiday – holiday! it was supposed to be fun! – and then return to your first thought: what a lot of fried rubbish and shop-bought confection we subsisted on. A strike at the Heinz factory would have killed us off.

We ate this food not because Mum was lazy or unimaginative, but because everybody did. It was the Seventies, the decade of

---

1. Rise & Shine was powdered orange juice, presumably straight out of the Apollo mission, yet advertised – and in our house, embraced – as the height of culinary sophistication. Just empty the contents of the sachet into a pint of water in a yellow Tupperware jug, stir, *et voilà*! Real orange juice which you only drank at breakfast. The best part is, we considered it exotic and special because you didn't have to dilute it.
2. One assumes she left it. Foodcrime!

convenience. New parents could still taste post-war austerity and wouldn't wish it on their kids. They could still hear the ghostly clucking of the hens in the back yard as they threw their tins of 'chunky chicken' into the shopping basket. (The joke of chunky chicken, which came in a nondescript glutinous sauce and just needed warming through, was that it was more stringy than chunky, but it was bloody *convenient.*)

Mum tried us on vegetables (including the harvest festival specimens Pap grew up his allotment), but to little avail. I wouldn't even eat the kiddy-vegetables, carrots and peas. I was against them.[3] They tasted suspiciously of ... what they actually were, roots and seeds. I preferred my food processed, rendered, shaped, flavoured, enhanced, dehydrated and reconstituted. And when the food scientists finally got their tardy arses in gear and invented Ice Magic, a chocolate sauce that set when in contact with ice cream, I wanted some of that on top.

I know for a fact that Mum and Dad ate vegetables.[4] They were brought up that way. Dig for victory and all that. Plus, let us not forget, Mum and Dad were adults, with palates sophisticated by experience and dinner parties – in other words, they'd eaten gammon with a pineapple ring on top. If they didn't at one point attend a fondue party, I'll eat my hat.

Presumably to make us grateful for what we were, or weren't, about to receive, Mum and Dad actually *boasted* about the dripping sandwiches they enjoyed as kids – just as I might now boast about drinking orange from a cup, rather than an individual carton with a bendy straw glued to the side. Mum even ate sugar sandwiches in her youth, and carried a yen for banana sandwiches into adult life, which was a bit unnecessary – we got the picture. We junior gourmets – Simon and Melissa were equally complicit in the great vegetable boycott – had already been spoiled by the individual Supermousse in a plastic jelly-mould-shaped tub, and the Dracula

---

3. Apparently I ate carrots when I was very little, too young to know where they came from. With knowledge came aversion.
4. By vegetables, I mean something other than potatoes. When mashed, roasted, fried – or on special occasions mashed *and* fried – we considered potatoes honorary processed food.

ice lolly (black, with 'blood-red' jelly filling). There was no going back for us. Only if there was a war would we eat dripping.

I know Mum and Dad ate vegetables because we saw them do it at least once a week: namely at Sunday dinner. (You have to understand that 'dinner' means lunch where I come from, and 'tea' means dinner. Think of it as Sunday lunch if helps you picture us eating it in the middle of the day.) For Sunday dinner, while Mum and Dad tucked into sprouts and crinkle-cut carrots, peas and broad beans, I would have the meat, the potatoes, the gravy and the Yorkshire pudding, and that was it. Meat and one veg. And if truth be told, it was only the meat I was interested in: I would methodically (and annoyingly) eat everything else first, as if ticking off chores, saving the beef/lamb/pork/chicken till last. Sometimes – if Mum was feeling munificent – I was allowed to put it between two slices of bread and margarine. (Try saying 'melted hydrogenated vegetable oil' without saying, 'Mmmmmmmm'.)

Sunday was the only completely traditional dinner we ate in a normal week, with everyone present in the same sitting, and no getting down from the table until Dad was finished. (Dad, perhaps aware that it was his *job*, ate loads more than anybody else, including the pieces of fat, skin, gristle and rind we'd wimpily left on our plates – the time-honoured 'best bit'. Well, it's hungry work in the police.) The reward for our obedience and for not sitting on our legs at the table would be some fabulous Sunday dessert, such as a trifle – made by Mum's own fair hand but using reassuring, packet-based ingredients: Swiss roll, jelly, tinned fruit, custard – or, when the convenience food industry really started to get into its stride in the mid to late Seventies, packet cheesecake (which was so easy to put together with its numbered astronaut sachets, Dad sometimes made it).

The Collins family feared no God, but Sundays were still sacred. Half a tinned peach with cream and a dob of jam became 'peach melba' on Sundays. (And 'Paul Melba' in my TV-centric mind.[5])

---

5. One of the original line-up on much-loved LWT impressions show *Who Do You Do?* (1972–76). See also: Freddie Starr, Faith Brown, Roger Kitter, Aiden J Harvey, Peter Goodright, Johnny More.

For the rest of the week, Mum had foolishly allowed herself to get into a routine of one 'tea' for us, and a separate 'tea' for them (dished up when Dad came home from work). This would have been more of a drag for her if cooking our tea involved anything more time-consuming than heating something up out of a tin and serving it with chips or a slice of toast. (I've checked and neither pasta nor rice were invented until about 1986.)

Still, at least we ate real chips, crinkle-cut by hand in the kitchen. None of your frozen factory fries, there was hard graft in our chips. Since 'the freezer' in those days meant a tiny compartment at the top of the fridge (one packet of burgers, a mousse and an ice tray and it was full up), Mum made chips from *potatoes*, peeling them with her metal knives and everything. Before the McCain mutiny, she, like every mother from Winsford Way to Winsford in Somerset, diced with the apparent possibility of a chip pan fire every other day, noisily reheating matured cooking oil in a spitting, fizzing cauldron of scalding death (wet tea towel, right?). Let us not then dismiss Seventies chips as either an easy option for her, or a processed food for us (they were neither spry, crisp nor dry, but they had at least come from the good earth originally).

What do I smell? ...

I know a lot more about nutrition now than I cared to know then (and more than most parents care to know now), so when I see other people's offspring behaving in an irritable, listless or hyperactive manner I immediately think: bad diet, overdose of aspartame, not enough vitamins. But can they really be eating as calamitous a diet as I did? (By which I mean me and every other kid of my age: Generation E120.[6])

Eating habits in the UK were transformed in the Eighties and Nineties, and as a result, consumers have become ever more demanding. In the Seventies – and you try telling this to those pesky kids of today – there *were* no diet versions of all the processed

---

6. E120, a Seventies classic: cochineal, red food colouring sourced from pregnant Central American beetles *Dactilopius coccus*. Registered charity the Hyperactive Children's Support Group (formed in 1977) recommends E120 is excluded from children's diets. Found, still, in alcoholic drinks, cheddar, pie fillings, biscuits, sweets and the rest.

foods. If you wanted to lose weight (and luckily no-one did, except the Slimcea girl), you simply ate less. There were no salad bars, or bottles of mineral water, or vegetarian options. Not in Northampton anyway. (I'm not 100 per cent sure Hawaiian pizzas have reached there yet.)

But choice only makes you anxious. Ask anyone with 200 television channels. We had it relatively easy. The market was still super, not yet hyper or mega or even mini. The breadth and selection of processed rubbish may have been expanding exponentially throughout the decade that taste forgot, but the only fast food to which we had regular access was fish and chips. And until Mr Cadbury invented 'fun-size' Milky Ways, the notion of having multiple chocolate bars *in the house* was a Willy Wonka fantasy. Perhaps, through all that Corona and cochineal we still ate better than our own kids do today. We ate as badly as we could, but within the means available.

I may well be retro-fantasising, but wasn't there simply more meat in the burgers then? After all, pre-McDonald's, mechanical recovery was less sophisticated, demand was lower, production was less pressurised and rocket science was still largely the province of NASA, not Asda.

The important thing is this: I ate whatever I wanted for the entire duration of my childhood – except perhaps for that single sordid *escargot* we had forced upon us by cultural bullies as the climax to a middle school French trip in June 1978. I was what I ate. But believe me I loved my food. The description of mealtime in my diaries is always lovingly inscribed: 'I had a smashing tea, it was the best tea I've ever had' (24 February 1973); 'lovely tea: cheese sandwiches, pork pie and crisps and fruit cake for afters' (21 September 1975); 'lovely dinner and lovely tea' (12 September 1976); 'Mum made a really fun flan! eg. flan and real strawberries everywhere + jelly + cream' (27 June 1980). Lovely!

Whether crap food was better or worse then, I still managed to thrive on it. I was, as we have seen, rarely ill. I was in fact literally full of beans. I was neither especially irritable nor clinically hyperactive. There was no noticeable deficit in *my* attention. Perhaps it was all that fresh air. No, really. Perhaps it's because there were no computer games to keep me indoors, soaking up radiation, making me violent and frustrated. I mainlined colourful processed rubbish and lived.

It's tempting to nod sagely at the sentiment in the slightly wordy chorus of that excellent Faces song 'Ooh La La':

'I wish that I knew what I know now, when I was younger.'

But do you really? I'm inclined to say the opposite. I'm rather glad that I went about my childhood business in total nutritional innocence, food unlabelled, E-numbers undisclosed. Quite honestly, it didn't seem to do me any harm. Except perhaps foul up my teeth and give me asthma. (Do you like the 'perhaps'?)

Back to that Pam Ayres poem:

If I'd known I was paving the way
To cavities, caps and decay,
The murder of fillin's,
Injections and drillin's,
I'd have thrown all me sherbet away

Would I really go back and eat my way through boyhood differently? Cast that floury sherbet to the four winds like ashes scattered at sea? I think not. Texan bars[7] tasted so good, and a man's gotta chew what a man's gotta chew.

* * *

The trouble with having grown up in the late Sixties and Seventies is that none of the food and drink is around any more. The custard tarts have changed. Walnut Whips don't have a walnut inside. Welfare orange has been phased out. Whither Kunzel Cakes? Blobs? Dimples? Freddo bars? Those biscuits with stick men playing different sports on the underside?

How are we supposed to enjoy a true Proustian rush? When

---

7. The *raison d'être* of these chocolate bars was that they were really hard to eat. The Texan dude in the animated adverts used his to duck a firing squad – it took so long to chew his way through the nougat, the Mexicans went to sleep. 'A man's gotta chew what a man's gotta chew.'? Gary Cooper died for these people.

Marcel Proust invented the concept in his novel *Remembrance of Things Past* the object of his nostalgic reverie was a Madeleine – the light, spongy cake French people dunk in tea ('I raised to my lips a spoonful of the cake ... a shudder ran through my whole body and I stopped, intent upon the extraordinary changes that were taking place'). This wasn't some vague memory of a cake, it was the cake itself that took his protagonist back.

Of course, Marks & Spencer did their own Madeleine in the Seventies. A typically heavy-handed interpretation, it was a sponge tower with a tablet of apricot-flavoured jelly in the centre, tarred and feathered with adhesive syrup and desiccated coconut. I scoffed a few of those in my time, leaving the jammy bit until last by eating from the bottom up. I'd love to think that eating one now – if only! – would take me back to Saturday teatime.

A la recherche des gateaux perdus.

Every generation has its food memories, be it bully beef, sugar sandwiches or Outer Spacers.[8] Generation E120 had – albeit briefly – Space Dust, a confectionary fad now remembered to death thanks to the nostalgia industry but still evocative for me. It was 1978 and the craze entered my orbit just as our year were setting off for Normandy in France for the aforementioned snail-eating school trip. Space Dust was the big hit of the ferry crossing. We all bought in bulk at a service station, and proceeded to walk around the decks with our mouths agape and our tongues orange, while the crystals crackled away to nothing.

It was like having a campfire go out in the back of your mouth, and was only food in the sense that it was taken orally. More akin to eating something out of your chemistry set. (I never had a chemistry set but I knew the drill: stink bombs, crystals, cupboard under the stairs.) However, with all that I know now and didn't know then, I'd still have to neck some Space Dust if you magicked a packet up and handed me some. As it snapped and crackled and dyed my tongue with foul tartrazine I'd be *there*, transported back to the ferry (it was called *The Dragon*) – my first time on a boat and

---

8. Unwieldy proto-Monster Munch 'corn snacks' in the shape of rockets and UFOs. About four in a bag.

the first member of my immediate family to leave British shores. A momentous occasion marked by a once-in-a-lifetime sweetmeat.

Food and drink played a small but significant part in this five-day Gallic odyssey, beginning when we reached our destination, *le colonie vacances* in drizzly Quiberville (it's not in my current Philips atlas – although there is a Thiberville in the approximate region; perhaps I misheard the teachers). *Le colonie* was an unlovely halfway house between school and campsite, with dormitories and washrooms. Anyway, they gave us all a bowl of tea. A bowl. Of tea. Why, was there a cupmakers' strike? (After all, those French really know how to do industrial action.) I reckoned it was a practical joke this phoney tradition, foisted upon English visitors by the staff of *le colonie* to throw us on arrival and make us think all tea was drunk this way *en France*. I mean, isn't a bowl of tea Chinese? We didn't argue at the time of course. If they'd fed us bratwurst and Welsh rarebit we'd have accepted it as the French way of things and sung 'Frère Jacques'.

I have no record of the meals we ate with our spurious *bols de thé* but I remember well the school dinner we had in Dieppe. As a means of getting our hands culturally dirty, we spent the day at a French school, highlight of which was finding out what their dinners were like. 'Nicer than ours!' would be the clichéd response, but they weren't really. I'm afraid I described the food as 'gob' in my diary. The dessert was especially curious: a plain yogurt[9] which you mixed with sugar. It would have been alright without the yogurt.

On the Wednesday I bought what I described as a 'French Cornetto' from the village, and on a day trip to Paris I ate a rock-hard baguette with cheese and ham by the Seine, though I was too shallow to appreciate the romance of the situation. I did buy a French stick from a market in Dieppe to take home (*Je voudrais une baguette s'il vous plais*), but my heart wasn't in it. I wanted Angel Delight and Dream Topping, with perhaps a little sugar mixed in, just to show how European I was.

---

9. I'd never encountered a fruitless, flavourless yogurt before. The whole *point* of a yogurt was the bits of fruit in it. Ask any of those skiers.

It took me three days of regular Northampton eating to remove the taste of that snail though. We were served *escargot* for our evening meal on the final day – mere hours before a coach ride and a Channel night crossing, more proof that sadists were at work here. 'They were vomit,' reads the review in my diary, and they were. But it wasn't the gristly little knuckle on a pin that tasted so foul and foreign to me, it was the *garlic* the snails were swimming in. I had never eaten garlic before. I was 13 years old.

(That's three brand new taste sensations in the space of a week: a mollusc, a pungent bulb, and a crystalline orange powder of laboratorial origin.)

It is fair to say that throughout the Seventies (and even into the Eighties) the Collins family enjoyed whatever the opposite of a cosmopolitan diet is. (Monopolitan?) No foreign holidays to broaden our culinary tastes, and Fanny Craddock was not much help.

Writing of our adventure-free tastes reminds me of the story a music industry friend of mine called Phill used to tell about his infamous dad – a conservative sort – visiting him at his first flat and refusing a cup of tea because Phill only had Earl Grey. 'I haven't got time for experiments,' he said. That should have been the Collins family motto.

There may have been no rice in our house, but then nor was there any Eastern cuisine to demand it. No curries, not even a packet Vesta with curly crisps, not even super-mild like the stew-with-curry-powder version we *very* occasionally got at school with sultanas in (school food was always essentially meat in gravy, what-ever they chalked up on the board – the first hot meal I ever ate at school was 'goulash': meat in gravy). There was no pasta in Mum's cupboard, unless you over-generously count the wheaten slop in tomato sauce canned by Heinz. Herbs and spices? The white pepper shaker was only there for symmetry.

I tried my first ever rice while walking home from town with Hayley Mayo,[10] Anita Barker and Chris Thompson in the summer

---

10. My 'girlfriend' at the time.

of '78 (about a fortnight after getting back from Quiberville/ Thiberville). Chris had bought a one-person Chinese takeaway, which we were invited to share, a decidedly tame dish but no doubt the most exotic thing you could buy on the Wellingborough Road in 1978: sauceless chicken in egg-fried rice. I took a few slickened fingerfuls from the foil tray and it neither converted me to Asian cuisine nor made me sick on the pavement. There were, I decided, easier ways to get at meat.

Neatly enough, the four of us had been on a double-date to see *Close Encounters of the Third Kind* at the ABC, in which electrical engineer Roy Neary makes contact with extraterrestrials and is whisked to another galaxy. A similar thing had happened to me: I had eaten my first ever 'Chinky' – as you were still allowed to call them in 1978 – and it had transported me to another world.

I ate my first-ever pasta at my friend Paul Bush's house, around the same time. (His was the first ever stepdad I'd encountered too. So many firsts.) I was pre-warned. Paul's mum had asked me if I liked spaghetti and I'd said yes, assuming she meant the real stuff, Heinz, out of a can. She meant this long, white Italian stuff I'd seen only in that clip from *The Lady and the Tramp*. Now it's stressful enough eating at someone else's table, especially when they all sit down together, even on weekdays (strict!). But to be served Spaghetti Bolognese – an Advanced Eating dish at the best of times – when I'd never seen any in 3D before; this was sheer torture.

I left almost half of it; I admitted defeat, having done my best to ape the practised spooling and sucking of Paul's family. What crazy Bohemian people they clearly were. (I hated leaving food on my plate. It was not the done thing. If I did it at home, Mum would say, 'Your eyes are bigger than your belly,' scrape my plate on to Dad's and I would be a pariah.[11]) I'm sure Paul and his folks worked out that I was a pasta novice.

It's a rite of gastronomic passage we must constantly repeat,

---

11. 'There's no shame in being a pariah,' as Marge Simpson once said.

ordering one thing and getting another.[12] So while I cautiously applaud my parents for allowing me to eat *exactly what I wanted*, it wasn't exactly preparing me for the world, was it?[13]

Here's a dinner table conversation from March 1983:

> *Dad* [to Simon]: What's in fruit cocktail that you don't like?
> *Simon*: Fruit.[14]

You see, that's what they were up against. They had created a monster with their non-interventionist food policy. Our relationship with food was broadly emblematic of our relationship with Mum and Dad: based on love, leavened by practicality, and governed by a selective discipline. By and large, we ate when we were told, at the table, with knife *and* fork, never on our laps in front of the TV, and

---

12. I was once at the house of some friends of Nan Mabel and Pap Reg where I was offered a 'toffee' by the host. I took it with glee, only to find on chewing that it was hollow and contained some gooey substance I wasn't familiar with (jam?). I spat it out. Never get out of the boat, as Chef (Frederic Forrest) advises in *Apocalypse Now*. And he's a *saucier*. On my first visit to an authentic diner in New York, about ten years after the Paul Bush spaghetti incident, I confidently ordered a lox bagel, unaware that lox is Yiddish for smoked salmon. I was a strict no-fish vegetarian at the time and, having laboriously extracted vast folds of salmon from my plate, I ended up eating the decorative salad leaves round the edge I was so hungry. In Chicago, almost ten years after that and no longer a veggie, I ordered a 'soft shell crab sandwich' and was dismayed to find three whole crabs under my bread. In their shells. They might as well have been scurrying about among the onions. The point is this: I never let my companions know that I was surprised by what I'd been served up, and gamely tucked in. We never grow up. (I left half of that too – my eyes were bigger than my belly.)

13. I was eventually taught how to eat vegetables by a girlfriend in the mid-Eighties. Indian food came in 1988, after which I started to travel for my job and the world became my oyster – or at least my soft shell crab.

14. This is quite shocking. If it's as late as 1983, Simon is on the verge of joining the Royal Anglian Regiment proper, and yet he is still refusing his greens (even *I* ate fruit). The army would make an omnivore of him. Or would it? For a couple of years, before and after joining up, Simon kept a diary. In 1983, just prior, he helpfully compiled a 'Food Chart' which tells us all we need to know. It reads thus:

1 Mr Men Fruit Gums
2 ET biscuits
3 Twiglets
4 Choc éclairs
5 Mars bars

we cleared our plates. We had a lolly from the ice-cream van only when it was decreed, and two biscuits between meals with a drink of squash, but *no more than two*. Mum didn't put the packet out, and we would never help ourselves from the cupboard.

However, within that rigid framework, we seem to have been the masters of our own diet.

The Alpine lorry brought with it a tantalising taste of autonomy, just like the Freedom Train imagined by poet Langston Hughes.[15] Other lorries had literally come and gone – the coal lorry, the vegetable lorry (made redundant by central heating and cars) – but the Alpine lorry was a signifier of modernisation, not a victim. Alpine, based I understand in Sunderland, made fizzy drinks in hefty, family-size glass bottles (these were anything but fun size; they were serious). They delivered them to your door like ill-health milk, and they took your empties away. It was the mid-Seventies so having screw-cap bottles of pop around the house was *ne rigueur* (Nan Collins sometimes had a bottle of orange Corona in, but nans do soft things like that). My childhood drink was squash, lemon or orange, with an occasional mania for Ribena (mixed strong and dark in the glass). I was never a milk-drinker – my teeth stand testament to that – but that was because an early experience with the skin that forms on hot milk had put me off it.

So, our family signed up to the Alpine deal and every week the lorry would bring brightly coloured carbonates – cherryade and limeade being my big faves – which would then 'live' behind the kitchen door. (No room in the fridge for these big boys.) It was risky, but we did sometimes sneak a glug of fizzy out of the bottle – a forbidden act twice over (you don't know where that bottle's *been*!) – thus breaking down the walls of parental control.

It was the Soda Stream that put Alpine out of business, and Mum back in control of pop consumption. She and Dad's resistance was finally broken by the purse-friendly prospect of cheap DIY fizzy drinks (an endless stream in fact), and as if to prove them

---

15. Forgive me the comparison. 'Freedom Train' by Langston Hughes ('the Poet Laureate of Harlem'), written in 1947, imposing a civil rights agenda on to the US government locomotive of the same name.

145

right we consumed no end of that sickly syrup with metallic-tasting self-carbonated water in it (especially the 'cola', which tasted so unlike Coca-Cola it was like discovering a brand new drink). It was of course virtually impossible, with all that clanking and shooshing, to sneak under the radar and make Soda Streams without Mum's blessing.

Once, as a much smaller boy, I'd hidden behind the settee (that's how small) at Nan Collins's house and eaten a whole packet of Jaffa Cakes. Mind you, these were the first Jaffa Cakes I'd ever seen and I treated them as if they might also be my last. Unbelievably, I was neither physically sick nor physically reprimanded, but I never ate cakes or biscuits without signed permission ever again.

Kids today (not them again!) don't eat, they graze. They chew the crud, steadily, round the clock, with an access-all-areas pass to the larder, eating sweets between sweets. It doesn't *spoil* their appetite, like our parents always warned us it would (you'll *spoil* your dinner), as child hunger doesn't work the way it used to. Kids don't work up an appetite, they have a continuous need for sustenance that ebbs and flows but never switches off – which is presumably why parents have stopped trying to control the food. Instead, a running buffet of sweets, crisps and biscuits is laid on, 24 hours a day (cupboard doors will be the next thing to go), and mealtimes involve the blasé moving around of items on a plate until it's time to get down and return to the games console.

I had a Winnie the Pooh lampshade in my bedroom when I was very young and I began to obsess over it, as you do. After hours of lateral thinking, I worked out that I could copy the familiar Disney characters on to paper and recreate all the colours needed to fill them in using ... foodstuffs. The brown of Owl could be made using Marmite, the orange of Pooh using marmalade, the pale yellow of Rabbit with lemon curd, and so on. I'd love to be able to tell you why I wished to do this thing, this edible painting, but all I can say is, the very act of discovering that I *could* was enough of a reason to have a go.

I'm sad to say, having plucked up the courage to ask Mum if she had all the ingestible pigments required (she did) I then chickened out. She asked me why I wanted them (was it for school?) and I said it doesn't matter. Pity. I could have made a profound statement about the links between processed food, Disney characters and pester power with my condiment art.

The irony is, if Mum had spread either Marmite or marmalade on a piece of bread for me, I would have refused to eat it. (Didn't *like* Marmite, didn't *like* marmalade.) Smear them on to a sheet of paper, no problem, but try them?

Don't play with it, they would say – but what else were we supposed to do with toy food? If it didn't have a face on, it was shaped like letters of the alphabet or zoo animals. Even the relatively grown-up tomato ketchup was, in our house, indulgently decanted into a roadside-caff squirter in the shape of a tomato. This stuff should have been found in the Kays catalogue under 'jokes and novelties'.[16]

My long epicurean journey from bib to enlightenment was thus free of obstacles. I ate nice things, and when I was presented with something green or simply bland, like the occasional frond of Seventies lettuce for Sunday tea or a bowl of Ready-Brek in winter, I smothered it – the former with salad cream, the latter with treacle. If I can't see it (or taste it), it can't hurt me.

Weetabix was a classic case: an adult cereal which Mum ate exclusively (a *surreal*, then, if we adopt her unique pronunciation). But we became frustrated at the leisurely rate with which she got through them, because Weetabix gave away premium gifts (always flat and card-based, so that they fitted in the box, but highly collectable, like *Asterix* characters, *Star Trek* or *Dr Who*). In order to speed up turnaround and increase productivity, Simon and I valiantly began to eat

---

16. As teenagers, my friend Paul Garner and I made an entire joke dinner – with Mum's weary permission – by adding lurid bottled colours to various foodstuffs and presenting them on a plate to be photographed with my new Instamatic camera. I have the photo here: the dish seems to comprise a potato dyed green, two types of slop (apple sauce? desiccated coconut?) dyed green, and some liquid dyed red, acting as a bright gravy. Chocolate sauce completes the plate, along with a green drink, which must be milk, in a wine glass and possibly a portion of trifle in a frilly paper case, also dyed green. Paul and I experimented by eating some of it, and the alimentary results were suitably vivid. I like to think of this meal as a spiritual fulfilment of the aborted Winnie the Pooh food painting.

Weetabix ourselves. It was vile. No, worse than that, it was boring, like eating sawdust bricks. There was only one thing for it: layer an inch of sugar on top of each 'bix' and drown in milk, creating a sweet soggy mulch which could at least be dispatched quickly.

And that, when it comes to the crunch, is how we regarded food: as a means to an end. Firsts were a way of getting at afters; savoury food a mere underlay for ketchup; meat a way of melting margarine; meals something you ate in order to get biscuits in between.

Just to prove that we did have a soul, some cereals were rejected as too unpleasant to contemplate, even for gifts: Shredded Wheat, Shreddies, Golden Nuggets,[17] Sugar Stars (they had Sweep on the front) and Puffa Puffa Rice (without doubt the finest source of plastic toys in the land but virtually inedible, like sunset yellow pellets). But we had a crack at them all, even the surreal cereals, at least once. If only some bright spark had thought of putting gifts in with vegetables.

* * *

Breakfast was a ritual meal, in that all five of us ate it at the same time, every single day – although 'getting ready for school' allowed you to leave the table at any time. Porridge made with hot milk in winter (central heating for kids), cereals in summer, and toast with the crusts cut off, I'm rather mortified to recount. (If we were lucky, at weekends Dad would cut our toast into the shape of a house, which sure made it taste nice.)

Where *this* started I do not know, but for a time in the mid-Seventies, I developed a habit of getting up before anybody else, coming downstairs and setting the table, like the breakfast fairy. Extending my own role in The Ritual, I would lay the tablecloth, put down the wicker mats, set out all the bowls[18] and cutlery and

---

17. Huge things, the size of conkers, advertised by cartoon gold prospector Klondike Pete and his mule. I think they gave away something desperately desirable when they first launched, like stickers or transfers. But the penance was too great.

18. We ate, and I mean all of us, from plastic bowls. Made from some wonder polymer developed during the space race, you could bounce them off the walls, drive a car over them. They'd come as part of a picnic set and somehow found their way into kitchen circulation. It was an unbreakable decade.

stand up the cereal boxes in the middle (Weetabix and Corn Flakes for them, Frosties and Sugar Smacks for us). If I'd been allowed to I'm sure I would have ironed Dad's *Telegraph* and boiled the milk, but I was only insured for the acoustic stuff. What I hoped to gain from this butler act – every morning – is unclear. Credits? Maybe I was just being nice. For what we are about to receive – crusts off, taste disguised by treacle – may the Lord make us truly thankful, amen.

It was nonetheless advanced and prescient domestic behaviour. I am now 37; as old as my dad was in 1978 when I was 13 – and guess what? – I get up before anybody else each morning, come downstairs, set the table, empty the dishwasher, replenish the cats' bowls, top up the bird feeders, set out the cups, get out the teabags, fill the kettle, lay out my vitamins and fillet the *Guardian*, placing the unwanted sections in the recycling ...

The world falls apart but some things stay in place.[19]

So what has changed, apart from the custard tarts? I have. I am now an adult and as such I eat my greens but it's a little more extreme than that. It's more than gammon and pineapple. I no longer eat like a sinner, I eat like a saint. My body is a proverbial temple, whereas once, in the decade that forgot taste, it was a chemical toilet. There's no processed food in *our* house, beyond a jar of mayonnaise and some tinned tomatoes; it's organic everything, wholefood surprise, wheat-free this and gluten-free that, a small pharmacy of vitamins and supplements, herbal infusions, sunflower seeds, oat milk, tofu yogurt and vegetables that I have to look up in a book.[20] It's a harvest festival every day, and I know the first names of the farmers who grow it all.

Thinking about this nutritional U-turn, it's more like penance, as though I'm eating my way backward until I reach my misspent, miseaten youth. I'm eating for two now: the grown-up me and the Supermousse me, trying to fortify us both before the carcinogens come knocking. While other areas of my life are a continuation of

---

19. 'Levi Stubbs' Tears' by Billy Bragg (1986): 'When the world falls apart, some things stay in place/Levi Stubbs' tears run down his face.'
20. *A Gourmet's Book of Vegetables* by Louise Steele.

my childhood, the way I eat now is an exercise in damage limitation, an attempt to rectify. Here's where I start paying: in swede.

Oh, I make a pie occasionally, not treacle or shepherd's, but fruit. (*What's in a fruit pie that you don't like?*) In fact, I made one for Mum and Dad only the other week,[21] heating it through at their house, turning the tables at last: their kitchen smelt of *my* home cooking. It was nice to put something back. We ate it all, and they were grateful and we sat back, sated. And here's the bombshell: *my* fruit pie was made with not a single grain of sugar. That's my secret non-ingredient.

Revenge – upon the decade, not upon Mum and Dad – is a dish best served at dinnertime.

---

21. Apple, pear, cherry and redcurrant. Mr Ambassador, you are spoiling us!

eight

Joy Rides

I'm allowed to get my vest wet!
Simon Collins, Black Rock Sands, North Wales (1975)

Oh, how we dreaded going on holiday. A cloud of misery hung over our heads for weeks beforehand. It was worse than having a dentist's appointment or an exam. We used to feel sick just thinking about it. Even the approaching end of term ('We break up, we break down, we don't care if the school falls down etc.') was tainted with a sense of doom and gloom.

It wasn't the holiday itself, you understand – that was a guaranteed two weeks of fun, fresh air and free gifts – it was the journey from Northampton to North Wales. Six hours it took us in those dark days before bypasses and Happy Eaters: two junctions north up the M1 then along the M6 to Telford where we were forced back on to soul-destroying A-roads for the rest of our grey odyssey, via Shrewsbury, Oswestry and Chirk; a faint cheer from within Dad's Viva as we passed the 'Welcome to Wales' sign on the A5, the traditional leg-stretching stop-off at a layby in Llangollen, then we pushed on into Snowdonia on the A494 past the glinting Bala Lake and towards Trawsfynydd via the even more windy A4212; triumphantly, we passed through the mental checkpoint of Porthmadog and rattled down the Lleyn Peninsula past Llanystumdwy to Pwllheli – just in time for breakfast. Sorry, did I not mention we used to set off at 3 a.m.?

A six-hour car journey would test the patience and digestive stamina of any kid, but having to be turfed out of bed at 2.30 a.m. when it was dark and cold and *wrong* was never going to start the holiday with a smile. You see, the Collins family always went to Wales on Day One of the school holidays, as if it were a race – this meant we were hitting the M1, M6 and A5 at *exactly the same time* as every other unimaginative family with a roof rack in the country. Thus, the only way to 'avoid the traffic' (every dad's dream) was to set out at such an ungodly hour that we only met lorries along the way. Lorries, and hundreds of other families with roof racks who'd had precisely the same idea.

The first year we went to Wales – 1972, when Melissa was still a baby – we ran slap bang into a carnival at Porthmadog, which must have doubled our already swollen journey time, and I'm sure Dad vowed there and then, gridlocked between floats, clowns and people in national dress, to leave a bit earlier next year.

Thus, 3 a.m. became our most extreme start time, although in later years it relaxed to 4 a.m. and even 5.30 a.m. Either way, the central heating would be off – I always remember my teeth physically chattering, which was at least good training for the fortnight to come – and we would have to whisper and creep about so as not to disturb Jean and Geoff and the kids next door, adding to the stark, Colditz-like unreality of the situation. In a game attempt to reduce the misery of this midnight flit, Mum and Dad would buy us a holiday special to read and keep it from us until the start of the journey, as an incentive not to dread the whole thing. Dad would tantalisingly place our holiday specials – a *Frankie Stein* and a *Battle*, let's say – on the back shelf of the car while loading up the night before, which meant we could look out of the kitchen window and see them, beckoning us. Did this trick make setting out on the miserable six-hour journey any better? Of course not. It was pitch black at 3 a.m. and we could only make out the pages by the yellow lights of the motorway moving across the comics – massively frustrating, and of course guaranteed to bring on motion sickness before Telford.

These days families travel in minibus-sized 'people carriers' with bags of ergonomically designed leg-room and luggage space. The 1970s Vauxhall Viva, though a family car, was very much economy class. A people crusher. Shoehorn three kids in the back, including one in a strap-in baby seat, and you've barely got enough room to stash the plastic potty and the I-Spy books. The potty was for throwing up in, although I don't recall any of us ever doing anything so neat with our unwanted guts.

Travel sickness blighted our every car journey. One out of the three of us was sick every time Dad drove more than 500 yards.[1] On major journeys – Wales, Yarmouth, Ilfracombe, Blackpool, Weymouth – Mum and Dad would carry a big bottle of water in the boot for the express purpose of wiping our inevitable sick off the upholstery. Mum recalls with a shudder the time Simon and I vomited in stereo, one out of the driver's side window, the other out of the passenger side. I can only hope that it looked spectacular to the driver behind us, like a display by the Red Arrows perhaps.

A chain reaction occurred if one among the three of us chucked – the smell would set the other two off. Sometimes it was like Charlie Caroli in the back seat of that car. They tried to get us to take nasty pink travel-sickness tablets – the sinisterly named Joy Rides – but none of us would swallow. Or indeed 'chew', as it laughably suggested on the box (the very box which described these acrid dots as 'pleasant tasting'). Dad once inventively gave me a Joy Ride sandwich, with the pill held between two chalky but much-loved Refresher sweets. I secretly flushed the Joy Ride down the toilet and noisily crunched the sweets in front of him. It fooled no-one, and I forever put myself off chalky sweets. Honestly, it's a wonder they took us further than Weedon.

One year, we made Dad pull over so early in the mammoth journey – because we felt 'a bit sick' – he furiously *forced* Simon and me to take a Joy Ride each, there and then on the hard shoulder of the M6 with the lorries whipping past us. I went first, chewing it like a man and insisting to Simon, 'It's not that bad' (oh, but it was). Simon stoutly refused and promised not to feel sick any more. We drove on. Neither of us was sick again, or at least not until the traditional layby at Llangollen. Simon and I piled out of the car and ran down the incline of the adjoining sheep field.

---

1. Dad tells me that on the long drive to Yarmouth in 1973 we made him stop the car at Thrapston, which can be no more than 12 miles out of Northampton. That was our record.

There, I surreptitiously removed the half-chewed Joy Ride from my shoe, where I had in fact secreted it back on the M6. The very sight of it loosened my lunch and I quietly vommed on the grass without Mum and Dad even knowing.[2]

Travel sickness was a downward spiral we could never escape from. The thought of Joy Rides made us sick; the thought of being sick made us sick; being sick made us sick. My guess is that the 'travel' and the 'motion' had nothing to do with it. Not one of us was even queasy on the drive home, even though the journey took just as long. Having said that, we generally left later: desperate to squeeze every last drop out of Wales on the way there, but not as bothered on the way back – one year we casually left on the Friday afternoon at 4.30, having been to the beach in the morning. Nobody felt sick; the miles flew by. The psychology of the return journey has never been satisfactorily explained to me, but it holds in adult life, and on other forms of transport: it always seems easier coming home, no matter where you are or how long you've been there.

Even if the car still smells of sick from the outward journey.

Wait a minute, we've been to Wales and we've come home already, bronzed only by the coastal wind and about half a dozen holiday specials richer. There was, mercifully, more to holidays than being sick out of car windows.

* * *

We self-catered on the same peninsula in North Wales from 1972 to 1979 inclusive, eating the same food we ate at home except for the occasional holiday-only treat like a burger in batter from the chip shop at Morfa Nefyn or a takeaway Wimpy on the seafront at Pwllheli. Cold beef sandwiches were the traditional extravagance on the days we went to Black Rock Sands at Llanbedrog. Kunzel Cakes were often broken out too. And flat eggs.

---

2. On the subject of secretion: I overdid it with some chocolate-covered fudge once in Wales and shoved the last piece behind Melissa's car seat rather than admit I had been greedy. It stayed there until Melissa was old enough not to need the seat any more, or Dad changed cars, whichever came first.

It might not have seemed like much of a holiday for Mum, self-catering – after all we self-catered all year round – but she didn't seem to mind. Yes, she was still cooking our tea, but she was doing so in a farmhouse nestled in the majestic vistas and clean air of Wales. For the first four years we stayed in exactly the same spot just shy of a tiny village called Llithfaen (found midway across the biceps of the peninsula). We stayed in two different properties rented out by English ex-pat Mrs Roberts on a farm called Tyn Cae – irresistibly close to 'Tin Can' in our heads, which is what we called it – first, the more modern, added-on bungalow, later the original farmhouse. Then, when she sold up after the summer of 1975, we moved down the lane to another farmhouse, Bryn Celyn Isaf, owned by Mr and Mrs Williams, an authentic Welsh farm couple we could barely understand. We stayed there for four more years running, each as idyllic as the last. Same place, same two weeks in July, same holiday effectively, but it suited us down to the ground.

Other, more adventurous, thrill-seeking families went on package holidays to Spain and came back burnt umber. Uncle Brian and Auntie Janis went to Disneyworld and Cape Canaveral and drove on the right-hand side of the road. The Caves went sailing.[3] Even Nan Mabel and Pap Reg flew to Canada to see Nan's sister Doll, and to the chi-chi Channel Islands too. But we were happy in North Wales, sitting in the car in the driving rain, looking out at the unyielding Atlantic, eating fudge and doing quizzes. And to prove our undying love for Llithfaen and Pwllheli and Black Rock Sands we went back every year for the best part of a decade. These were the best holidays in the world.

To start with we hedged our bets and went on two, shorter holidays, a week in a caravan park in Yarmouth on the tacky east coast in June, and a week at Mrs Roberts's in Wales in July. A year later, we sensibly threw our lot in with the sheep and put the slot

---

3. Remember that Uncle Allen Cave was a builder and self-made man who was encouraged to spend large sums of money before the end of the tax year. Somewhat conspicuously, he had a boat, and in later years a Jaguar XJS for dry land. And a full-size snooker table in a full-size snooker room (which he had, to be fair, built himself).

machines behind us. We made our own entertainment in Wales, and that's why it was such a valuable experience every summer. The family that plays together, and all that ...

Compare and contrast a day in Yarmouth – a breathless round of fairground rides, pennies in slots and ticket stubs – with a day in Wales – perhaps a game of cricket on the beach at Pistyll and *The Fenn Street Gang* before bedtime – and you start to see how character-building the Welsh holidays were. We wanted for very little: some stumps, a tennis ball, a stick, a bucket, a kagoul, a deck of Top Trumps.[4] It was like being down the field, except it was *up* the field and the allotments stretched for as far as the viewfinder could see.

Directly behind the bungalow was a serviceable hill walk with a rocky outcrop at its peak which we christened The Crag. We went up The Crag every year, a family expedition captured on the grainy Instamatic. Simon and I would naughtily sing the words '*in and out the sheep shit/in and out the sheep shit*' (trad. arr.) as we dodged the pellets, running ahead of Mum and Dad – and Nan Mabel and Pap Reg if they'd joined us for a few days, as they habitually did, as if to make it seem even more like home from home.

At the peak, action man Simon would play at mountain climbers on the imposing Crag itself with his jeans tucked into his football socks and a length of rope slung manfully over his shoulder. I threw bits of slate off the top and watched them smash.

The sun did occasionally shine in July in North Wales, but it was wise not to rely on it. We spent a lot of the fortnight in the car, as I remember it, or else sheltered behind a windbreak on the beach, poles knocked into the ground with rocks. Even during the apparent long, hot summer of '76 it rained and I caught a chill. But we didn't care, as long as there were fish fingers for tea and the prospect of dam-building tomorrow at Aberdesach or Dinas Dinlle.

It would seem pertinent at this point to admit that in eight years we didn't ever really fully embrace the Welsh language. Instead, we mashed its evocative, lyrical beauty to fit our unsophisticated Northampton mouths. Llithfaen was simply 'Lithvan' for as long as

---

4. International Super Cars and Tennis Aces I recall being particular favourites.

we stayed there, Pwllheli was to us the rather comical 'Puwelly'. Not once did we pronounce Nefyn correctly as 'Nevun' – it was Neffin to the Collins family for two weeks every summer. I daren't tell you how we pronounced Trawsfynydd and Llanystumdwy for fear of sinking further still into a caricature of imperial ignorance. Alright – Transfinnywinny and Lanstuddymuddy.

Let us off. I don't imagine a Welshman could pronounce Cogenhoe,[5] Towcester[6] or Duston.

* * *

We were in love with Wales. The hills, the crashing waves, the tell-tale snags of wool on wire fences, the treacle toffee, a bottle of Coke and a packet of crisps on the wall in the garden of the Victoria Inn, the Welsh words for gents and ladies,[7] the walks, the drives, the white sand, the card games, the occasional jellyfish, the tiny cinema in Nefyn where Dad took us to see *Live and Let Die* in 1975, the walk across the golf course at Morfa Nefyn, a drop scone from Mrs Williams, feeding the chickens with Mr Williams, playing on the rope swings, running with Meg the sheepdog, eating steak and kidney pie at the Sparta Café, reading James Herbert's *The Rats* and being too scared to have it on my bedside table at night, the glow-in-the-dark Moonlighter Frisbee, rock pools, Mum seemingly having her hair done every other day in Pwllheli, rain cascading down the spiral stone staircase like a waterfall in the tower at Caernarfon Castle, Simon being told by Mum he could 'get his vest wet' at Black Rock Sands and charging into the sea wearing it ... these are all memories made in Wales.

Smashing place, but how did we justify going back to the same map reference every year? (In 1980 we went mad and tried Jersey for the first time. It was so good we went back there every year for the next decade!) First, everybody went on holiday to the same place in the Seventies. I have anecdotal evidence of this. After all,

---

5. 'Cooknoe'.
6. 'Toaster'.
7. *Dynion* and *merched*, I think. The only Welsh – apart from *croeso* (welcome) – we learned in eight years.

who except for the rich could afford to experiment? In 1975, just to be adventurous, we decided to stay for one week on the island of Anglesey, then move on to Mrs Roberts's farmhouse for the second week. OK, so Anglesey was in North Wales and it looked out on to the same bay as Nefyn and Aberdesach, but it was still new, still a relative voyage into the unknown. On arrival that fateful Saturday morning, it quickly became apparent that Mum was far from satisfied with the house we were to stay in (I remember there were flies all over the lounge window – I described it as 'tatty and horrible' in my diary), so the decision was made. We drove away, back over the Menai Strait and into the Wales we knew. It was as if this was our punishment for trying somewhere new. We ended up calling Mrs Roberts from a phone box and she put us up in the bungalow.

Two years later, we attempted once again to go off-piste, booking a second self-catering holiday in Ilfracombe, Devon. Same story: arrived (after a six-hour drive, during which Melissa won the sick cup), inspected the place, deemed it uninhabitable, turned around, drove all the way back to Northampton. It's not that Mum was picky: compared to the homely farmhouses in Llithfaen, this place was cold, musty and unlived-in with ugly bedspreads. What's worse, it had been recommended to us as a nice place to stay by a friend of Mum and Dad's. This was a holiday with all the good bits taken out, leaving just the six-hour car journeys, with a short break between to view a damp house. Melissa was sick on the way home too.[8]

When we made the momentous decision *not to go to Wales* in 1980, we might have been compensating for all those years conservatively pounding the same tarmac on the way to the same beaches

---

8. Our reward on the drive back was a consoling sit-down Wimpy. The Wimpy hamburger remained magical to us because we so rarely had one. How can a Big Mac hold the same spell today? It can't. I have a feeling the burgers we ate on the front at Pwllheli weren't Wimpys *per se*. We called them Wimpys just like people call vacuum cleaners Hoovers. I ate my first ever true Wimpy in 1973, when we were taken out for one as part of Paul Cockle's birthday bash. (I rather sweetly describe the place as 'the Wimpy bar' in my diary.) It was here that I first encountered the mouth-watering menu: the Wimpy Brunch, the Shanty Brunch (fish and chips), the Brown Derby (doughnut and whipped cream) and that coiled sausage (never had one of those). The 'Wimpy' we had in Pwllheli was from an outdoor stand, cooked on a flat grill while you salivated. It was eaten sitting on a wall or a bench, and tasted all the better for that. And at least Mum didn't have to cook it.

with the same sandwiches packed in the same beach bags. In fact, we were beaten into submission by Nan Mabel and Pap Reg, who had been singing the praises of Jersey for some time. Plus, Dad had a decent bonus from work, so we could afford to go a little upmarket. It was the start of a new decade, and we were going to cross a major body of water for the first time in our lives. (Actually, I'd been across the Channel in 1978 for that French trip, but this was our first time abroad as a family.[9])

Perhaps fittingly, it began with a four-hour car journey, from Northampton to the port at Weymouth (so far, so familiar). Then a seven-hour ferry trip, during which something magical happened, as if to mark the paradigm shift: only one of us was sick, and it was Dad.

Crisps and grapes mainly. 'B' deck. I'm sure it was as much of a shock to him as to the rest of us, and it revealed a welcome chink in his mortal armour. No longer was he a god, he was a man. A man who smelt of sick. When we arrived, exhausted and crumpled by what was the best part of a day's travelling, at the Merton Hotel in St Helier, Jersey, we didn't feel like the sort of family who would stay at a hotel at all, but this feeling of inferiority (alright, inappropriateness) soon passed. We settled into our new lives almost immediately.

On the face of it, Jersey wasn't so different to the Lleyn Peninsula – it was rural, they had animals in fields (albeit cows), it occasionally rained (although less occasionally), and what we did in the daytime was drive to beaches and sit behind a windbreak banged in with rocks. I was 15 now, so holiday specials held less allure – transplanted by *Mad* magazine and horror novels – but Simon and I continued to play together, tennis balls and frisbees. However, the change in our holidaying pattern was profound and irreversible. We were staying in a hotel. Waiters brought us food with French names. There was a pool. There were *other people*.

---

9. Simon and I were the first Collinses to travel by air. In 1983, Mum and Dad decided in their customary benevolence that the pair of us could *fly* to Jersey while they took the car over on the ferry. ('Twats!' as I rather unkindly wrote in my diary.) I had a Bacardi and Coke on the plane and thought I was Spandau Ballet.

Dovetailing perfectly with my hormones, Jersey proved itself a place to meet girls.[10] Holidays suddenly got sociable. Mum and Dad – for the first time ever – made friends on holiday, buying rounds in the ballroom, swapping addresses, that sort of caper. In other words, from 1980 onwards, our tastes became more sophisticated. We demanded more from the fortnight. Nightly cabaret in the ballroom, bingo, discos, the hotel photographer laying out his wares on a trestle table each morning in the lobby. We never looked back. We stayed at the Merton right through the Eighties – I even joined them there when I was at college – and it's such a family-friendly place, always improving, that Simon and Melissa have been back with their kids. Three generations having a great time. Pampered. Corrupted by luxury.

Me? I've reverted back to type. My idea of a perfect holiday now is a rented cottage in Ireland. Driving, walking, reading, sitting outside pubs. I even mispronounce the place-names. I expect I'm trying to recapture the cut-price, easily-pleased, self-catering, all-weather paradise of Wales. But that would take a plastic potty, a *Buster* holiday special and some Refreshers. Some things are best left in the past.

---

10. See Chapter 14.

nine

A Sip of Tonic

I warn you not to be ordinary,
I warn you not to fall ill, and I warn you not to grow old.
The best speech Neil Kinnock ever made, Bridgend, 7 June 1983

Pap Reg died while I was writing this book, the last of my grand-parents to go. The angina got him in the end, aged 85, but at least he spent these last few years with all his sensory and mental faculties – indeed, Pap could remember stuff from as far back as the early 1920s, like the address where his headmistress lived (the corner of Forfar Street and Harlestone Road) and the specific Meccano set his parents bought him while off school with whooping cough aged six (the A1 set).[1] A lot like me really. I have the

---

1. Early in 2001, Pap wrote a piece about his schooldays for an anthology published by the National Organisation For Adult Learning. It makes fascinating reading. He writes vividly of life in the 1920s, his father a clerk in the goods yard at Northampton Castle Station but still unable to afford to take the family on holiday every year. His mother 'cried all night' when their landlord told them he was selling the house they rented on Glasgow Street, but his father decided to buy it. He recalls in great detail a holiday on the Isle of Bute – travelling there by paddle steamer and visiting a sugar factory at Greenock – and taking his father's flask to him during the General Strike at his temporary office in a house 'against the old Star public house' (he was secretary of the Railway Clerks Association). 'On Fridays my mother got me to call at the Maypole shop which was close to the school, to buy a piece of currant, rich fruit or cream cake plus a pound of fresh butter. Also on Friday after school, we used to visit Agutters at the corner of Talbot Road and buy a 1d hot sausage.' Pap sent me a copy of the booklet, *Learning Now and Then: Memories of Education through the Years* in June 2001, obviously proud of being in print. He should have been writing a book, not me.

same instinct to collect, horde and map, make sense of it all by keeping things close, knowing where to lay my hands on them.

They talk about putting your affairs in order. Pap left not a single loose thread. He died before Christmas 2001, but he'd already written out his Christmas cards and passed on the most recent minutes from his Pensioner's Voice meetings. We all had him down as an organised man, but we had no idea. He had folders and boxes and files back at the house in Lovat Drive, neatly packed with papers and effects, all awaiting collection, as it were. But one of these folders was especially interesting, bulging as it was with memorabilia and cuttings relating to his grandchildren.

Well, grand*child*. Me.

This folder seems to confirm what I already knew: that I loomed large in the lives of Nan Mabel and Pap Reg. It's a regular *This Is Your Life*: every single hand-drawn birthday, Christmas and Easter card I made for them down the years, letters and postcards I'd sent them, programmes I'd designed for sixth-form productions, local newspaper clippings about me and my drawing ('Losing out on his art class',[2] 'Budding artist', 'On-the-Spot Caricatures'[3]), me in the

---

2. 11 March 1980. 'Losing out on his art class' was the subheading to a letter printed in the Northampton *Chronicle & Echo* written by my dad. In it he railed against the education cuts that spelled the closure of Nene College's Saturday morning art classes: 'My own son is affected by the discontinuance of these classes and I know that he has benefited greatly from the teaching and encouragement he has received not only from the staff but also the opportunity he has of mixing with other children from a wide cross-section of the community ... One suggestion is that in future perhaps parents may be prepared to pay on a fee basis ... this would be an example of discrimination both on the grounds of ability to pay and also against children gifted in what is perhaps a less publicised pursuit as compared, for example, with sport.' Way to go, comrade!

3. My rise to fame in the *Chronicle & Echo* continued thanks to my friend Paul Garner, another Nene Saturday boy, and a far more naturally skilful and fluid caricaturist than I, although we did spark off one another and with so many shared interests – *Mad* magazine, films and much later, the music of Talking Heads – we formed a symbiotic partnership. Paul had already had some cartoons in the paper, but in June 1980, his dad, who worked in the print room at the *Chron*, got someone up there interested in the ambitious caricature project we were working on, our 100 Favourite People. They printed 20 of them, all film stars, as a name-the-faces competition. This led to an appearance on BBC1's *Look East* – and the 'Budding artist' article, in which I was cast merely as Paul's 'school-chum' – and a commission from the paper to draw the entire Northampton cricket team. In June 1981, they printed a sequel to our 20 faces, and we have noticeably improved our strokes. Pap kept that one too.

early Eighties local rock band Absolute Heroes ('This school band is hoping to graduate ...'), and me getting my first radio series in 1993 ('Pop writer's adventure on the airwaves'). There are even pages from the *NME*, including my debut in print – a film review of the yachting thriller *Masquerade* – from October 1988 (something I hadn't even got in *my* files), and the handwritten notes for my best man's speech at Simon and Lesley's wedding, 23 March 1987. I don't know how Pap got his hands on those, but when he did, he probably thought, 'I'll put these in the folder.'

There are items relating to the other grandchildren – a cutting about Dean and his radio-controlled cars, one about Simon qualifying as a soldier after 42 weeks' training at Shorncliffe, and the announcement of Charmaine's birth – but I'm afraid the bulk of it is me. Now you might say, well of course it is – I'm the one whose cartooning got me in the *Chronicle & Echo*, I'm the one who knuckled down and made all those Christmas cards for at least ten years – but the truth is not so easy to explain away.

Nan Mabel and Pap Reg systematically spoiled me for the better part of my formative years, not with expensive gifts and lavish feasts (they didn't have the money) but with attention, quality time and special interest. As the first grandchild of four, I had automatically earned a special place in their hearts without even lifting a finger. For that we can forgive them: it happens, I was a novelty. But I always assumed that the newborn snatch the limelight from the already born. Doesn't parental – and grandparental – affection unconsciously shift on to the youngest, the freshest, the cutest? Not in our case. Nothing could convince Nan and Pap that Simon or Melissa were as cherishable as me. Pap called me his 'pidge'. It was short for pigeon: 'Alright, m'pidge.' I didn't hear him call anybody else this.

Unfortunately Nan was in hospital when Simon was born in 1967, and as such she never really bonded with him as a baby in the way she had with me, or so Mum reckons. Perhaps Nan was unconsciously bitter that the new baby took up so much of Mum's time when *she* was unwell. Either way, it led to a more remote relationship with Simon as he grew up. Again, can't be helped. Circumstance.

But the fact remains: blatant and immovable favouritism held sway in the court of Collins. Nan and Pap made no secret of the fact that I was the anointed one in their eyes. It started out harmlessly enough – buying me my first watch, taking me to Blackpool – but ended in black farce, with Nan 'whittling' to all and sundry about me living down in perilous London, while all along Simon was on patrol with his unit in Northern Ireland, many years before the ceasefire, something that didn't seem to concern her. (I won't implicate Pap in this – he wasn't the whittler.)

As the Pet Shop Boys pointedly asked: what had I done to deserve this?

* * *

I was lucky enough to have all four grandparents around while I was growing up, and although I didn't appreciate them as *people* until I was out of my teens (which kid does?), I enjoyed their presence throughout my early years, and not just because they bought me comics, although that was a factor.

It was Dad's parents who got to be called Nan and Pap Collins, family name and all that, but in a way Nan Mabel and Pap Reg were the lucky ones: they got to be identified by their given names. More personal, they were Mabel and Reg. The other Nan and Pap weren't Bill and Win, not to us. However, here's a bombshell: when we were younger, we preferred Nan and Pap Collins to Nan Mabel and Pap Reg.

I am filled with the deepest remorse at the memory of this defining incident, but here it is. It happened on the doorstep at Winsford Way back in the days when the estate was still a building site. Mum and Dad were taking Simon and me to Nanny and Pappy's (to use the juvenile). Simon asked which Nanny and Pappy. They told him: Nanny and Pappy Collins. He asked which ones they *were*. I told him:

'The *nice* Nanny and Pappy.'

Clang! Mum soon put me right on my *faux pas*. Both Nannys and Pappys were nice. And of course she was right – they were – it was just that Nan and Pap Collins were more *obviously* nice:

rounder, sillier, less tidy, more chaotic, and they had pets: a sweet little dog called Sally, replaced by Butch, who we think was abused by its previous owner as he hid whenever he heard the swoosh of a golf club on telly.[4] Nan and Pap Collins lived in a late Victorian terraced house, slightly worn and jerry-built (Pap had literally fashioned his own lean-to 'extension' out of wood and corrugated plastic sheeting). This was a fun place, full of stuff, with a musty, scary cellar where Pap made ramshackle things and effected make-do repairs. Once, on *Play Away*, they showed you how to make a dynamic-looking bouncing marble track out of jam jars with old pieces of balloon stretched over them. Pap Collins had made one for us the very next day.

Now it's not that Pap Reg *couldn't* make us toys, just that he *wouldn't*, and *didn't*, repressed perhaps by the iron rule of Nan Mabel.[5] He had been a tool-maker by trade, don't forget, and his first ever job, aged 14, was producing and assembling parts for model trains at Wintringhams, but at Lovat Drive he had no cellar full of junk like jam jars and old balloons.

Nan and Pap Collins did not whittle. Their house at Adnitt Road was clean but not fussy like Lovat Drive (blimey, even the street names spoke volumes: one hard and bruiserish, the other fragrant and idyllic). Both sets of grandparents were of stout, working-class stock, but only Mabel and Reg had gone up in the world, with Pap's union job. Pap Reg drove, he had vehicular independence and they took themselves on holiday to Wales, Exmoor and Minehead (they even flew to Jersey and Canada).

---

4. Pap told us he'd trained Butch to bark whenever a black person went past the house, which was patently untrue, if a disturbing boast.

5. Mum tells me that Pap Reg was very much the master of his own house when she was a girl, but somewhere along the line, Mabel took over his duties. He wasn't henpecked, he just preferred a quiet life. I discovered from a speech at his retirement party in 1981 that he could have moved up the ranks at the AEU, but Mabel wouldn't countenance moving house, so he stayed put. This was said as a testament to his loyalty, but there was a tinge of regret here that I picked up and never forgot. She held him back. She was no dragon though, simply a persuasive and strong-willed woman, and he *was* loyal. I'll bet he never *looked* at another woman. He once controversially went to see *Emmanuelle* when he was in London on business, but this was common family knowledge, and rather amusing to us too.

Nan and Pap C went on holiday by coach to the Isle of Wight and Bournemouth, or else Dad drove them.[6]

The house at Lovat Drive, a trim 1939 bungalow, had a front and back garden, with a hedge and a wall and a garden path and a side entrance. The front window at Adnitt Road looked out on to the street and the back garden was more of a yard. Guess what – we played in the back yard, we rarely *went* into the back garden. Pap C, true to form, even made us a slide from scratch.

This is not to say we didn't enjoy going to Lovat Drive. We did. Nan and Pap kept some really nice Dinky toys there for us, and of course, they were first in the family to get a colour television! It just wasn't a place where much *matter* was displaced.

Nan Mabel could be uptight, Nan Collins seemed to have a constant smile on her face (what a great dinner lady she must have made), and she would greet us all like homecoming heroes the minute we stepped through the door. Nan Mabel would be worrying that we were 'bringing dirt in'. Symbolically, the front door at Adnitt Road was always open (until Dad subsequently convinced them that they should probably lock it).

So, even though it was sinful to describe one set of grandparents as the *nice* Nanny and Pappy, their open-door policy said something inviting about their world. Nan and Pap Collins had lots of seven-inch records, things like 'Little White Bull', 'March of the Mods' and 'The Laughing Gnome', and what's more, we were allowed to 'put them on fast' by switching the dansette to 78 rpm. To be at Adnitt Road was very heaven.

So why did I spend a lot more time at Lovat Drive?

'I came to Nanny's house to sleep' is a recurring phrase in my diaries. It was a tradition: I would go to Nan Mabel and Pap Reg's house, on my own, and sleep over, usually for two nights in a row, creating a mini-break. In effect, I would get to be an only child for a couple of days, see what Dean's life was like. It was a fact of my

---

6. It seems crazy this but Pap C was having trouble walking due to an unpleasant but fixable ailment he refused to see a doctor about. In June 1979, Dad drove them 140-odd miles to Bournemouth and then drove back, repeating the process a week later. I went along for the ride actually, and enjoyed the quality time with Dad. He bought me a *Mad* Super Special for the three-hour home journey, and a *Penthouse* for himself (tucked under the *Mad*).

life: come the school holidays, I would be packed off to Lovat Drive, where, among other things, I would be allowed to stay up late and was usually bought a gift of some nature, an Action Transfer or later an Airfix model. It was a hermetically sealed little world. No harm would come to me here, no siblings would encroach upon my limelight, and the chances are, one of Nan's jolly neighbours like Mrs Brinclow or Mrs Hanson would come to visit and tell me how good my drawings were.

In February 1973 (half-term), I stayed with Nan and Pap for three days and I was allowed to stay up till 9.00, aged seven, to see *Bless This House*. In 1974, I note that I 'came to Nanny's house to sleep' twice in one month, for the weekend 8–10 February (during term-time!), and from Sunday to Tuesday, 24–26 (half-term). 'I stayed up till 9 o'clock,' says the entry for the 25th, 'and played cards with Pappy.' It'll have been Rummy or Draw the Well Dry, and a sip of tonic will have been involved.

Pap Reg gave me my first-ever taste of beer. He called it tonic, and I liked that. Didn't like the beer, but I took it anyway, perhaps aware that it was a rite of passage. In the summer, Nan and Pap would invariably drive me out to a pub, and we would sit in the garden and I'd have a bottle of Coke with a straw in and a packet of crisps. At a time when neither Coke nor crisps were the kind of thing you had in the house, this was a rollercoaster ride of extra-curricular pleasure.

In April 1974 I was back again (this time at the Easter holidays), doing 'some Spirographing' on Sunday, visiting Oakley Garden Centre on Monday, and coming home on Tuesday. Dean would often come up to Nanny's too, although he rarely stayed overnight. You'd think Lovat Drive was miles away from home – but it's only the other side of the town centre. Ten minutes by car.

In July '75 I came down for a record five days during the school holidays: Lego, yogurts, Rummy, *two* Cokes at a pub, and staying up till 9.30 to watch *The Squirrels*.[7]

---

7. Office sitcom from *Rising Damp* creator Eric Chappell, set in the accounts department of International Rentals with the fabulous Ken Jones and Bernard Hepton in the lead roles (although aged ten I went for the more obviously humorous characters played by the younger Ellis Jones and smooth operator Alan David). Lasted three series, 1975–77.

This was not a case of my own parents trying to get rid of me – I'd long since stopped being the little sod – though I expect they were happy enough to have one less mouth to feed for a couple of days. No, the Lovat Drive arrangement seems to have become routine because it suited Nan and Pap and it suited me. On the face of it, Simon seemed to benefit too – after all, no Andrew meant more attention for him from Mum and Dad. Knowing that I would inevitably be spoiled while I was away, they spoiled Simon in return (to a sensible degree, of course). For instance in August 1973, when I got back from a four-day stay he'd been allowed to start collecting football stickers in my absence. He nearly had the page of Arsenal already. He *was* still bitter of course (not that he expressed it at the time), partly because he couldn't understand it.

I was a Nanny's boy. Since Pap would be at work if I went there on weekdays, it was Nan who had the lion's share of me. Even if she was pottering in the kitchen making treacle tart and listening to Jimmy Young ('What's the recipe today, Jim?') she still had me about the place, like a surrogate son I suppose, a surrogate angel. Don't all grandparents subconsciously treat their grandchildren as their own? It would make sense. All the advantages of being a parent again, without the hassle or the commitment or going up the school.

I was happy: if it meant missing my friends for a couple of days, at least I got lots of drawing done at the little fold-out table in the living room (I considered it *my* table, just as the spare bedroom was *my* bedroom). Here at Lovat Drive was *a bit of peace and quiet*, something you don't usually appreciate as a kid, but I soon learned to. There was plenty of time to go down the field and ride my bike when I got back to Mum and Dad's. I think being packed off to Nanny's was a sophisticating influence on me. When we weren't playing Scrabble (they had the Deluxe), we watched grown-up telly like *Columbo*, *Kes* and – a strangely ultra-vivid memory, this – *The Shoes of the Fisherman* (a 1968 epic starring Anthony Quinn as a Russian bishop who becomes Pope, which taught me about the white smoke).

I bonded with Nan over mid-afternoon telly like *Houseparty*,[8]

---

8. A ladies' lifestyle show from Southern TV from the days when the concept of 'daytime' hadn't really been invented.

and with Pap over the strawberry nets at the allotment. I was their pidge. They even took me away for long weekends to Blackpool, easily the most glamorous place on earth, where we stayed in a *hotel* (years before Jersey). We rode on a tram, thrilled to the illuminations, went up the Tower and saw Mike Yarwood and Freddie Starr live. I ate my first toffee apple in Blackpool (and promptly threw it all up again). It was like a filmed montage designed to convey fun, leisure and abandon.

So it was a win–win situation – at the time. I only became self-conscious about the bare-faced injustice of it all vis-à-vis Simon when I grew up a bit and stopped going down Nanny's. How they must have hated that day, when I was suddenly too grown-up to want to go down Lovat Drive any more – when I didn't 'lovat' any more. The day my voice broke. That was the day they had to wave parenthood goodbye for ever and accept mortality's fate.

The ritual continued through 1976 (a four-day stay in August: 'Pap got me a load of paper, a *Whoopee* and three Tempos'; three days in October: 'I had four fresh cream chocolate éclairs today'), 1977 (February: 'Had chocolate éclairs for tea'; August: 'I helped Pap do the potatoes') and 1978 (January: 'Nan, Pap, Mrs Hanson and I went up Harlestone Furs for a blow';[9] August: 'We watched *Out*,[10] it was magic'). But in 1979, it was suddenly and without ceremony all over. My age – 14, a *funny* age – had caught up with me, and the allure of cards, *Columbo* and tonic ran out, superseded by punk rock, girls and hanging round the shops.

Without any of us realising it (although Nan and Pap must have sensed it coming), the Sunday to Tuesday I spent at Lovat Drive in August '79 was my last ever stopover. It had it all: trifle, a visit by Dean, a trip to Auntie Jean's, *Moving Target*,[11] and Litchborough

---

9. 'Blow' was a Ward family colloquialism for a bracing walk.
10. Gritty ITV six-parter from Euston Films about Frank Ross (Tom Bell), just out of nick, and bent on finding the slag who shopped him.
11. Paul Newman in a 1966 Chandleresque private-eye thriller written by the great William Goldman, called *Harper* in the US. According to my diary, it made a considerable impression on me: 'Good and excitin' ... with kidnappings, busting big woodfiles into people's heads, lobbing people off balconies, driving cars off cliffs ... goodies turning out to be baddies, etc.' A career in film criticism awaited me.

Garden Centre. But that was it. Goodnight, Nan, goodnight, Pap. They were my own personal grandparents no longer, their privileges were taken away, no more access, no more weekends. I was off to chat up Cindy Offord, listen to The Ruts and get hot under the collar when Sarah Brightman and Hot Gossip came on *The Kenny Everett Video Show*.

It was a difficult time, especially for Nan. I started to wear my hair spiky, a very real cause for concern. I still visited Lovat Drive, but only with the rest of the family, and like any teenage Kevin, I could think of about twenty places I'd rather be than at my grandparents' house. Boo-oring.

* * *

Where had the *nice* Nanny and Pappy been all this time? (Talking of whom, it's clear to me now that I innocently distinguished them as *nice* because it's Simon who wanted to know – to him, they probably were the *nice* ones.) Well, even though we never once slept over at Adnitt Road, we were there without fail every Wednesday during the school holidays for dinner and tea and a walk in the park – more ritual, more institution. Though of course I had to share Nan and Pap C with Simon and Melissa, and share we did. No dangerous favouritism here. A comic for one, a comic for all.

Was it dangerous though? In the final analysis, did the routine act of spoiling me actually *spoil* me? (As in: you'll spoil your dinner.) I think not. It drove no wedge between my brother and me – we were great mates through it all, even though he admitted to me recently that it did trouble him as a child. It didn't turn me into a little public schoolboy, demanding a hand of Rummy and a glass of beer at all hours and greeting every parental injustice with a snivelling cry of, 'Well, *Nanny* lets me!' In fact, my regular disappearances seemed to help maintain the equilibrium of the Collins household. No lasting harm was done. Not even the two Blackpool mini-breaks in '73 and '75 – on both occasions much play was made of buying everybody presents while I was on the Golden Mile (soldiers for Simon, a book for Melissa, a flower holder for Mum).

My special relationship may have pushed Pap C and Simon closer together (what use did he have for a Pap who watched the war go by from a factory in Jimmy's End?). But they were old combat-buddies to start with. Pap C saw some of himself in Simon.

Nan Mabel and Pap Reg saw some of Brian in me. Uncle Brian was the proverbial apple of their eye, the eldest and their only son (Mum and Auntie Janice used to have to share a bed as kids, while Brian had his own room – the room I would eventually come to think of as *mine*). It was a hard day for them when Brian finally got married and left home. Though older than Mum and Janice, he was the last to fly the nest; he had been a resident of Lovat Drive for 30 years. He also worked within walking distance at the Express Lifts factory as a draughtsman and he would still pop back to Nan's for lunch when he was married. The force was strong in this one, and he clearly left a big hole, particularly for Nan. I was a substitute Brian.

It all makes sense, as these things invariably do. Philip Larkin advised to 'get out as early as you can' in 'This Be the Verse', but Brian obviously never read it. He did it in his own time.

I 'got out' of Nan and Pap's at exactly the right time. Our relationship never really soured, even during punk. Nan would whittle about my appearance, especially when I discovered hair dye at 16, but I remained her favourite to the end, and Pap and I belatedly bonded over our socialist ideals, his deep-seated, mine 'discovered' at college. We were very much isolated within the family, but that made the bond stronger.

I carried on making birthday cards for the both of them right through college, because to have stopped would have been taken as a snub. (I was under no pressure to make cards for the *nice* Nanny and Pappy, although I drew them a cracking caricature for their golden wedding which I hope compensated.)

I'll be honest, some of these cards I made for Nan M and Pap R are pretty good. They are surprisingly satirical, many of them gently taking this piss out of Nan's ways. After some impersonal early efforts, with Top Cat ('love from Andrew, Boss Cat, Spook, Fancy, Brain, Choo Choo and Benny and Officer Dibble'), *Monster Fun* influenced spooks and Peanuts characters on them, they begin to feature cartoons of Nan and Pap themselves. For instance, on the occasion of Pap's 60th birthday I have pictured him addressing a union meeting; 'What do we vote, brothers?' he is asking the assembled flat-capped 'workers'. Open the card and he is being blown off his platform by their response: 'We vote that we wish a happy 60th to Brother Reg!!'

The Christmas card for 1979 lampoons Nan's recurring fantasy about me being a choirboy. In the drawing, spiky-topped, I am singing from a book marked 'Punk Hymns by S. Vicious'. Inside there's a PS under the greeting: 'Don't forget to show this card to Mrs Brinclow and Mr and Mrs Burt and all the girls at Guild and all at Lovat Drive.' A cheeky reference to Nan's tendency to show me off which became postmodern when, presumably, she showed it to Mrs Brinclow and Mr and Mrs Burt and all the girls at Guild. (Perhaps she never did!)

In 1981 I have combined Nan's 60th and Pap's retirement into one huge card – with a poem for each occasion (what am I, the Poet Laureate now?). In Nan's half there's a Marks & Spencer gag ('I hope you like this card – you can't take it back!!'), and in Pap's it's more union laughs ('Now Brother Ward/Will never get bored/If you want to see Reg/He'll be cultivating veg'). I have by now turned them both into serviceable cartoon characters. They were flattered of course, and despite her reputation for being highly strung, Nan took all this ragging in good spirit. The same year's Christmas card sees the pair of them snowbound, inching along in Pap's car with Nan giving it the full whittle: 'Ooooh, Reg. Careful. Watch this bit. Oooh-er. There's no salt on this road. I'm all worked up. Watch it, Reg. Be careful!! Slow down a bit. Not so fast. I shall get no sleep tonight. We're late, Reg. We're missing *Blankety Blank*, Reg.'

What fun we had at Nan's expense. By 1982's birthday card I am mocking her neuroses relentlessly, comparing myself ('the arty one') with Simon ('the army one'). In cartoon form we stand side by side, me with my henna, drumsticks and rolled-up jeans, Simon in cadet uniform and 'smart regulation haircut', saluting if you please. 'In a few years,' runs the legend beneath my likeness, 'when he's a star you'll be proud of him.' Under Simon it reads: 'In a few years when he's an officer you'll be proud of him. What more could you want?'

It borders on the tragic, this card. Simon and I have both signed it ('from your two lovable grandchildren'), and yet of course, it's all my own handiwork, so I was in line for all the praise anyway. There's so much hope and optimism in this card – not that I would be a 'star' (doing what?) or that he would be an officer, but that Nan Mabel would be equally interested in our fates. I'm desperately trying to make her proud of my brother, pushing his very real achievements like a PR. It would all be for naught.

She was proud of me when I became, if not a star, a published journalist – although she'd have preferred it if I could have managed this without leaving Northampton and the family's immediate orbit. As I said, Simon moved to Folkestone, then Colchester, then Hanover with his job and not once did Nan lament the distance. He made Corporal, but she wasn't proud of that.

She also denied her own passing years after 60, which I always thought was deeply sad, although we made a big joke out of it at the time. 'Don't throw away this piece of work,' says 1981's card, 'I'll re-use it next year (and the next)!' If only. '62 again?' asks her 64th birthday card. 'And you don't look a day over 64 ...'

The message inside also hints at something subtly heartbreaking to me now, as I sit here moist-eyed and return everything to Pap's folder:

Simon's in the army, I'm in college and Melissa's growing boobs!!
We're growin' up.

Had I no empathy for an elderly lady's feelings? Was I intent on rubbing salt into Nan's inner wounds with all this loose talk of things past? Was this my under-the-counter payback for what she and Pap had done to me with their undying love?

Or was it just a set-up for the punchline?

Could be worse – I could be growing boobs.

1977

Selected Extracts From My Diary

The Queen's Silver Jubilee, and a sturdy, black WH Smith Desk Diary with handsome, embossed '1977'. Somewhat ruined by the overenthusiastic application of decorative tape to the cover – purchased with tokens off the back of Sugar Smacks packets in March – and a little Jubilee sticker.

I have filled the so-called 'Memoranda' section before the diary starts with many wonderful things, including another aerial view of our Action Man barracks, an in-depth questionnaire for all six of our Action Men (in which we discover that, for example, Captain Steven James Livingstone is nicknamed 'Libby', enjoys motorcycling and fish and chips and is best friends with Rodgers – honestly, it's like backstage at the National), and a self-penned, quasi-Pythonesque Dictionary Of Useless And Silly Words (sample text: AGGRO *– laying in the boot and dobbing over;* BOGEYMEN *– stupid, green, sticky blokes who get you when you come home from Cubs;* PUNK ROCK *– heavy 'music', Stranglers etc.;* POUFF *– a bit that way, queero;* UGLY *– Donny Osmond … and so it goes).*

A further series of questionnaires have been filled in by non-fictional people, from Simon to Paul Milner. In my own, we discover that my favourite film is The Spy Who Loved Me, *my favourite food is beans, my pet hates are vegetables and haircuts, and my favourite book is* Airport '77.

Joined-up writing lasts like a New Year's resolution until 5 January, from whence it's back to comic-style capitals. The drawings improve but a mood of couldn't-care-less takes over towards the end of the year with very brief and scribbly entries. Funny age, 11–12.

Saturday, 1 January

Made a Lego house in the morning. Watched *Swap Shop*. Watched *Willy Wonka and the Chocolate Factory* in the afternoon, after playing Monopoly. New series of *Jim'll Fix It* and *Dr Who*. Watched *Starsky and Hutch*.

Sunday, 2 January

Did drawing in the morning. More to my *Target* comic. Went to Nan Mabel's for tea and the tea was lovely. Won 12p in bingo.[1] I started doing a great picture of seagulls with my inks.

Saturday, 8 January

Went shopping this morning. I bought a fab Britains cowboy on horseback. Got some library books. Si went to the Cubs fancy dress party as Dracula. Dad mended my record player. We watched a new series of *Mike Yarwood*.[2] Dad, Simon and I made our model planes. By the way Simon came second in his fancy dress party. Mum wouldn't let us watch *Starsky and Hutch*.

Sunday, 9 January

Went for a 'blow' in the park. It was raining. We saw a squirrel. We saw some mice in the bird cages. Then we popped in Pap Collins'. I got two weeks of *B&MFC*.[3] Pap gave us two a transfer

---

1. Nan M. and Pap R. had a home bingo set, pre-war, which would frequently come out at family gatherings and keep us all transfixed like the decent working-class people we deeply were. (We called out 'House!' – or '*Hace!*' in Northamptonian – what further proof do you require?) The set consisted of a metal board (metal!) with all the numbers etched in by Pap himself in his old job, a cloth bag containing 100 wooden numbers, and a good thick book of paper bingo cards. It was all there. Just add a motley clutch of pens and half-pencils. The old ones are the best.
2. That'll be *Mike Yarwood in Persons*, the first of four series he did under that imprint for the BBC between '77 and '81 (plus specials). Then he crossed the floor to Thames, where, like Morecambe & Wise before him ('78), his decline began. Why do they do it? Can the money matter so much? Or is it just a comedians' graveyard, a resting place to which all dying stars are drawn? (I don't blame Thames, that lovable warren by the river in Teddington: the Goodies went not to Thames but to LWT the same year as Yarwood defected and the diminishing effect was the same.)
3. *Buster & Monster Fun Comic*, whose merger was as easy to swallow as its new title. I read in the paper this morning that there's an advertising agency called Abbott Mead Vickers BBDO. If you insist.

each. Dad hung Simon's plane up on the ceiling. I cut a load of faces out of the *TV* and *Radio Times*. And I've drawn cartoon bodies for them.

Tuesday, 18 January

Mum got us three a toothbrush each. Mine's white. We had to draw a god for RE. I did Collius, God of Drawing! Mrs Goodall is away yet again. We had Mr Bates. No homework. Jes, Angus and I did a brill sequence in PE. Saw *Spot On*.[4] Si went to Cubs.

Thursday, 10 February

I am getting brill at drawing figures now. In art I painted a footballer. I got 18/20 in the French test. Quite a bit of homework. It was our last lesson with Mrs Watling today as she is having a baby in April, she's leaving tomorrow. I drew loads of figures tonight. I saw *Just a Nimmo*. Simon did his length at swimming.

Tuesday, 22 February

This morning I 'lost' my two Parker pens and so did Gibbons at the same time. Kim and Cameron also 'lost' theirs some weeks back. Very suspicious. I've been round all the classes.[5] Choir's back on again. A bit of homework. Mum cracked her false teeth and is using her spare ones.

Saturday, 26 February

This morning *Swap Shop*'s Swaporama came to Northampton. Si went. But in vain. And he got his shoes covered in thick mud.[6]

---

4. Possibly (I have no sources) a regional magazine programme. We certainly seemed to like it. (I even bothered to reproduce its logo in my diary: concentric circles.)

5. I think we know what I'm getting at here. I learned a valuable legal lesson while coping with the evident theft of my two Parker pens (I think one must have been a propelling pencil – I wouldn't have had two ink pens): you must never accuse anybody, not even an unnamed pen-thieving ghost. Crime investigation is entirely euphemistic: my pens have gone missing; I have lost my pens.

I also learnt a more practical lesson: to use biros and Pentels at school in future. Pens are not meant to be of sentimental value. There should be no whodunit after the loss of a pen. Not even the 'loss'.

I stayed at home. Dad and Mum bought: a picture for the hall, a doormat and a mat for the kitchen. Mum and Dad went over the road to Mel and Margaret's[7] and Si and I stayed here and watched *Thunderball.*

Sunday, 27 February
Si went on the Cub cycle-cross at Overstone. We watched him. He came fifth. Very good. Nan M and Pap R came. I started a mad magazine called *Ferret's Own.*

Friday, 4 March *MY BIRTHDAY*
I got ... cassette recorder, two Parker pens, Concorde picture, Asterix book, money (about £7.50), Tempo. Went to the dentist's in the afternoon. Had a filling. Si had couple out. A bit of homework. My party tomorrow sort of. Just Angus and Soardsy. Melissa is a bit off and was off school.

Sunday, 13 March
Si and I went down the field. Cor. Interesting. Sorry. My days are getting a bit boring these days.[8]

---

6. Our maiden brush with the painted whore of television. Swaporama, the town-hopping roadshow part of *Swap Shop*, always looked enjoyably chaotic on TV, with battered toys being passed across the crowd for barter – but it was only when Simon went down to Abington Park the week the circus came to Northampton that we discovered just how unenjoyably chaotic it was. I remember the call-out at the start of *Swap Shop* that morning: Keith Chegwin up the familiar, nay iconic climbing frame shaped like a space rocket. At that delicious moment I tasted the thrill of seeing a piece of playground apparatus I'd ascended, *on telly*, with *Cheggers up it*. The Swaporama may have been local that Saturday – less than a mile from where I was sitting – but for me, at home, the experience remained remote: clean and annexed. For Simon it was mud-caked and humiliating, and when he got back and related his woes, the screen came down: the real Wizard of Oz was revealed.
7. New arrivals in Winsford Way: the popular Mills family, from the West Midlands. Mel (bald and gregarious), Margaret, elder son Martin (went to agricultural college where, one hopes, he was able to properly cultivate that bum-fluff moustache) and daughter Sarah (had a lot of problems with her legs or was it her back?). We liked them so much, when they moved away to Crowborough in East Sussex, we went to visit them. I fell in a river, possibly the Ouse, and Mel entertained us with a road sign he'd spotted locally bearing the place-names BALLS GREEN and BLACOMBE (which doesn't exist, so perhaps he'd misread BALCOMBE, or tweaked it for comic effect).
8. First sighting of 'onset teenage ennui'.

Monday, 14 March

Dad got us a Matchbox track from Green Shield Stamps. Went to the library after tea. Got: *Heritage of Horror, Dad's Army, Vision On* and *Asterix*.

Wednesday, 16 March

Normal lessons. Usual stuff. It rained. No drama. Boring. Boring. (I mean today's diary was boring.)

Thursday, 17 March

It rained a bit. Normal lessons.

Sunday, 20 March

Made a *Jaws* play kit (including rubber Jaws, Lego *Orca*, Quint, policeman and Professor Dreyfuss, two drunks, wreckage, boat).[9] Played Newmarket.

Monday, 28 March

My denim waistcoat is well and truly finished. It snowed a tich bit but didn't settle. Played with Carl. He gave me a load of *Krazy*s and I've cut them out. Marbles are back in craze.

Friday, 13 May

Did athletics in games. Gained two Habitat marbles. Did drama and missed French. I had a brill scrap with Simon. I really bashed him in.

Wednesday, 18 May

Everyone went down the field, including: me, Angus, Dash, Kate, Taf, Gibby, B Jnr, Ally, Westy, Argy, Chris, Gibs, Si, Roobarb, Hirsty, etc. etc. etc.[10] Argy and Gibby had a great scrap.

Saturday, 28 May

Went shopping. Melissa is being a twit. It was brill at swimming. It was sweltering. Poufter Dad won't let me watch *That's Life*. Maddo.[11]

Monday, 30 May

Played an ace game of stony for about two hours with me, Angus, Jes, Doyan,[12] Little Paul, Doboe,[13] David and Dashfield. Si gave me two marbles, two Habitats, one gobby and one ball bearing. Ace! Brill!

Sunday, 5 June

Looked at Dad's *Mayfair* magazines. Wahey! Ssssh![14] Saw *World About Us* about a zoo doctor. That's about all I spose. Si and I went on a Jubilee tour of the estate on bikes. We saw all the decorations.[15]

---

9. I have by now seen *Jaws* (18 March with Dad, Simon and Angus). Though an 'A' certificate, it is by far the most frightening film of my 12 years on earth, and thus, I am now obsessed with it.

10. Some of these names are just that: B Jnr, Ally, Westy, Argy, Chris, Gibs. Who were these abbreviated souls? I can identify the following: Dash is definitely Chris Dashfield (who also had a Soda Stream); Kate possibly Katy Prout (but I wouldn't put money it); Taf and Gibby the aforementioned Givelin brothers; Roobarb – Paul Roberts; and Hirsty – David Hirst. And that's ignoring 'etc. etc. etc.' whoever in God's nickname *they* were.

11. The epithet 'maddo' is so me and Simon. I don't think anyone else has ever said it.

12. Self-styled nickname for John Lewis, tenuously derived from the fact that John is 'Johan' is Dutch. I never understood it either, but I idolised the long-haired Lewis so much at this stage I would have called him anything he'd asked me to. Daddy, Sir, anything.

13. Another Incomprehensible nickname, this time for Stephen Tite, tall blond kid with bee-sting lips. (Often shortened to Dobs.) He and Lewis had come from the same ecosystem at another lower school where these bizarre names had originated. At least Dave Watson was just Watto.

14. Another disappointing but inevitable slide into proto-adolescence. Dad kept his frankly tame soft porn mags – *Mayfair* and *Penthouse*, none of your tat – in the garage. Mum wouldn't have them in the house, but she seemed to know he kept them, which is interesting. (For instance I didn't have to smuggle the *Penthouse* he bought in Bournemouth into the house inside my *Mad* Super Special.) Poring over these soft-focus, undressed but mostly knees-together 'rude ladies' – as we called them – was certainly a necessary voyage of anatomical discovery, but I was more interested in *Mayfair*'s monthly comic strip 'Carrie', in which the heroine would lose her clothes in a variety of inventive ways. These gave me my first 'confused' feelings.

15. I'm looking at a photo taken on Jubilee Bank Holiday, 7 June. We seem to be in the spirit of this great royal occasion: Mum, Simon and I are wearing identical red, white and blue 'Jeans' T-shirts with Union Jacks on the sleeves, and Jubilee-styled party hats (Simon has fixed an Action Man Union Jack to his and it is hanging down over his eyes, the wag). Melissa is waving a flag. Not a trace of irony here, but it's difficult to convey to people how royal the nation was in 1977. Winsford Way's 'street party' took place not in the street (it was a through road) but in a large tent in Jean and Geoff's back garden. I have decorated my diary by writing each letter in alternate red and blue Tempo. As I write it is the Queen's Golden Jubilee year and I feel I am in good company not giving a fuck.

Tuesday, 14 June

We were all woke up at 6.30 because of loads of thunder plus rainrainrain. The garden was flooded, the roads were flooded and most of all, the school was flooded. It was about 24 inches deep in places. We nearly had to swim in the playground, but the spoilsport caretakers pumped it up.

Tuesday, 28 June

Simon went to Coombe Abbey. I got a Jubilee Crown presented in assembly for being 'highly commended' in an art comp. in which I painted the Muppets. I've joined the Dance and Movement Club.

Wednesday, 29 June

I got through to the second round of the Carol Barratt Art Prize and with the title 'Wave After Wave' in which you could do anything to do with the sea. I did a *Jaws* painting. Had loads of French homework. There was a car crash up the top of the street by the pub. One bloke got killed in it.

Tuesday, 12 July *HOLS IN WALES*

I got extreemly sunburnt. We went to Black Rock Sands. Congratulations!! You have won 'Sentence of the Year 1977' with the most interesting sentence ever written: 'We went to Black Rock Sands.' Wow! The way in which the words flow together. It is stupendous. (What does stupendous mean? Eh? Wot's it mean? I dunno.)[16]

Wednesday, 20 July

It was quite nice and sunny. We discovered the hay barn and Mr Williams said we can climb on it so we did. We went to Black Rock Sands and in a café in Porthmadog I had a knickerbocker glory (45p).[17] Si had a strawberry ice cream milk shake and Melissa had a strawberry whirl.

Sunday, 24 July

It was pretty sunny. But it was windy. I shot down an enemy

Russian nuclear sonic guided missile anti-tank gun plane with a supersonic anti-nuclear plane double-barrelled triple-magazined anti-plane 59 vector gun. (You believe that don't you?) Saw *The Intelligence Men* film. Wot 'orrible writing.

Monday, 25 July

It was quite a nice day. We played on bikes and on Simon's 'skateboard' (bit of wood screwed on a roller skate!!). Tonight I went up Becky's house to give her the fudge I got from Wales. But she wasn't there so I'm going tomorrow maybe.

Tuesday, 26 July

This morning I cycled up Becky's house and she was there this time. I gave her the fudge.[18] I played with Carl after dinner and we made a *Rollerball* go-kart. (It's only got a bit of wood on the front with 'Rollerball' written on it.)

Thursday, 28 July

Dean came down. Simon is being the most stupid git. He keeps being a bum. He is mad. He is thick. Simon smells. He is a slimy toad. He's loony. He has the brain of a backward, demented chimpanzee.

---

16. Irony and sarcasm have arrived, like unwanted, boorish gatecrashers at a party. There'll be trouble.

17. I'd wanted one of these ever since seeing *The Punch and Judy Man* (1962), in which Tony Hancock and child actor Nicholas Webb methodically devour a 'Piltdown Glory' each, one rain-soaked seaside afternoon: 'two scoops of luscious vanilla, two scoops of tasty chocolate, a succulent slice of banana, juicy peach fingers in pure cane syrup, topped with super-smooth butter-fat cream. Oh – and a cherry!' (Mine wasn't that elaborate but it was good enough for me.)

18. A tragic tale of unrequited interest. Becky was Rebecca Warren, befreckled, buxom star of the choir and in the year above. I took a shine to her, mistook her polite reciprocation for encouragement and bought her fudge from Wales. She accepted the gift gracefully but I was simply not ready for boy-girl friendship with the new undertones of pre-teenhood 'confusion'. It was awful, like something out of Mike Leigh. I became obsessed with a small hole in her jumper as we sat there in her mum's front room, eyeing the time. She looked better in school uniform I thought. I never went back. Married to a man called Tim now.

Saturday, 30 July

We went shopping this morning. It was quite hot in the afternoon. I painted my British Infantry Support Group soldiers. They look brill. I've now got the set of *Dr Whos* (free in Weetabix) after a bit of swapping wiv Jonathan next door. Tonight we went up the park to see the paintings.[19] We had an ice cream. Then we popped in Nan C's. I got *Action* wiv an ace Spinball booklet. Wow! *Action* is the brillest comic in the universal solar system. So is *Krazy*.

Friday, 5 August

I painted the Afrika Korps and German soldiers. They look ace. It rained, but it soon cleared up. Gibby, Si and I played Tiggy Off Ground but Si was a bad sport. He is an absolute idiot. He's a bum.

Saturday, 6 August

Wowee! I sent an alien drawing to Si's comic *2000AD* ages ago. Now it's been printed and I'll win £2.[20] Wowee! It rained. Bum.

Tuesday, 30 August

Usual stuff. Skateboards. Si and I played Colditz. Watched *The Rise and Fall of Reginald Perrin*. I have now gone mad on crispbread.

Monday, 2 September

Started doing proper timetable. It was pretty simple. Had games. Wow! Is my scout car model looking great? You bet. I am

---

19. The 16th annual Abington Park Art Exhibition, a pleasant diversion in any year. Anyone could enter a painting, and red stickers were applied to those that had been sold. In later years, I entered pictures of my own, slightly inappropriate caricatures of film stars that always got hung inside the museum in a dark corner (1980: the cast of *The Poseidon Adventure*; 1983: Donald Sutherland and William Atherton from *Day of the Locust* – which I actually *sold* to someone whom I was heartbroken to learn hadn't a clue who the two men were; 1984: a pair of Marlon Brandos, as Vito Corleone and Walter E Kurtz).
20. Fame at last. The issue was dated 13 August ('Prog 25', as they called them in *2000AD*) and I received a letter of notification from the editor Tharg with the traditional salutation, 'Borag Thungg, Earthlet'. It came of course from Kings Reach Tower in Waterloo, London, the home of publishers IPC – where I would later work.

now an honorary fan of the Fonz.[21] He is cool. Fonz is very cool.

Monday, 12 September

The bad news: loads of homework. The really good news: we went to the library. We had chips. We went to Pap's and he had bought me the Airfix 1/32 scale Crusader III tank. Wow, it is just too fantastically brilliantly ace for words.

Thursday, 15 September

I've finished my model. Hardly any homework. Angus came down. I am now a member of the Airfix Modellers Club. I sent away for it. I got a certificate, badge, sticker, membership card, voucher, stamps, letter and kit price list. Wow! And just for 35p. My number is 106339.

Sunday, 25 September

We went to Uncle Pete's and Auntie Wendy's at Wisbech. Uncle Pete gave us some plums, a load of old model planes and a load of lollies. There I did my *Prinz Eugen* model. It's really detailed. It looks brill though.

Sunday, 9 October

Usual stuff. Played Lego. Si and I played around the building site on the dirt heaps. Ace fun. Also saw *Flight Into Holocaust*. A mini plane smashed straight into a skyscraper and it was all about rescuing the passengers.[22]

---

21. The most significant thing about my love (at first sight) of *Happy Days* was the fact that I didn't realise it was set in the 1950s. I just thought it was what America was *like* – and in terms of high school and ice cream parlours I was right. *Happy Days* must have been into its second 'season' by now, having taken two years to cross the Atlantic. (It began in 1974 in the States after the success of the film *American Graffiti* convinced ABC to pick up the rejected 1972 pilot *Love and the Happy Day*.)

22. I wonder if the terrorists who flew into the World Trade Center on 11 September 2001 caught this TV movie? It starred Patrick Wayne (son of John) and Christopher Mitchum (son of Robert); also Lloyd Nolan and Sid Caesar for disaster movie ballast (*Airport* and *Airport '75* respectively).

Thursday, 13 October

Usual lessons. No homework. Before Carl mended his wooden skateboard and gave it to me, he wrote off to the company. Today, they sent him back some new wheels so he gave them to me. Now my board really goes.

Wednesday, 19 October

Played hockey. In the game I came tearing down the wing, burning up the track. I did a 20mph hot shot which burned through the air at the speed of sound and tore through the back of the net and made an eight foot crater in the grass bank. To put it in a nutshell, I didn't play very well.[23]

Monday, 24 October

This morning I went round Watto's and we had an ace H0/00 war game. I had another war game with Si in the afternoon. Watto gave me an unfinished Buffalo Amphibian H0/00 Airfix model. He also lent me a *Mad* Don Martin book. It is brill. Dad went to London. Uncle Brian baby-sitted while Mum went out.

Tuesday, 25 October

This afternoon we went to Auntie Margaret's new big house.[24] They have got a baby retriever called Jack. He is really nice. Saw *Charlie's Angels* wiv a new Angel – Kris.

Wednesday, 2 November

Another stupid power cut. For two and a half hours. Power cuts are bum. So is Simon. He keeps playing with this loony friend of his: Paul McBride. What an idiotic pouf.

---

23. I actually discovered a moderate ability for hockey, quite out of step with my Eddie 'The Eagle' Edwards performance in every other school sport. Never played for the team or bought my own stick or anything but the fact that I wasn't bad is worth noting.

24. As coincidence would have it, two of my uncles are called Alan (one of them spelt Allen). Both are self-employed builders; both built themselves big houses in posh streets. Uncle Alan and Auntie Margaret (Dad's sister) did it first.

Monday, 14 November

Nothing happened today. Well obviously something happened but it's so boring it's not worth putting in. I mean, you would not be interested if I told you that we studied the industrial areas of France in geography or that we started to talk about Edward III in history. Or was it Edward II?

Tuesday, 15 November

I have finished making my skilful teddy in needlework. He is called Arthur.[25]

Saturday, 17 December

Went shopping. Angus came in the afternoon. He gave me a Christmas present: a Honda CB450 motorbike Airfix model. It is ace. He also gave me a ginger beer plant. Nan C baby-sitted again. I am mad.

Tuesday, 20 December

Wrapped up loads of presents. So did Dad. I started making my Honda model. It's so fiddly I feel like smashing it up. But I won't because it is too fabulous.

Saturday, 24 December *CHRISTMAS EVE*

Magic. Dad took me to Binleys and got me all the skateboard padding (helmet, elbow pads and knee pads) for a Christmas pressie to go with my skateboard. Went to the park after dinner. It's Christmas tomorrow! Magic.[26]

Sunday, 25 December *CHRISTMAS DAY*

I got: £18.00 Newporter plastic deck skateboard, all the padding, Boeing 747 model, drawing book, *Goodies Disaster Movie* book, model knife, glue, 11 model paints, 64 Crayola

---

25. After the Fonz, Arthur Fonzarelli.
26. Blame Selwyn Froggitt for this, eponymous Scarsdale halfwit off the Yorkshire TV sitcom, by now into its third rip-roaring series. I don't know why it took this long to start using his catch-phrase.

crayons, *Krazy* annual, Gambler, *Bert Fegg's Nasty Book, Psycho*, mini-stapler, Concorde model, Bugatti model, Lifeguard model, loads of pencils, diary, rubber, RAF refuelling set model, two monster jigsaws, Quality Streets. Magic! Magic! Magic!

Friday, 30 December *MUM'S BIRTHDAY*
More skateboarding. Dad bought me two good paint brushes. Dad took me with him when he played squash. It was a brill match. Dad lost against Les Hull 3–2. Dad played magic.

ten

Big Boys Don't Cry

– Is it bad?
– It's a fire. All fires are bad.
Paul Newman and Steve McQueen, *The Towering Inferno* (1974)

How many people can honestly say that Roger Whittaker gave them nightmares? I can. By the time I'd turned ten – and this seems to be a pivotal year for me, fearwise – anything could put the frighteners up me. Not that I was walking around in a constant state of paranoia, jumping out of my skin every time a car back-fired or a dog barked, it's just that fear definitely *set in* at this time. I expect it was all part of growing up.

Roger Whittaker's 'The Last Farewell' was the song that broke him in America in 1975, though he was already well established in Europe. A moving declaration of love from a sailor about to go to war,[1] it has the heartfelt chorus, 'For you are beautiful, and I have

---

1. The lyric was written by Mr R.A. Webster, a Birmingham silversmith and fan who had entered it into a 1971 competition on Nairobi-born Whittaker's radio show. The winning entry was actually 'Why' (a minor hit in 1971), but Whittaker liked 'The Last Farewell', recorded that too and put it on an album. Four years later it was picked up by the radio station WSB in Atlanta, Georgia, as it captured the mood of the Vietnam era. 'The Last Farewell' went on to become the most requested song on their playlist and within weeks it was a hit not just in the States but all over the world, selling over 11 million copies. Way to go, Mr Webster.

loved you dearly/More dearly than the spoken word can tell.' But never mind that.

I heard the song for the first time on Radio 2 at Nan Mabel's during one of my special-relationship jaunts. I expect Jimmy Young was playing it. For some reason, the following couplet caught my ear, almost without me knowing:

'I've heard there's a wicked war a-blazing/And the taste of war I know so very well.'

And the taste of war I know so very well ...

That very night I had a bad dream. About war. This line from the song kept repeating in my dream like a mantra or the quote at the start of a chapter in a pretentious book. It was otherwise an abstract canvas, this dream, the thrust of which was me being alive during wartime. Jackboots marching past in the street outside, sirens, searchlights, that sort of thing. In my dream, I knew the taste of war so very well, and it frit the life out of me (as they say in Northampton). It was as if actual war had been declared that night.[2]

There's no doubt about it, a trigger had been pulled. The phoney war was over. From that moment onwards, I somehow realised that war was real. World war had happened twice, maybe it could happen again and if it did, this time it would happen to me. None of this was based on information, simply intuition. Black storm clouds had suddenly gathered on my horizon, signalling the end of the age of innocence. All thanks to Roger Whittaker. Bastard.

Now, I enjoyed my black and white war movies on TV – *Ice Cold in Alex, The Wooden Horse* – never missed an episode of *Colditz* or *Dad's Army,* and of course we lived for Action Man, but war up to that point was a setting, not a reality. It was *not a problem.* Even the

---

2. By 'war' of course I meant one that impacted directly on my life, saw me evacuated to Wales in a Mickey Mouse gas mask, that kind of thing. Unbeknown to the ten-year-old me, war raged all around the world in 1975. South East Asia was in turmoil, with South Vietnam falling to the Communists and the Americans hauling ass out of there. Cambodia fell too after a bloody battle, with the Khmer Rouge announcing in Phnom Penh, 'We enter as conquerors and are not here to talk about peace.' (That much was clear, as tales of appalling genocide emerged.) Anarchy reigned in Bangladesh. Civil war in Angola. Christians fought Muslims on the streets of Lebanon. Spanish embassies were bombed and set alight in Holland and Turkey when Franco executed five Basque separatists. Revenge killings erupted across Northern Ireland. But things seemed peaceful enough in Northampton.

grave and devastatingly non-fictional *The World at War*, which we would gather around every Sunday before tea, seemed remote, grainy, boxed-off, defused. The footage of the concentration camps chilled my blood, but it was all so surreal – bodies in a pit, bodies in a cart – my mind wasn't capable of being *scared* by it. Amazed, appalled, but not directly worried. This was clearly never going to happen to me, or my family. It was unthinkable, so I didn't think it. The little boy's haunted face at the end of the programme's credits gave me the willies (as did Carl Davis's solemn theme music and Sir Lawrence Olivier's narration), but only in the same way that *Dr Who* did. A plate of crisp sandwiches and a piece of haslet[3] would soon banish my unease.

We had been watching *Dr Who* since 1972, much of it through our fingers, so the thrill-ride aspect of fear was well known to us. It was a good game. My preferred comics were ones with a ghostly theme, *Shiver and Shake* and *Monster Fun*. One of my favourite *Shiver* stories was 'Scream Inn', about a haunted hotel. 'We're only here for the fear' ran its tagline. That was me.

However, this new post-Whittaker insight, vague as yet, that *some* scary things were real, marching past in the street outside, was truly head-turning. We didn't really believe that Dr Who's Silurian foes the Sea Devils were going to rise up out of the surf at Pwllheli – although Simon and I teased one another that they might – and we didn't really think that the Jerries were coming.

But what if they did? What would I do if they did?

This horrible, dawning realisation was some kind of early, unconscious acceptance of mortality, even though it wasn't death that scared me but suffering, disruption and sirens. I suspect it's a trait I have partly inherited from my more anxious mother's side – just as I'm certain my hoarding and cataloguing come directly from my dad. But I also suspect it's programmed into us somehow. Perhaps all ten-year-olds have a lucid moment of understanding: we're doomed.

I didn't exactly see dead people *all the time* from the moment I

3. Cooked minced pig's offal, eaten cold and sliced off a loaf. We also ate faggot, which was made of minced pig's liver and breadcrumbs, I now learn. Yum.

heard Roger sing, 'the taste of war I know so very well', but it definitely marked the onset of the spooked years.

* * *

Simon's birthday is on 29 May. However, in 1975, when he turned eight, I was the one who got the gift that goes on giving. The gift of mortal terror. Dad took us, as a treat – ha! – to the ABC in town to see a double bill. A perfectly mismatched double bill as it happened, and a sign of those random, pre-video times: *Please, Sir!* and *The Poseidon Adventure*. A tenuous big-screen adaptation of a popular sitcom[4] and the godfather of 1970s disaster movies, both enjoying a second run (*Please, Sir!* had originally come out in 1971, *Poseidon Adventure* in 1972). I expect Dad fancied seeing them – or else they were simply 'what was on' at Northampton's only cinema – and Simon and I were up for it, as going to the pictures meant Disney and James Bond up to that point, and we had yet to be disappointed.

Please, Sir! was amusing enough (I think some kids swore at Hedges and Price at the beginning; very 'A' certificate), but I was captivated by *The Poseidon Adventure* – the stunts and the high adventure, the rising water and the heroic Gene Hackman, the horror, the horror. And it literally changed my life; the world looked very different afterwards.

The waterlogged tale of ordinary people trapped in a capsized liner on New Year's Eve, it is now recognised as the film that kickstarted a box-office cycle. In fact, by May 1975 the cycle was spinning fast: *The Towering Inferno* had opened, and *Earthquake* and *Airport '75* were almost upon us in the UK. Fire, flood and devastation were all the rage, reflecting a public appetite for catastrophe in line with the general precarious state of the decade thus far.

Very much the age of the jumbo and the balaclava, it seemed

---

4. As Graham McCann notes in his invaluable book *Dad's Army*, 'It was considered more or less *de rigueur* in those days for a British situation comedy to attempt this hazardous transformation – during the first three years of the decade alone, the likes of *Up Pompeii!*, *On the Buses*, *Please, Sir!*, *Steptoe and Son*, *Father, Dear Father*, *Bless This House* and even *Love Thy Neighbour*, aided and abetted by an ailing and risk-aversive British film industry desperate to tap into television's mass audience, would all spawn at least one cinematic spin-off.'

that planes were crashing or blowing up every week in the early Seventies: Palestinian terrorists destroyed three airliners in Jordan, a British Trident crashed in Staines (118 killed), a Libyan Boeing 727 was shot down in the Sinai desert (74 killed), and a Turkish DC-10 crashed in Paris (341 killed). Meanwhile, smoke billowed out of the *Queen Elizabeth* in Hong Kong harbour, 35 were killed in the appalling Moorgate tube crash, 30 died in the 'Summerland' holiday camp fire on the Isle of Man, and 10,000 perished in an earthquake in Managua, Nicaragua. The bodies were piling up, the temperature rising.

It's a fire. All fires are bad.

The day before we went to see *The Poseidon Adventure*, Britain recorded its worst ever road crash (all road crashes are bad), when a sightseeing coach plummeted 16 feet off a bridge in the Yorkshire Dales killing 32 passengers. Not that the ten-year-old me would have noticed or cared. In my world, nobody died. All fires were somewhere else.

Then I saw *The Poseidon Adventure*: 117 minutes that shook my world. In it, most people died. The whole point of it, and of all the other copycat disaster movies, is that you can count and identify the survivors. Six. Mike Rogo, James Martin, Nonnie Parry, Manny Rosen, little Robin Shelby and his sister Susan. ('Is that all?' asks the rescue worker in the film. That is all.)

Now, the Whittaker watershed is something that's been buried deep within my psyche all these years; I didn't pinpoint it at the time. But I knew *The Poseidon Adventure* had changed my life from the moment I emerged back into the light that dusky May evening. It opened my eyes to the possibility that everything could go belly-up. Like the passengers of the ss *Poseidon*, I could be singing 'Auld Lang Syne' one minute, and drowned out by the wail of the ship's hooter the next, while the boat listed to one side. It's the classic disaster-movie narrative structure: happy equilibrium established and disturbed; a motley band of survivors organise themselves to escape, and we place bets on who will make it and who won't. Bad luck if your money was on Mrs Rogo, Mrs Rosen, Acres the ship's steward or their valiant leader Reverend Scott. The film may be taken as a metaphor for the journey of life and the arbitrary nature of natural selection, or else as a metaphor for a load of people getting burnt and drowned in a ship.

I will always cite *The Poseidon Adventure* as one of my all-time favourite films, never mind how unfashionable or dated it looks. This is a film that has lived in the very marrow of my bones for over 25 years. In the four-year gap between seeing it at the ABC and it being premiered on television at Christmas in 1979, *The Poseidon Adventure* grew and grew in my mind, forming new shapes in my memory, until the myth of it was, for me, far greater than the reality. More real, in fact. It still gives me a memory rush when I see it:[5] the spectacle of all those gallons of water pouring into the ballroom, the statutory shock moment when we glimpse a scalded kitchen worker, the climactic boiler room which so acutely illustrates the film's tagline, 'Hell, upside down'.[6]

Was this what Hell looked like? Twisted metal, slippery gantries and burning oil? It was good enough for me. I lived the rest of the Seventies in fear of fire and water.

My wife Julie was raised as a good Catholic – the first I have ever had a sensible conversation with about the subject. She also grew up fearing fire, but the kind that comes with brimstone. Her Hell

---

5. Another instant transportation device to this period is the song 'I'm Not In Love' by 10CC, which was Number One during *The Poseidon Adventure* aftershock period, entering the charts the week after we saw the film and staying in the Top 10 for a month. It more than reminds me of the time – the famous female-whispered interlude ('Be quiet, big boys don't cry, big boys don't cry') struck me then as an apposite soundtrack to the film. It might have been Mrs Rosen reassuring little Robin, telling him to be brave in the face of watery doom. Perfect timing by Manchester's 10CC boys and the great British record-buying public – it could so easily have been 'Whispering Grass' by Don Estelle and Windsor Davies (lovely boys don't cry).

6. An interesting allusion, especially as the souls trapped in the *Poseidon* work their way *up* through the concentric circles of torment, counter to Dante's vision. Religious suggestions run right through *The Poseidon Adventure* – even the ship is named after a Greek god, and the Bible of course is chock-full of disasters: flood, fire, plague. The *Poseidon's* survivors are led by a fire-and-brimstone priest who sacrifices himself so that his flock may live, and the final rescue by the coastguard sees them whisked away into the sky, blinded by a bright light after being trapped in the darkness. And the meek – Martin, Nonnie, Manny – inherit the earth. I love this shit. I once encountered a 'reading' of *The Guns of Navarone* which involved Oedipus and castration (disabling those phallic guns) and I loved that too.

BIG BOYS DON'T CRY

was not a movie set, it *was* Hell. As such, she didn't worry too much about being trapped in a sinking ship or a burning building – there was a good deal worse in store at the other end if you didn't behave yourself. Because I was raised without fear of damnation for my sins, I suppose I was subconsciously casting around for something else to believe in. A secular society will always find its own devils. Mine was the disaster movie.

These films, major cinematic events, haunted my waking days. I had looked *The Poseidon Adventure* in the eye; I had sat through it, counted the survivors into the helicopter and jumped at the scalded cook, and I had no intention of putting myself through that sort of distress again. *The Towering Inferno, Earthquake* and the rest would never get me. My image-filled head had no room left to spare. While on holiday in Blackpool later that year Nan, Pap and I would walk past a cinema showing *Earthquake* every day, and I noticed from the dramatic poster that it was being shown in something called Sensurround:

'Please be aware that you will feel as well as see and hear realistic effects such as might be experienced in an actual earthquake. The management assumes no responsibility for the physical or emotional reactions of the individual viewer.'

What responsible advertising, I thought. If only *The Poseidon Adventure* had carried such a warning. There was no way you'd get me into that cinema. What if there was 'an actual earthquake' while the film was showing, and nobody noticed until it was too late?

I began a rigorous programme of disaster-movie avoidance. (You might like to call it denial.) When the kids' movie show *Clapperboard* ran a feature on disaster movies, with on-set footage from *The Towering Inferno*, I actually left the room (it was at Nan's house, so nobody else knows this). That's how vigilant I was about not glimpsing further Hollywood disaster. Another junior film programme *Screen Test* shattered my fragile defences by running a clip of *The Towering Inferno*, and because I was at home, with Simon, I couldn't very well admit my demons and leave. I watched it – the bit where a screaming woman is winched off the top floor in a breeches buoy – and it had the predictable effect of deepening my fear of fire.

Shipboard peril could easily be avoided by remaining on dry land, but I had become so genuinely frightened of dying in – or being dishevelled by – a house fire, I developed my own foolproof psychological defence. Every night in my bed I would deliberately think about the house burning down. That way, I reasoned, it wouldn't actually happen. Because if it did, I would be able to say to the firemen as they wrapped me in a blanket, 'I knew the house was going to burn down: I thought about it just before I went to sleep.' The probability seemed so remote, I actually found comfort in this bizarre piece of provincial voodoo.

But I'm more struck, retrospectively, by the way I exorcised the demons of *The Poseidon Adventure*. Mature and focused, I faced down my fears. I may have been running away from the disaster movies I *hadn't* seen, but not from the one I *had*. My obsession initially took the form of a project. I saw the film on Thursday; by the weekend I was making a book about it, methodically drawing all the characters and key scenes from memory in a pad with biro and coloured pencils.[7] On the Monday Dad, having noted my fixation with the film, bought me the original novel by Paul Gallico when he took Simon to Birmingham for his allergy tests (I think we all know what *I* was allergic to). I still have the book, dog-eared to within an inch of collapse – but then, unlike every other film and TV tie-in book I bought, I actually got a lot of use out of it.

Originally published in 1969, this is Pan's 1974 paperback edition and it bears two stills from the movie, which I pored over even more than the text: a happy, pre-'Auld Lang Syne' line-up of Rev Scott (Gene Hackman), Linda Rogo (Stella Stevens) and husband Mike (Ernest Borgnine); and a sweaty, precarious boiler room scene featuring Nonnie (Carol Lynley), Mr Martin (Red Buttons) and the Rogos. You can also see the high-heeled feet of Susan (Pamela Sue Martin).

What's more, the book listed the principal cast on the back under the obligatory now-a-major-film blurb. Having it seems absorbed every chronological detail of the film in a single sitting,

---

7. I've seen them since. Not bad at all.

I was now able to guess which actor played which part simply from the hierarchy of the cast.

I devoured the novel, though it was resolutely not a kids' book. Most of the characters had been retained in the screenplay by Wendell Mayes and Stirling Silliphant, though Rev Scott had the nickname 'Buzz' in the book and 'looked like some primitive tribal priest at invocation' at the climax, 'all but nude, the lantern strapped to his back, the fire axe still bound about his middle'. Mayes and Silliphant had thinned out the band of survivors too (a common novel-to-screen trick, but one to which I was not yet accustomed): no Hubie Muller, no Miss Kinsale, no Kemal, no Beamer. And no Susan Shelby rape scene, understandably ('a hand tore at her underclothes', all that). But the novel was close enough to the film for me to relive the pain, discomfort and degradation of those survivors. It was my mid-Seventies way of getting the video.

The self-administered psychotherapy was going swimmingly. Talking of which, there's a key scene in the film where our embattled band must swim through a flooded corridor to get to the boiler room, and they are asked to hold their breath for thirty seconds. (Actually, if you time the sequence in the film, Scott and Mrs Rosen are underwater for at least three minutes of elastic screen-time.) In accordance with my healing programme, Dad, Simon and I would practise holding our breath for thirty seconds at Kingsthorpe when we went swimming on Saturdays. We called this game *Poseidon Adventure*, but I knew it wasn't a game. It was preparation for the worst.[8]

I didn't know at the time that it was what Freud identified as 'repetition-compulsion' (the tendency to relive unpleasant or traumatic situations), but I knew it helped. It's helping right now. It is, as Freud spotted, anxiety that prepares us for danger. In other words, whittling is a good, useful emotion. Nan and Mum had it right all along. Because *The Poseidon Adventure* was a shock – I wasn't prepared for it – I subsequently used repetition-compulsion (the swimming, the drawing, the reading, the all-purpose fixating)

---

8. The irony is, I couldn't swim, not without a polystyrene float. But then neither could Dad, and he was our swimming teacher. I feel he taught me everything he knew.

to prepare for the next such shock. I was building my defences. Live in fear, be prepared.

I had conducted this elaborate dance with dread before. When I was much younger, aged five or six, I experienced coulrophobia: I was scared of clowns. Not their painted faces and big shoes, although it has been long established that these are very scary things, but by the possibility – I think – that they might drag me out of the audience and make me a part of their show, perhaps throw water at me. (So, there's a link between this and my later disasterphobia: dishevelment; loss of dignity – is someone taking notes?[9]) It was a big day when the circus came to town, either Billy Smart's or Chipperfield's, and Mum and Dad would always take us along to watch the sad animals and the high-wire spills and then ... they would send in the clowns. At no point did I express any displeasure at this torture: I just sat and laughed with the rest of them, willing it to end and for some sedated lions to come on.

I recall, one year, making eye contact with a clown who was waiting to enter the ring. He saw me looking at him and raised his eyebrows twice for my benefit (everyone else was watching what was going on in the ring). It was my private clown moment, and it sent a shiver down my spine.

However, if you go through my childhood drawings from the time,[10] you will discover that they are virtually all of clowns. Endless

---

9. I wonder now if this all dates back to the time my mum pulled my trousers down in public: the Adam and Eve moment of shame. We were off somewhere in the car and on the doorstep of Winsford Way she simply and practically took my shorts down to tuck my shirt in properly. However, this coincided with Jack the policeman from the top of the road walking by. I was not just embarrassed, I was fearful that he may arrest me for what I couldn't have known was indecent exposure.

10. The complete artistic works of the young Andrew Collins are stored in a suitcase in my parents' attic. I went through the whole lot in researching this book, an exhausting delight (boy, did I get through a lot of National Provident Institution paper). My desire to be published was strong from an early age. I made a very early book based on the Disney version of *Alice in Wonderland*. It's primitively drawn but I have clearly remembered the whole story, in order, from seeing the film at the pictures. The spelling, however, is rudimentary: 'Alic in wudland et the bisgs wich mad her vere big.' (Alice in Wonderland – her full name – ate the biscuits which made her very big.) There is a comic based on the Harlem Globe Trotters – or at least the Hanna-Barbera cartoon – which has a slack narrative structure but guess what, our heroes are playing basketball against a team of clowns (the story is called 'Clownball').

clowns, many of them in various states of dishevelment, jumping out of their trousers to reveal spotted pants, or wearing torn trousers after some comedy explosion, the spotty underwear showing through.[11] This was my revenge on the clowns for potentially endangering me. All the slapstick and violence and humiliation would be visited upon them, not me, in my pictures. The clowns would be contained, they would stay in their ring.

When the Italian clown Charlie Caroli became a Seventies children's TV star, I watched without fail every week, entranced by the relentless slapstick. Because there was no live audience, I felt safe.[12]

It was this safe distance that was broken down by Roger Whittaker and *The Poseidon Adventure*. Just because something was on television or in a film no longer meant it couldn't happen to me.

* * *

Nothing did happen to me, of course. Auntie Janice had that chip-pan fire but the damage didn't extend any further than the blackened kitchen. There were flames when Dad 'found' a Misfit in the toaster (Misfits was a children's card game), but beyond that, through all my childhood, nothing truly disastrous happened. I was never dishevelled or blackened. The Jerries never came. Whenever we had high winds, I was convinced the windows would blow in, but they didn't. The back fence blew down in a gale in September 1975 but that was as cinematic as the weather got.

The disaster movies got me in the end. By which I mean I was forced by circumstance and the idiocy of my fear to watch some of them. (This is just as well actually. I had enthusiastically drawn up a 'disaster film survey' at the back of my 1975 diary and it fizzles out quickly, because of course in 1975 I had only seen the one.) In 1976, we were bought *Big Terror Movie Themes*, an LP by Geoff Love and his Orchestra, containing the foreboding music from *Jaws*,

---

11. I have created some crazy characters called The Clown Gang – Noddy, Big Ears and Ugly. Ugly, though male, wears a bra. Don't ask.
12. We saw Charlie Caroli and his gang (Jimmy the Frozen Face, Charlie Jnr among them) live in 1978, by which time I had obviously got over my fear of being pulled out of the audience, even though a pantomime, which is what it was, is fertile ground for audience participation.

Airport '75 and *Earthquake*. Good therapy, even though it was only orchestral cover versions. In 1977 I braved a number of made-for-TV disaster movies, the nursery slopes of any genre – *Flight to Holocaust, Smash-up on Interstate 5* – and subsequently some lesser-known pre-cycle pictures like *The Last Voyage* and *Skyjacked*. I also saw what was according to Geoff Love an honorary disaster movie, *Jaws*, at the pictures. My fear was subsiding. In 1978 I went on a ferry, which didn't turn over. In 1979 I saw *The Poseidon Adventure* for the second time, on TV.

Everything was fine.

And then in the Eighties, I found out there might be a nuclear war.

eleven

Leeds Mug

It's such a fine line between stupid ... and clever.
David St Hubbins, *This Is Spinal Tap* (1984)

I fear my own *Fever Pitch* would be a slim volume. When Nick Hornby talks in the book of his footballing life flashing before his eyes, it reaches back over a quarter of a century to 1968 when he was 11 and takes in Cup Finals, League Championships, internationals, replays, non-league games, cup ties and 'all those terrible nil-nil draws against Newcastle' (actually, there were only two of those but it felt like more).

Me? I went to see England play twice, and that's it – once in November 1979 against Bulgaria (we won 2–0), and again in November 1980, a World Cup qualifier against Switzerland (we seem to have lost 2–1 but the match report in my diary is a little impenetrable: 'well-known Hans-Jorg Pfinster scored the second-half Swiss un-own goal'). I loved being in the crowd at Wembley both times – the atmosphere walking into the place the first time blew me away, as it would any boy. But I never once went to the County Ground to see the Cobblers play – thus I missed out on the rain-lashed romance of local allegiance.

Because I drifted away from football in the Eighties and never truly went back, I sometimes forget what an avid follower of the game I was, albeit restricted to games on TV, football stickers, Subbuteo leagues, playground chatter. I didn't read *Shoot!* but I knew all the grounds in the first four divisions and could draw many of the club badges from memory. I never missed an FA Cup Final on telly, and neither did Dad (we ate salted peanuts from a bowl on that special day each May, sometimes the kind with raisins in). If you'd asked me between the ages of 10 and 13 which team I supported I would have said Liverpool (I had found my brand), but that all changed when I started Weston Favell Upper School in September 1978. A lot did.

As we have seen, I sailed through Abington Vale Middle School a star pupil, top of the class or thereabouts for the duration.[1] I left there in the summer of '78 with my head held high: 169 credits falling out of my pockets, not a mark under 72 in my final exams, confident, unselfconscious and ready to take on whatever life threw at me.

Unfortunately, it threw life at me.

* * *

Weston Favell Upper School was a nice enough place. Well-stocked, modern and mixed, and reasonable cycling distance from home. It was where I wanted to be. I had spent much of the final term at Abington Vale in pathetic hypothetical terror of being forced by numbers and circumstance to attend 'the boys school' (crash of thunder, horses whinny). Northampton School For Boys, or the NSB, used to be the town grammar school – the one my dad had attended in the Fifties. They had dragged it into the Seventies of course, but I still feared it because it was a St Custard's-like institution that struck me as the sort of place which had bullying and canings and the blue goldfish. (Jasper Carrot did a routine in the Seventies about having his head flushed down the toilet at school: 'Have you seen the blue goldfish?') Also, aged 13, I didn't want them to take all the girls away. I was getting to like the girls.

I needn't have worried. The cards fell in my favour, I was granted my first choice, and thus avoided the single-sex path –

---

1. My school reports for Abington Vale Middle make me blush. I appear to have had two days off sick in three years, and the teachers' comments vary all the way from 'Andrew has worked with great enthusiasm and skill throughout the year' to 'Andrew has worked conscientiously and consistently throughout the year'. I am commended for my uniform by form teacher Mrs Dennison ('Excellent. Neat and tidy appearance') and they even say I am 'making steady progress' in PE!

which I still maintain is an unhealthy one, engendering suspicion and myth-making between the genders at exactly the wrong time. To reiterate: Weston Favell Upper School was *where I wanted to be.*

Unfortunately, many of my chums went off to the blue-blazered NSB (Eddy, Griff, Johnny, Kim, Nivek). Not all of them, but enough to reduce my chances of ending up next to someone I knew. So my first shock at the new school was finding myself in form 3CN, bereft of any other Abington Vale kids. No Angus, no Hirsty, no Lewis, no Doboe. No mates. I was on my own for the first time since day one of primary school, separated from the pack, and as if to rub salt into this particular wound the wheel of fortune sat me next to the biggest spaz[2] in the class on day one: we'll call him Burns.[3] He didn't know anybody either. Wide-eyed, pale-skinned, jittery and cursed with a limp, Burns was the runt and he was sat next to me. What chance did I have?

I didn't spend the whole live-long day with 3CN – we were streamed for maths, and art and design saw us split again into

---

2. I use the insensitive vernacular only for evocative effect. Spastic was the accepted term for the mentally and physically handicapped at the time, and kids are cruel, cruel bastards. We also used 'flid' as an insult, derived from Thalidomide, often accompanied by a short-armed mime. Joey Deacon – handicapped, book-dictating hero of *Blue Peter* – greatly influenced the generic playground impersonation for 'spaz', tongue behind bottom lip, that sort of drill. If I could go back and live my childhood again, I would, but I fear I would exhibit exactly the same shallow, unhelpful view towards the disabled. At least by Weston Favell I had faced down my *fear* of the handicapped. At primary school I was literally frightened of spastics. It was a basic aversion to something I didn't understand, a form of innate xenophobia, I guess. I was scared of my own human fallibility. Mrs Munro's boy, Steven, frequently came to school (he went to a 'special school'): partially sighted with huge milk-bottle glasses, he was deaf too, which meant he spoke in a foreign tongue and loudly. I as good as hid from him. More fool me.

Then, at middle school, by befriending Nigel Wilson I was forced to deal with my irrational distaste. He had an older brother, severely handicapped by cruel palsy, whose life was spent in a wheelchair being fed, watered and changed. His was a constant, dominant presence in Nigel's house, but not a negative one. I learned from him some important lessons about humanity and dignity. Mrs Wilson understood him alright, so why shouldn't I? He was just Nigel's brother, not some kind of special case, and not a monster.

I think he died, but not in vain. It's a pity I forgot all about him when I used the word 'spaz' at Weston Favell.

3. I have changed his name. I hope he grew up to be happy. He deserves it after what must have been a hellish time at Weston Favell. He once actually wet himself while doing long jump – that's in *white shorts* everybody – and no kid should have to go through that.

random sets – but for the most part, these were my new school-mates. And they all knew each other; these kids seemed tight, tribal, as if they went back a long way together. What's worse, they were naughty, irreverent, scruffy. They were an element. The male ring-leaders – and I will never forget their names – were Bill Jeyes, Lee Masters, Simon Triculja and Gaz Smith, a walking clique of in-jokes, back-chat and swagger. They were the family, with geographical satellites like Chris Bradshaw and Kev Bailey as honorary *caporegimes*. All came from the other side of the Wellingborough Road: Parklands, Lumbertubs, Boothville. By opting for the coeducational utopia of Weston Favell Upper School, I had entered a new gene pool. None of their dads did something indistinct in an office.

It's not like my previous school had been a genteel academy for Fotherington-Thomases, but it was quite a culture shock for me, moving due north to a school whose catchment area extended beyond the estates named after places in Somerset and Devon. I look back on it now as a character-building social mix, the bedrock upon which comprehensive schools should be founded, but at the time, I just wanted there to be less hardos in my class.

To them, looking spruce and carrying a briefcase was an admis-sion of homosexuality. For the first time in my life, I was a swot. I hadn't changed, of course, but the demographic scenery had. That which had made me top of the class just one short summer ago now made me a creep and a poof: a target. The scales had tipped: being clever was now uncool, and I was subsequently forced to readjust.

I didn't want to be lumped in with a deadleg like Burns. Sadly, for most of the first term, I was. Academic excellence held no sway here. The portcullis of cool had come down, and I was on the wrong side of the bars.

It was like being exposed as a stabiliser-assisted cyclist by Anita Barker, except the pain and humiliation were stretched out across weeks. Weeks without end. I had flirted with the Molesworth dictum but the truth is, I used to *like* school. Now it really was 'the jug'.

My diary, as we know, generally presents a united front, favour-ing upbeat sheen over the brutal truth. I hated Weston Favell Upper School so much I actually wrote it in my diary. You can see the positive spin draining away in my first week there. On Tuesday

I'm putting on a brave face ('Our form teacher is nice Miss Chapman ... today wasn't as bad as I imagined'), by Wednesday I'm telling it like it is: 'There is no-one in my class I know or want to know. I hate my class.' Tellingly, I have crossed out the last comment but you can read through the scribble. I hated my class.

What I didn't write was that I cried at night that first week. I even voiced my anxiety (boiled down to the simple fact that there were no Abington Vale kids in my class) to Mum and Dad, and they contacted head of year Mr Bowden. He had me in his office and – without crying – I told him why I was unhappy in school, hoping it was not too late to put me in a new form, perhaps the one with Angus in. No chance. The rotund, sausage-fingered Bowden placated me like a true diplomat (he really did have a tweed jacket with leather patches on the elbows, incidentally) and sent me on my way. I was a condemned man.

Clinging to after-school and Saturday morning art classes for salvation, I made a big decision. To rise above the myopic 'cool' of the northern-estates kids and forge my own academic path through the next three years of school, immune to their sneers. Not really. I decided to pretend to be thick and try and get in with them.

Thus began my quest for cool.

* * *

All thoughts of academic excellence were pushed aside in favour of this much more important campaign: to move among the hard kids and gain acceptance. I scored an early own goal by joining Mr Bowden's ornithology club – Gaah! What on earth was I thinking of? – but this was short-lived and only involved one field trip which took place at the weekend, so Bill, Lee, Si and Gaz never knew about it.[4]

---

4. As a born-again birder and RSPB member, I look back on this brief ornithological flirt with pride, although it had little precedent. My only field trip, to Ecton Brook on 24 October 1978, has been vigilantly recorded in a xeroxed form, with the following bird types ticked off: grey heron, red crested pochard, mute swan, quail, moorhen, coot, lapwing, herring gull, black-headed gull, skylark, carrion crow, hooded crow, great tit, blue tit, wren, mistle thrush, song thrush, blackbird, robin, dunnock, pied wagtail, grey wagtail, starling, greenfinch, goldfinch, bullfinch, chaffinch, reed bunting, house sparrow, tree sparrow. Bloody impressive, although I'm prepared to put one or two of those down to overenthusiasm and misidentification.

Bill, Lee, Si and Gaz were my heroes, or more accurately my antiheroes. I wanted to be like them: cheeky, stylish, obdurate ... thick. It was impossible to separate their cool from their ignorance. They had little interest in learning. They would happily martyr themselves on the altar of failure rather than bow and scrape to authority, even nice Miss Chapman. To be like them I would not only have to denounce the class spaz and answer back to the odd teacher, I would have to regress to an uneducated state to prove my manhood.

In the lessons I shared with 3CN I actually pretended to be dimmer than I was. I put my hand up less, volunteered never, and cranked my knowledge down a few notches. As Les Dawson always used to say, pretending to play the piano badly takes as much skill as playing it well. It takes a smart kid to affect stupidity. You need to know all the answers in order to deliberately get a handful wrong. It became second nature to me to throw in a couple of wrong answers in tests, thereby ensuring I would never again come top.

In an English test with Mr Gilbert we were asked who wrote *To Kill a Mockingbird*. I put 'Lee Harper', secure in the knowledge that it was Harper Lee. I got it wrong as planned, and I secretly awarded myself two points: one for knowing it, the other for looking good. I wonder if Mr Gilbert knew.

I was leading a double life. In school I was this new, damaged version of my old self: tie in a big Windsor knot (as was the fad), sports bag in place of the old briefcase, and the beginnings of an attitude (when I was picked out of a line-up in PE by the dreaded Mr Blogg, I made such a do-I-have-to? meal of the walk to the centre of the gym he asked mockingly if I needed an injection). Meanwhile, at home, I was a proud member of the ELO Fan Club and a regular reader of *Look-In*, playing squash with my dad, and hanging out with Hirsty and Angus (both of whom would be branded 'bum chums' by Bill, Lee, Si and Gaz). Of course it's a pathetic, cowardly way to live your life, but to me at the time it was a necessity.

This was growing up, albeit a ruthlessly accelerated kind. That Christmas, one of my main presents was Lego. Alright, it was a 'technical set' but it was still interlocking plastic bricks. It would be my last toy. When we got back to school, Mr Sharman asked our group in 'building craft' (a self-explanatory design option) what we got for Christmas. Unfortunately there were two relative hardos in my group, Wayne and Tarry, and I realised on the spot that I simply could not admit I'd had Lego. I frantically ran through my present list in my mind for something 'cool' and the best I could come up with was a Leeds United mug.

'What about you, Andrew?'

'A Leeds mug.'

'A Leeds mug?'

There was much sniggering. The other kids, including Wayne and Tarry, thought I must be some kind of pauper. Tiny Tim with his Christmas cup, and grateful for it.

Another own goal in the cool play-offs? Actually no. Being poor was obviously cooler than being rich, and anyway, I had publicly confirmed my allegiance to Leeds United. And guess who supported Leeds United? Bill, Lee, Si and Gaz ...

Switching my loyalties from Liverpool to Leeds was no great hardship. (Good thing I wasn't a proper football fan, eh?) Liverpool may have been top of the table, but at least Leeds were in the first division. The true glory days of Billy Bremner and Norman Hunter under Don Revie may have been over but they still had a degree of cool, not least since the new badge came in, which was a rounded, cartoon-like 'L' with the 'U' tucked inside it. (If they lost a few games, and they did, you could always blame manager Jimmy Adamson.) Now, looking back, I'm sure Bill, Lee, Si and Gaz didn't all support Leeds at the outset – I'll bet a couple of them fell into line. It may have even been a conspiracy – who shall we support at the new school then? – but it played so well in a gang. Kev Bailey and Chris Bradshaw were Leeds too. Well they had to be. And so did I.

The big day came on 29 November (quite a way into that all-important first term). Dad bought me home a Leeds scarf. Yellow with blue and white stripes, it cost £2.20 and was pocket money well spent. This was my ticket to acceptance. I remember the first day I wore it, a frosty Tuesday, walking from the bike sheds to class flushed with a mixture of self-conscious guilt and genuine pride in my new colours. I had changed my stripes.

Miss Chapman groaned and said, without malice, 'Oh you don't support Leeds as well do you?'

'Yes,' I replied, aware that the tribal council were watching me. They were unable to mock. They didn't exactly proffer me an approving nod or kick Chris Bradshaw off his seat and offer it to me, but their artificial allegiance to the yellow, white and blue was so strong, they had to respect my choice. (They had no idea I supported Liverpool a few weeks earlier, as I had never worn a red scarf. For all they knew I had been an LUFC man all my life.)

This was an important stage in my development. I was now a Leeds fan for the sake of cultural homogeny and it felt good. I covered one of my exercise books with a picture of a Leeds player (I forget which, possibly Parlane or Hird) and monitored their progress each week in case I should ever fall into conversation with the firm.[5] I never did – it wasn't that kind of acceptance. It's not as if they had been bullying or picking on me before – Burns took all that heat with his dodgy leg – I just needed to be able to hold my head up in their company; to not be a poof or a creep or a swot. I saw Kev Bailey after school once or twice, but that was as close as I ever got to the hard kids' manor.

Offering up my Leeds mug after Christmas had marked a new dawn. At the start of 1979 I put all childish things behind me. I started buying seven-inch singles with my pocket money, and grown-up magazines like *Film Review* and *New Musical Express*. I made new schoolfriends from outside 3CN, like Pete Sawtell, Matthew Allen, Craig McKenna, Andy Howkins, Dave Griffiths – real and lasting friends, among whom I could be myself.

Once O-level options dominated the timetable, my time spent in the same room as Bill, Lee, Si and Gaz became limited to registration, PE and the odd design class. I could handle that. They even started talking to me when they discovered I could draw scurrilous

---

5. My devotion to Leeds continued long after my desire to get in with the hard kids. I doggedly recorded their scores throughout 1979, 1980 and 1981, even noting cancellations, such as the match against West Brom on 25 April 1981 due to snow. This was a genuine, healthy interest (12 September 1981: 'Leeds ****ing lost 4–0 to Coventry. It's a joke! Paul Hart has got appendicitis') although it seems to fade in 1982. Mind you I *was* gay that year.

caricatures of the teachers to order. Alan Evans, a behemoth[6] who operated in their anti-authoritarian orbit, and ruddy sidekick Dougie Lines once asked me to help them with their maths homework (they were in a lower stream) – they probably thought they were *getting* me to do it for them, but they weren't. There were no heavy manners. I did it as a favour. I think they even thanked me. Probably called me 'Collins' but I could live with that. Chris Bradshaw and I bonded at the shallow end of the swimming pool – neither of us could swim. He proudly showed me that he had hair on his toes. What a man.

In fact, all this bare-faced assimilation actually loosened me up a bit as an individual. Wearing trainers for lessons even though it's against school rules, for instance (what harm is there in that?). Forgetting to do up my top button. Getting caught reading *Cracked* magazine by Mr Twinn in maths. Going to school discos and only dancing to the punk songs. After all, nobody likes a square.

Ah yes, punk rock. It came to Northampton late, predictably enough. And can you guess who Weston Favell's first punks were? Bill, Lee, Si and Gaz.

---

6. The first boy in our year to show pubic hair. Any bodily hair, in fact. But any latent pubescent jealousy was curtailed by the fact that he was the school fat lad.

1978

Selected Extracts From My Diary

I suppose I thought I was being clever when I took to the cover of this bright red Collins diary with a hole punch Dad had brought home from work. It is subsequently full of holes. I have tried to justify this act of self-abuse by writing 'It's a holy diary, lads' in black marker (very funny) but that only makes aesthetic matters worse. There is also a nature sticker depicting a rock wallaby.

It's a tatty artefact all round, 1978. Scribbly entries, lazy, rudimentary drawings, torn pages, felt-tip smudged by spit, and a sinister new development brought on by the onset of the teen years: dishonest tampering with the text. Stalin, however, would not have been proud of me – these rewrites are generally done in a different coloured pen! Who was I intending to fool? Myself? The police? They start to occur in May, when – and there's no way round this – I become really interested in girls. My ever-changing loyalties, from Jackie Needham to Hayley Mayo, Anita Barker and back again, necessitate some glaring felt-pen revisionism. For the purposes of record, I shall transcribe the original words.

It's all in capital letters now, and a declaration before the defaced title page lists some of my favourite things: rock wallabies, wombats, The Boomtown Rats, ELO, RSPB, girls, Grease, Lynda Carter, Roots, Monty Python, Olivia Newton John, kangaroo mice, hare wallabies, etc.

Saturday, 7 January

Went to Pap Collins' party. Jane and Paul also went. We did a show to all the grown-ups, including: impressions (I did Shirley Bassey and Uncle Punk),[1] Miss World 1978, plus Cinderella (I

---

1. See Chapter 12.

was the Fairy Godmother and the Prince). Dad got me *Mad* magazine. Pap bought me a Northampton diary and an invisible ink pen.

Wednesday, 25 January
Yahoo! A fab day. All the 4th year went in four coaches to Coventry to the Belgrade Theatre to see *Mother Goose*. Sounds pouffy but was absolutely ace. Reg Dixon, Ellis Jones and Carol Cleveland were in it. Then we came home at 6.00. I had some snack soup and Dad took me to squash. He beat the other bloke 3–1 easy.

Tuesday, 26 January
Yesterday Heidi got Ellis Jones's autograph and I chatted her up today[2] and she gave it to me. Ha. Did it ever occur to you that I am made of gold?

Friday, 3 February
Attempted to chat up Anita more. Not much use though. I'm getting her a Valentines card. That might help. No heating on at school. Everyone went around with their coats on all day. Brill laugh.

Sunday, 5 February
Played Lego demolition derbies but when I cut my finger really badly I went all dizzy and nearly passed out. Swoon. Started making a new comic called *Ace!*

Thursday, 9 February
I started chatting up Tracey Allen.[3] Much better than chatting up Anita. Lots of homework. Huh! Mum and Dad went to the school this evening to get our reports.

---

2. We get this phrase a lot in '78. Don't be fooled. It means 'chatted to'.
3. If I may say so, Tracey Allen was out of my league. I had not yet turned 13. She had, in a big way. She had a curly perm, breasts and one of those Afro combs, and she wore a skirt down to her ankles. *Way* out of my league.

Wednesday, 22 February

Oh goody! Because of no oil we've got tomorrow off school as well. Ace! Angus came this morning. Dad took us three to the library. I got a skateboarding book, a book about mammals, a book about film make-up and a Tony Hancock book. Magic. Magic.

Sunday, 26 February

Great! Dad cleared our room out completely and rearranged it and it is fab. Here is a news flash ... I have gone mad on *Star Wars*. Luke Skywalker rules! Darth Vader lives. See-Threepio is king. So is Artoo-Detoo. Chewbacca is magic. *Star Wars* is ace!

Saturday, 4 March

It is actually my birthday. World celebrations. Magic! I got: *Monty Python* LP, *Star Wars* poster, *Star Wars* transfer, *Star Wars* book, *Star Wars* badges, skateboarding book, Asterix book, two cassettes, cassette cleaner, autograph book, *Clapperboard Film Quiz Book* etc. and £2.00 left. Angus came for a late night meal (gammon, duchess potatoes,[4] gooseberry fool, cider) and he slept.

Wednesday, 8 March

Mrs Dennison took our form (4–1) to the Lings cinema to see *To Kill A Mockingbird*. It was in black and white and it was crap BUT I sat next to Tracey Allen. Didn't do anything though.[5] Huh!

Wednesday, 13 March *MARBLE SEASON STARTS*

We had no homework. Good. The teachers are on a 'work to rule' strike this week. They HAVE to leave the school premises at dinnertime or the coach will turn back into a pumpkin and there is no school dindins. HOOOORRRAAAYY! Once more innocent school children may live.

---

4. Mum's bought a new cookery book! Basically mashed potatoes out of an icing bag, browned under the grill.
5. What did I expect to 'do' on a school trip? Put my arm around her? Sheer fantasy. I would achieve even the most innocent physicality only intermittently during the first year of girls.

Saturday, 1 April

This is not an April Fool. Went shopping. Dad and Mum bought an ace Sony (£300) music centre. It is fabdiferousti-clousant. It has a cassette deck, two speakers, headphones, radio facilities, stereo control, ace controllability, Dolby etc. etc. It is great. I have mastered the instructions already. I am clever. (That *is* an April Fool.)

Sunday, 9 April

STAYING AT MARGARET AND MEL'S IN CROWBOROUGH

Took the dog for another walk. I got in a mess with a stream, some holly and some barbed wire. Hmmm. Luvly dindins. Came back home from Margaret and Mel's. Journey took four hours. Bought a Nutty at service station.

Wednesday, 12 April

The day has arrived at last. I asked Tina[6] to go out with me to the pics to see *Star Whores* when it comes. Magic. She will think about it. Had a filling at the dentist's.

Thursday, 13 April

Success! Tina said she will come! Hooray. She is brilliant. Our art'n'craft group did our project displays. Angus and me's was 'Terror Movies'. Tina kept sneaking me bits of her peppermint cream from the cookery class. It was nice.

Sunday, 16 April

Brill. Tina went down the field. Ace. I think she will come to *Star Wars* if Jackie Needham[7] goes! So I am trying to pair up Angus and her so that they can go with me and Tina.

---

6. Tina Woods was certainly *closer* to my league, in that I'd known her since primary school and she lived on the estate (Crediton Close). I think it was in 1978 that she had her head bandaged up to stop her ears sticking out.
7. Jackie was another girl I'd known since early childhood: she lived over the back in Huntsham Close; her parents were part of the old school-run rota. She was a nice girl (in the same way that Tracey Allen was a *naughty* girl).

Wednesday, 19 April

Yawn. Boring day. No homework. Bollocks. I suspect Tina does not want to go out with me any more. Flipflipflipflipflipballs. Aaaaw!

Thursday, 20 April

Snotsnotsnotsnotsnotsnotsnot. Tina is going out with Mark Walsh.[8] You can't trust girls. Huh! I'm in a right mood now. Had haircut.

Wednesday, 29 April

Ace. Jackie and I went round to Joanne Flanders' new house which they haven't moved into yet. And we ate our packed lunches there. It rained. Walked home with Jackie. Tonight Dad and Mum took me to Whitehills squash club and I watched them play. Had quiteabita homework. Well ...

DISASTERS 0
TRIUMPHS 3

And a fantastic win for the Triumphs in their first match.[9]

Monday, 8 May

Simon's being a right bummer, lolling about all over my bed like a demented dead armadillo. Doing well wiv Jackie[10] (so wot else is new?). Went to a parents/children meeting about the trip to France we're going on. Great doss.

TRIUMPHS 2
DISASTERS 0

Tuesday, 23 May

What a fantastic day. Triumph 1 – made a lovely *jalousie* (fruit

---

8. No memory of this guy. I bet he was in the school team. I seem to remember Tina was a bit of a netballer.

9. Not sure where this triumphs vs. disasters thing came from. It's very Bridget Jones, isn't it? Notice how disasters almost never win – that's the kind of spin doctor I was. Not such a bad trait really.

10. Read nothing intimate into this. I didn't even kiss her on the cheek.

pie) in cookery 10/10. Triumph 2 – tonight I went out wiv Jackie to see *Star Whores*. Ace. It was absolutely brilliant. We had a great time. AT LAST I HAVE BEEN OUT WITH A GIRL. Jackie is wonderful.

Wednesday, 24 May

After school Angus came down. We had grate fun. No homework. By the way, I am now Han Solo. Great, kid, don't get cocky. Don't worry, she'll hold together. Hold together, baby.
  TRIUMPHS 2
  DISASTERS 0

Thursday, 25 May

Doesn't it smell? Yes. I don't think Jackie wants to go out wiv me any more. Huh. Snot fair is it? No it isn't. But I'm gonna keep working on her.
  TRIUMPHS 0
  DISASTERS 5,822
Wot a bum day.

Tuesday, 6 June

A grate day. Made chocolate cake in cookery 10/10. After school Paul came round. (By the way Jackie is ill and woz away from school.) So Paul, me and Anita walked round the lake, across a field, cross the motorway, up Thorburn Road, down Church Way and down Bridgewater Drive. Put my arm round Anita. And we held hands.[11]
  DISASTERS 1
  TRIUMPHS 4

Friday, 9 June

Grate stuff. I had thoroughly gived up with Jackie and I asked

---

11. I've been in touch with Anita and she doesn't remember this. (Or else she *chooses not to*!) She was going out with Paul at this stage – whatever that means when you're 13 – so I suspect it was an act of benevolence to allow me to put my arm around her. Paul obviously believed in sharing.

Tina, Lindsey[12] and Hayley[13] out at school. Three refusals. BUT Hayley rang me up after I'd had my hair cut and said she WOULD go out wiv me, and so it was all arranged. So me, Hayley, her brother Vaughan and Liz Carr went round the field, up the pub and round Liz's house in her bed(room). Ho ho. Hayley is grate. AC4HM

> DISASTERS 0
> TRIUMPHS 4

Saturday, 10 June

Wot a grate day. First of all I was going out with Hayley to see *Crimebusters* at the ABC but ... she couldn't go, so we went down the field. (By the way Margaret, Mel, Martin and Sarah came to sleep so Mum and Dad had a party with all the street.) I was just getting involved in this wild party when, after two sherries, Hayley's brother rang up and said that their Mum and Dad had gone out. So I went up Hayley's until 10.30. When I came home, had a few more sherries and I am stoned. It is now 11.30 and this sherry's gone to my head. Really.[14]

> TRIUMPHS 6
> DISASTERS 0

Tuesday, 13 June *SCHOOL TRIP TO FRANCE*

Got up at 4.30 in de morning to go to France. The channel crossing was good. Got to the *colonie* at 9.30. Had a bowl of tea and went to beddy-byes in the dormitories. Our coach driver is Derek. Our ferry was called *The Dragon*. French people are greasy.[15] Ah please![16]

---

12. Lindsey Best. Daughter of former Cobblers player Billy Best, which put her – guess where? – out of my league.
13. Hayley Mayo, the girl with whom I later tried my first Chinese takeaway. I suppose you could go mad and call her my first 'girlfriend', in that we went around together a lot that June (usually with her older brother Vaughan in tow – although I hero-worshipped him). Hayley was my first kiss. Much too tall for me, but then who wasn't?
14. Not really.
15. Travel certainly broadened my mind.
16. Inadvertent catch-phrase of one of our French teachers, Mr Eschalier.

TRIUMPHS 3
DISASTERS 0

Wednesday, 14 June

Had a coupla boring lectures from Mr Yates who runs the *colonie*. Went down the village. I bought two postcards and a French Cornetto. Went to a Benedictine Monastery. It was a dead bore. Lovely meals at this *colonie*. Had an ace disco till 9.30.
TRIUMPHS 3
DISASTERS 1

Thursday, 15 June

Went to Dieppe. We visited a French school. Had gob for school dinners there. Made friends with and talked in greasy French to Sophie, Natalie, Bob, Geres, Phillipe and Anne. Went to Mammouth Supermarche (greasy version of Tesco's). Lovely evening meal. Had 'nother chronic disco. Didn't go. Played table tennis.
TRIUMPHS 4
DISASTERS 1

Saturday, 17 June

It rained again. Went to Dieppe to the market. I bought a French loaf, some liqueurs and a pen set. Then it poured so we came back to the *colonie*. Sang French sweaty songs. Had anuvva lecture and had snails for evening meal. They were vomit. Left for home at five to eight. Slept on the ferry. Crossing very rough.
TRIUMPHS 1
DISASTERS 3

Friday, 14 July

Paul came to my house after school and we went to Nina's disco[17] at 8.00. Loads of kids went including Anita, Keith, Angus, Colin, Liz, Sally, Tracey, Neil etc. I had a grate time drinking whole bottles of Coke and tipping orange over Jackie.

---

17. It was a party at Nina Thadani's house, except with the music turned up.

Came home at 10.30. On the way I ripped my pinstripes as I fell over. I also had a nose bleed. Paul slept at my house tonight.
TRIUMPHS 4
DISASTERS 1

Friday, 21 July
Sniff! It was the last day at Abington Vale Middle School for me ... EVER! Sob sob. All the girls were crying. I won the Carol Barratt Art Cup. I gotten a certificate. I'll also get a cup presented. Anita was crying all the way home. Isn't it very sad? Went to bed early as we are going to Wales to Llithfaen tomorrow.
TRIUMPHS 2
DISASTERS 2

Thursday, 26 July *WALES*
We went on a lovely brisk walk to the Deserted Village but ... for one thing the walk itself is really really long and it is all uphill on the way back, and it bloody poured wiv rain and even hailed and it wuz absolutely a hurricane. So wot. We enjoyed it just de same. Sent all my postcards. Played in the hay barn again. Come on, weather, you'd better buck your ideas up a bit.
TRIUMPHS 3
DISASTERS 2

Saturday, 12 August
Went to town in the morning and I bought some straight-leg cords and a pair of ace Levi's boots. Tonight saw the film *Them* on TV. It wuz grate.
TRIUMPHS 3
DISASTERS 0

Wednesday, 30 August
Went to Nan Collins' for dindins and tea. Dad got me a *Film Review 1975-76* from the jolly old library. Reading *Dr Who and the Auton Invasion*. Grate. Saw *Z Cars*, wiv a stripper. Woohoo. Nipples.

Tuesday, 5 September *BACK TO SCHOOL*

To my new school, Weston Favell Upper. Well we (the new third years) didn't have to go to school till 1.15. Here is de details: Mr (Billy) Bowden is head of our year. I am in form 3CN (room M2). Our form teacher is nice Miss Chapman. We had a history lesson with Mrs Hadkins (who is also nice). Mr Bowden is fat. Wot a bum. But certainly today wasn't as bad as I imagined. (Saw *Goodies*.)

TRIUMPHS 3
DISASTERS 1

Wednesday, 6 September

Today had some good aspects and some bad aspects. Good: I am in top set for maths with Duncan and Stuart Skelton. Most of our teachers are nice. School dinners are lovely. Bad: there is no-one in my class I know ... or want to know. I hate my class. Also ... PE is absolutely nasty, like the teacher Mr Jenkinson. Oh dear.

TRIUMPHS 2
DISASTERS 2

Friday, 22 September

Grate day. For a start we didn't have any really bad homework. Dad bought the *Grease* album. I received my ELO Fan Club membership. Dad took me to Lings cinema to see *Monty Python and the Holy Grail*. It was the best film I've seen. It wuz really dead magic.

TRIUMPHS 5
DISASTERS 0

Wednesday, 4 October

Got a letter from Anita. There wuz a whole bunch of Smurf stickers in *Look-In*. Went wiv Dad to the Old Wellingburians Squash Racquets Club. He won 5–1 against a bloke called Whitcombe.

TRIUMPHS 3
DISASTERS 0

Monday, 9 October

Had a boring Monday at school. Usual stinkin' lessons. Paul[18] and I are probly joining the bird watchers club which will be a larf. Mucked about round at Hirsty's[19] place tonight listening to his magic 10CC single 'Dreadlock Holiday' etc. Saw *Till Death Us Do Part* film on TV.

    TRIUMPHS 3

    DISASTERS 0

Tuesday, 24 October

Went on a grate bird watching field trip organised by Mr Bowden and Mr Gilbert. About twelve went. We went in the school minibus to the Ecton Brook sewage farm. I spotted a heron and a kestrel and 25 other species. Just saw de final episode ob *Roots*. It wuz de greatest programme of all time.[20]

    TRYUMPFS 3

    DIZARSTARS 0

Wednesday, 1 November

Yesterday Mum got me a grate *Confessions From the Pop Scene* from her 'Wives' bazaar. I would've told you yesterday only Mum came back at 11.00 and I only got the book this morning etc. Clear! Good. Had a new telly. Boring day at school. Had gym. Hirsty came round tonight. Dad got me a (37p) black Pentel.

---

18. Not Paul Bush (who had gone to a different school by now, the Wrenn in Wellingborough) but Paul Price, a briefcase boy I would soon be forced to deny when I became hard and thick.

19. David Hirst came out of virtually nowhere and turned into a good mate at Weston Favell, largely because he was one of the few Abington Vale kids there (he lived on Bridgewater Drive; car porch). Tall kid with an unfortunate sticking-out top lip, he lent me some brilliant grown-up paperbacks like the novelisations of *Young Frankenstein* and *The Omen*, which broadened my palate. Again, I would be forced to distance myself from Hirsty when I changed my spots. Sad really. His Friends Reunited entry invites good cheer though: 'Now living in Southport (though still in Northampton regularly visiting family). Have acquired since school one wife, three children, one cat, a Baptist Church to run and greatly increased stress levels.' (Clearly cast aside *The Omen* then.)

20. I know, I know. See Chapter 13.

This is it. Didn't see *Monty Python* tonight. Probly because it's on Mondays.

TRIUMPHS 3

DISASTERS 0

Thursday, 23 November

Hallo, lads. I'm going to write my diary normally today. Sorry about that. Oops ... today we studied agriculture in India in geography. Also permanent chemical changes in chemistry. We were taught how to pass the ball in rugby and we looked over some revision in German. I had beefburgers for tea and after completing my chemistry homework at 6.52 ... oh crumbs. Now you can see why I write my diary silly. That is boring.

TRIUMPHS 0

DISASTERS 0

Sunday, 26 November

After dinner, Mum, Dad, Si, me and Melissa went to Overstone squash club. And after a load of absolute skill games ob squash Dad got me an early Christmas pressy: a grate, magic, good new Ascot 2070 squash racquet.[21]

Tuesday, 12 December

It's the exams tomorrow. Normal lessons. (Hey! Exams tomorrow.) Did a lot of revision in lessons (it's exams by the way). Hirsty came round tonight. (It's the exams tomorrow.) He gave me a card (exams don't forget). So did Liz and Jackie (exams you know). Saw *Man Alive* about fears (like the exams).

T – 0

D – 1

Exams, look ...

---

21. Though not a natural sportsman, I did give squash a run for its money, inspired to take it up by watching Mum and Dad play. It became a valuable father-son bonding time: we sweated and showered together and drank in the bar afterwards (I had orange and lemonade). He had always been vocally disappointed that I hadn't turned into a little footballer – and I think Simon had taken up fishing in the park by now – so this was the next best thing.

Friday, 15 December

Exams end. Phew. Flippin' what an ace day. Exams:

Biology: okay

History: okay

Maths: not bad

Also had a cross-country (inter-form). I came 135th out of 300. Not bad. But (here's the good bit) there was a third year Xmas disco at skool (7.30–10.00). It was reel cool. Everyone freaked out. I did the twist with George, pogo with John Lewis, a real good footsie with John, Bill, Lee, Si and George,[22] and an ace smooch with Liz.[23] Grate.

T – 5

D – 0

Tuesday, 19 December

Exam marks I got today:

Geography: 72% (2nd)

Biology: 84% (1st)

History: 78% (4th)

Hirsty gave me my Xmas pressie (*The Sentinel* paperback, about the Devil, evil etc.). Got the Christmas *Look-In*. Fairly good day at school. Saw *Carry On Matron*, an ace film about maternity wards. Also Dean came.

TRIUMPHS 4

DISASTERS 0

Thursday, 21 December

Dean came today. It snowed again but went all slushy. Tonight ... Dad and Mum took Si, Melissa and me to the New Theatre in Oxford to see *Aladdin,* starring Little & Large, Norman Collier, Charlie Caroli etc. It was ace. Charlie Caroli did a real larf slapstick bit and Little & Large did the usual. A brill panto. We came back at 12.00.

---

22. The Leeds scarf was working ...

23. Liz Heathcoate I think, a girl I would never 'go out with' although she was a good friend in later years.

TRIUMPHS 3
DISASTERS 0

Sunday, 24 December

Christmas Eve. Just thought I'd mention it, y'know. Absolutely brill. Flippin' it's Christmas tomorrow. Brill. I helped Mum and Dad make the fresh fruit salad: apples, pears, nanas, melon, pineapple, grapefruit, grapes, oranges etc. Luvly, gorgeous, brill. Went to Auntie Margaret's. Nan and Pap came tonight. So did Uncle Brian. Brill. Brill. Brill.

TRIUMPHS 4
ABSOLUTELY NO DISASTERS

Monday, 25 December

And the brill 1978 Christmas pressy rundown is as follows: £4.50 in vouchers, Lego technical set,[24] magnetic chess, giant drawing pad, George & Mildred game, Game Of Dracula, horror movie book, *Birds of Britain* book, *Jet Journey* book, *Star Wars* annual, *Sci-Fi Now* book, stapler, Radio 1 diary, *Mad Look at Old Movies*, *Grease* paperback, Spike Milligan's *Military Memoirs*, page-a-day diary, German dictionary, *Boy's Handbook*, Quality Streets, Pisces pendant,[25] Britain stencil, sketch book, ten-colour biro, letter stencil, hankie, plus mini Shell Lego set, Leeds mug. It wuz the brillest Christmas ever.

T – 8
D – O
SUPERSCORE

---

24. My last toy, although I didn't know it.
25. Mum's idea. Simon got a Gemini one. I never wore mine. Hated the feel of metal against my skin and still do.

1979

Selected Extracts From My Diary

The big time. A walloping page-a-day Boots diary – in unfetching dog's-muck brown – whose sheer size marks a turning point in the daily record of my life. More space, but don't expect more insight and detail (if anything, after a gung-ho start I end up writing less than ever as the novelty wears thin). Of all the diaries so far, 1979 most resembles a drawing book; an art happening; a repository for creative energy and half-formed ideas.

By the end of 1979 I drift into fantasy, creating an ecosystem of cartoon characters (the Talented Ten) who inhabit the diary's pages and play out a continuous narrative, whimsical then rather dark. This is bad news for anyone interested in what the 14-year-old me is doing day to day. It may be a big book, but the latter entries often consist of one, bald line:

'Had last haircut of 1979. O boy.'

Punk has arrived in the provinces, which explains the ransom-note lettering stuck to the front of the diary, reading: ANDY COLLINS. PRIVATE! *(Note: I am now officially Andy.)*

The traditional questionnaire – filled in at the very end of 1978 – reveals that I like Monty Python, Clapperboard, *wombats, girls and* The Rats.

I'm afraid the deliberately quirky spelling continues.

Tuesday, 2 January

Paul Bush came for dinner and we generally mucked about, taking the pee out of these two women sitting in front of us on the bus going to town, buying Scalextrix bridge for him and a pack of three Pentels for me, getting cold because it snowed, having to stand next to Sarah Gribble in the bus queue, playing a game of Scrabble using only slang and rude words, getting oil on my t-shirt as I fixed my new Smoker skateboard wheels on in my bedroom, writing pointless things in this new scribbling diary, getting a late Christmas card from him, trying very hard to arrange when to see each other again because he's got rugby and I'm going swimming, making lots of footprints in the virgin snow, reading yesterday's diary and thinking, 'How could I possibly fill up yet another day with just one visit from Paul Bush?' And Paul forgot to take home: his Christmas present from me, one Status Quo single, and his Chelsea scarf which I shall burn, mangle, mutilate, rip and wipe my bum on.

Si and I had a late night slipper fight and it was a magic larf. I didn't in fact do my diary, I wrote this today (tomorrow) and this day is yesterday (I think ...)

Sunday, 7 January

Nothing particularly fantastic, outrageously interesting, over-whelmingly fascinating, wow, zow, powie, zok, thrillsville happened. I lolled around on my bed, sorted all my drawers of drawings out a few times, lolled around on my bed, lolled around in the lounge, lolled around in the loo, wandered about, tried to start a colossal drawing project, completely read the *Radio* and *TV Times*, plus the *Sunday Mirror*, and this diary, lolled around on a living room chair, and lolled around on the floor until it was dinnertime, After dinner I read a crossword puzzle book a few times, cleared out my paperback collection and studied my *Mad* magazines and then something really WOW happened!! ...

We had tea. But ... I did have gorgeous crumpet with jam and two cakes. Luvly. And then we watched *It'll Be Alright on the Night* and *That's Life* after playing Scrabble.

And now I've gotta think of something to fill up this space. I've just gotta, you know ... Simon and Melissa have got no school because the lorry drivers' strikes and oil dispute mean there is no heat (along with 90 other Northampton schools NOT including our school).

Monday, 15 January *OFF SCHOOL DUE TO OIL DISPUTE*

I had a super enjoyable fun-day in the morning as I did my biology and French homework. O what fun. As a matter of fact, it was bloody boring. But I went to Pete Day's[1] and Simon and me had ace fun, smashing the odd spare room light, chucking teddys and pillows and chairs at each other, burying me alive, digging me up dead, drinking 'Peter Specials' (concoctions of any liquid he can lay hands on tipped in a glass with Coke, also including orange, gin, tapwater, rainwater, Vigor, Dettol and a spot of Domestos).

We're still on parole off school, jolly ace, flippin' brill show, good etc. And Dad took Melissa and me to sleep at Nan Mabel and Pap Reg's and I had to miss *Monty Python* as it annoys Nan and bores Pap. So I watched *Danger UXB* (which stands for Useless UneXplainable Bore) but it was bearable. And Melissa slept in the spare room and I slept on the settee with continental quilt filled with gravel and it was comfy with two pillows and I got to beddy-byes supa-quick and I wrote stacks too many 'and's. Awful English, Andrew. 5/10 could try harder.

Wednesday, 17 January

We were shovelled out of bed at 8.30 and Dad took us kids to Nan and Pap Collins'. We actually woke up at about 11.00 and then I did some drawing, I did my *Film Review* and it's a larf. I thought about my physics homework but that's about all.

We had a nice luncheon of chips, bacon and apple pie (in separate buckets of course) and then Mrs Day plus Pete came to collect Simon to go and see *Bambi* at the flicks. Well, *Jaws 2* really. Same difference, just as gory.

And I've now got three things to look forward to ...

1. Dad has ordered the *Rocky* LP from the record library and I'll get it in three weeks.

---

1. Peter Day was a friend of Simon's. Odd cove. He claimed (on this very day) to have whittled a stick of wood using what was clearly a butter knife. Simon expressed disbelief, so Peter set about trying to cut his finger with said knife to prove how sharp it was. We fetched his mum.

2. Dad has ordered the *Rocky* paperback from the bookshop at Wellingborough and I'll get it in two weeks.
3. I have sent away 70p for two back issue of *Mad* (*The Omen* and *Obsession*) and I should get them in two weeks.
4. I have sent away for the mafia kit in *Twinkle* comic. You get a pinstripe suit, shoulder pads, a pizza, a ready-rolled mafia-type joint cigarette, a horse's head, three car bombs, a book on how to talk like Marlon Brando, a machine gun and a mafia club pin-on badge and letter bomb. Oh sorry, I've gone again, slap me out of it someone, give me a glass of water ...

Saturday, 20 January

It snowed yesterday and so it wuz all slushy this morning when I went to art school. At college we made set-ups of apples, pencils, flower pots, tins and anything else we could get hold of (eg. small dead mammals, mortar bombs, lungs) and then we drew them and coloured them and shaded them and smudged them. By the time we got out and Dad picked me up the slush had melted.

Dad got me the single 'Baby Lay Your Love On Me' by Raccy.[2] It is ace. And Melissa got Olivia's latest single which is everso ace as well.

Uncle Pip, Auntie Val, Pete, James and Edward were supposed to have been coming for tea from Solihull but it was too foggy and they couldn't get through to good ol' Northants.

Wow! I haven't drawn a picture in my diary since January 7th. Amazin'. Anyway ... We played roulette and bingo in the afternoon and I lose a fortune every time. I did this time.

Tonite, after half a can of meths ... well, Coke, plus some crisps and chicken feed, Simon and me watched *The Iron Maiden* (a film) about nude ladies and sharks and spies and Dracula and (traction engines really).

Thursday, 25 January

Good ol' Mother Nature had toughed up the slush all day by

---

2. Punk has not yet arrived.

covering it with another three inches of snow glorious snow. It came down from 7.00 in the morning till 5.00 at night.

Mr Goldthorpe was away. Hence: no proper chemistry work. Hence: no no no no no no no no no homework. Hence: mucking about for a double lesson conversing about snow, slush, chemistry (occasionally), sweets, snow, telly, girls etc.

At breaks plus dindins time all (well most of ...) Weston Favell re-enacted World War II with snow against Nene College.[3] It was a good, wet larf and everyone was late in after dinner. Had a rugby test in games (yes! I did get 29/50).

Walked home. After tea, did homework, read *Mad*s, saw *Top of the Pops*, saw *Blankety Dankety Crankety Yankety Blank*.

Thursday, 1 February

Bloody boring, dull, limp day at school and I'm getting sick of writing whole pages of diary every day and that's why I always put boring-dull-limp for wot I did at school. But we had no homework at all and (you see it's all coming back to me) both Mrs Dee and Mr Goldthorpe were away, hence: no proper double chemistry or geog. And me and Wayne got 6/10 for our wall we knocked up in building craft.[4]

And it rained and covered all the melting slush/ice and the weather does get to be a bit of a drag nowadays, but at least we had just a quiz in games. Our class came joint third (last in other words, oh I'm sorry).

Tonight Dad took Liss and me to see *Watership Down* at the ABC. It was a cartoon film all about rabbits moving warrens and it was a pretty gory, thrilling 'U' certificate eg. one rabbit got bloodied up when caught in a snare, and the hero rabbit had a 'rip apart blood and saliva scar tear scratch' fight with the general baddie rabbit with one eye. It woz good tho' and I did get a *Film Review*, February, with *The Omen II, Jaws 2, Capricorn One, Superman Nil* (and Leeds – 82).

---

3. Nene College of Further Education adjoined Weston Favell Upper School by the playing fields.
4. Oh yeah, be impressed, we did actual bricklaying in building craft. And wallpapering. Girls did it too, naturally. This was very much the modern world.

Thursday, 8 February

Design. Building crap. Me, Wayne and Tarry made a massive tower of bricks and Wayne sat on it and I slopped mortar over Tarry's hand and Tina and Liz mixed the cement up all runny and cowpat-like. We got 6/10. Messy.

PE. Games. Rugby. But it was too hard'n'treacherous-death-trap on the pitches so we done swimming and Chris Bradshaw and me did our 15 and 25 yards. O ace. Spit and chlorine.

Dinnertime. Dinner was OK. It was bearable. But the curry was like volcanic lava with gravel.

Chemistry. Mr Goldthorpe is still away 'cos of a moped crash so we had Mrs Greene with no h/w.

Geography. Mrs Dee was still away so we kicked around and Phil, Si and me ate Polos during a film strip about lava and school curry. No h/w.

After skool. German.[5] We got sick of writing down all the German foods. Cold sausage with coleslaw and pickled cabbage and schnitzel and a bowl of fresh cream with Lego bricks or something.

After after skool. Before bed. Did drawing, saw *Blankety Yank*.

Wednesday, 14 February

Prat Poems No.4[6]

I looked out of my bedroom
My heart was full of woe
I had to go to Weston
Only it had been pouring with soft, flaky snow
We started off with English
And French was looming near
And even maths was not as bad
As reading crap Shakespeare

---

5. This didn't last long. What was I thinking? Swot.
6. I include this only because it is so very awful. I'm aware that much of the boyish charm has now trickled away and my diaries exhibit a teenage smugness that can irritate, but hey, as Bruce Hornsby would later observe, that's just the way it is. The *Goodies* books and *Monty Python* have a lot to answer for, stylistically.

Dinnertime was normal
With snow coming down, not rain
We had lava pie, with potatoes
And custard right out of a drain
And then we went swimming for double
I marked off the bronze survival
But I can still only swim 25 yards
And the only word that rymes is 'rival'
And then we had technology
And old Mr Archer's away
And it's a good job that it wasn't poetry
Because I am not too good
This is becoming quite boring
But I've got to write diaries somehow
Tonight I done some drawing
And the word that will ryme here is 'cow'
I don't think poetry is for me
Because for a start I can't spell ryme
And I reckon it's not exactly *Macbeth*
Or *A Midsummer Night's Shrew The Third*
Or something
By Andrew Coleridge Samuel Collins, aged 3

Sunday, 4 March

Magic ace brill, it's my 14th birfday. If you'd worked out from yesterday's diary, you'd have realised Angus slept. That meal last night was luvly. Plus gallons of cider, then a cup of coffee as we played Scrabble and I had a nose bleed.

Angus gave me a quid, Si gave me the *Jaws 2* paperback, Melissa gave me Violinski's single 'Clog Dance' and Dad'n'Mum bought me a magic Kodak 32 camera with handle, telephoto lens, ten flash cubes plus case and film. I've taken four pics already. It's magic. Nan M and Pap R got me a skill cassette box and an autograph book. Ace. Auntie Janice got me a *Mad* book and a magic photo album. The other Nan'n'Pap gave me £2, Brian and Janis £1.50, Auntie Margaret £1, Sue and Jon £2 (for my baby sitting) and Pete and Wendy £1. Plus an extra £1 from

Nan and Pap. I'm rolling in swag. Flippin' I'm gonna spend it on various Monty Python books and paperbacks.

Angus went home before dinner, but what an ace birfday eh? And ... our bog got bunged up. Dad squirted a hose down it, blew down it wiv a bike pump, put his hand down and generally said, 'To hell wiv it, ey?'

Wot a skill ace magic brill birfday.

Thursday, 15 March

Double building craft doesn't rule OK. But getting paste all over you during it does. Geography is really kinda eeuuur. Chemistry stinks OK. Chemistry h/w smells OK. Games in this cold weather is really kinda brrrrr. *Animal House* film was ace skill magic OK. You bet. It had nude ladies and a college and naughty kids and a carnival and larf slapstick comedy and it was my first 'AA' OK? [7]

Friday, 23 March

Had a disco at school. Ace it waz.
Bill Jeyes
Lee Masters
Si Triculja
Jon Ward
Paul Wallace?
Mark Emery
= punks
Ace music, Sex Pistols, Skids. Boring music as well. Kev never went, Hirsty looked a puff. [8]

Wednesday, 28 March

I got *Look-In* this morning delivered. It's got the Bee Gees in it. Chris lent me a *Cracked* mag and I got caught readin' it in maths

---

7. A true rite of passage from the pre-video age: your first 'AA' certificate film, aged 14. *Animal House* did not let me down, boasting three scenes with bare breasts in. I'd seen my dad's *Mayfair* ladies, but you can't beat moving pictures.
8. The denial begins.

by Mr Twinn. He said it was trash. It's not. It rained really wet all day. Listened to my new singles a lot tonight. Technology was as bad as ever and in PE we had Mr Blogg for volleyball. It was a bit pratty but not too bad. Tonight saw *Play for Today, Dwarf On Giant's Shoulders*. It was good 'cos it was on till 11.00.

Thursday, 12 April

O boy, wot a funny weather day. It poured, then slowed down, then poured again, then stopped, then dried up, then rained again, then poured, then stopped, then we had dinner*, then it started, then thunder, then lightning, then hail, then (after tea**) it dried up and stayed like it till now.

    * dindins = shepherd's pie, lemon meringue pie
    ** tea = tomato and cheese omelette, pineapple mousse.
I did go out on my bike when it was dry. I saw Lowey. Mum got a brand new brown Leyland Mini. I got my Sheffield photos delivered. We saw *Blankety Blecch*. I had a game of darts with Si and Dad. I won again with a skill double-five.

    Tomorrow is Good Friday. Let's hope it's good weather. Lesley Judd left *Blue Peter*.

Saturday, 28 April

Went to art class this morning. We sketched models in pencil. I was one model. It rained hard this morning. Quite sunny this afternoon. Got my *Mad* magazine, plus 'Mork' *Cracked* magazine, and the Sham 69 single 'Questions and Answers'.[9]

    This afternoon Angus's Dad took Angus, his brother and me to see *Death on the Nile*. It was absolutely skill. 'A' certificate because it had five murders:

      One throat slit with pools of blood
      One shot right in the head point blank
      One shot in the forehead, splurting blood
      One shot herself through the head
      One shot right in the side of the face

---

9. Not in a picture sleeve. So I stuck ransom-note lettering on it. I was that *Blue Peter* punk.

Grate.[10] Tonight I started a spoof of it, *Death on the Nail.* I painted my bike chain-guard black and fixed on my rack. Then played Scrabble wid Mum'n'Dad and saw the news and Roald Dahl's *Tales of the Unexpected* (till 11.15).

Tuesday, 1 May

Dad wouldn't let me do my diary tonight. He said, 'Lights out. No diaries. No talkin'. No snorin'. No whisperin'. No writing. No singing – or you will get it.'

Friday, 4 May

Didn't rain. It was dry'n'sunny. No h/w. Oh yes there was ... geography. Nice dinner: pineapple sponge. Metalwork in design. Walked home with Chris. Meatballs for tea. Game of soccer and cricket with Chris and Steve tonite.

Off to Uncle Phil and Auntie Eileen's at Blackpool for the weekend. Got packed.

Maggie Thatcher won. Oh. Hmm. New Prime Minister. A woman. Ooh dear.[11]

Saturday, 5 May

Got to Uncle Phil and Auntie Eileen's near Blackpool at 11.30. They've got two girls: Anne-Marie and Angela-Louise (seven and three). Uncle Phil's a linesman.[12] He had to go to a match this afternoon. Blackburn v West Ham (at Blackburn). Score = 1–0 to Blackburn. He got me two grate programmes from the match, one for me, one for Doug at school.

---

10. That career in film criticism moves ever closer.

11. A rare glimpse of the outside world from my diary here. Perhaps even through the thick fug of self-absorbed teen angst I sensed that something momentous was happening when Mrs Thatcher entered Downing Street and promised to bring harmony where there was discord.

12. Phil was a very cool honorary uncle, what with the linesman's gig and a very dry Lancastrian sense of humour. We once went with him to some Beazer Homes League game and he sprayed Ralgex muscle-rub on his legs in the changing room, telling us it made him run faster. We believed him. Looking back, Phil and Eileen must have been my first Catholics – they had religious pictures and crosses around the house, which I thought creepy at the time.

Si and me are sleeping in Anne-Marie's normal room. This afternoon the Tower (at Blackpool) (Blackpool Tower, you burk) was closed. So we went to the Pleasure Beach. Si and me took Anne-Marie on the Noah's Ark fun house. It was all dark, the ark rocked about, there was loads of moving floorboards and steep stairs and luminous moving animals and it was pretty ace. Si, Dad and me went on this skill firing range with loads of models that work if you trigger them off. And we saw the haunted mine and ghost train from the outside.

Walk on the beach at sunset.

By the way, Simon was sick on the journey.

Sunday, 6 May

It was Melissa's birthday today. She got tonz of prezzies including a cuddly bunny. We had a grate day today. We rode down into Blackpool (me, Si, Liss, Anne-Marie, Angela and Uncle Phil) and went in the BBC *Dr Who* Exhibition. Oh it was real magic. All the monsters, original sound effects, K-9, the Tardis, moving models, ace little scenes and original masks, plus flashing lights and dark corridors. I bought a 10p big *Dr Who* badge and a 'Welcome to Blackpool' Tom Baker postcard. Reeeally ace.

Then we went up the Pleasure Beach again. I took loads of good photos.

Fry-up lunch eg. bacon, egg and tomato. Then we drove up to Fylde for a birthday dinner/tea/meal at this great country/homely restaurant. Me and Si sat on a separate table as there was nine of us and we had gammon, egg, chips and ice cream and mint choc. I had four cups of luvly tea. Came home at about 7.00.

Melissa got a luvly cake from Uncle Phil and Auntie Eileen. Good day wasn't it eh?

Our car still smells of Si's sick.

Sunday, 3 June

We went to Coventry for dinner and tea to Uncle Jim, Auntie Christine's, Lorraine and Sandy's. Luvly dinna: chicken, spuds, gravy, sausage meat, stuffing, pie. Luvly tea: Scotch egg, tomato, salad cream, cheese, bread, onion rings, raspberry meringue.

We went for a walk round de park, losing tennis ballz etc., playing their croquet. Home at 9.15. Saw *That's Life* + drink of shandy. Oh I can't help it ... Sham 69, Skids, Buzzcocks.

Friday, 8 June

No rain. Amazin'. Bit of h/w. I've dunnit. Had metalwork. Went up de library. I got: *Guinness Book Of Names, Guinness Book Of Soccer Feats, Exorcist* book, *Vampire Films.* Really ace books.

Saw *Are Yer Bein' Served.* Read me books. Into the valley, betrothed and divine, realisation's no virtue but who can define ... sorry.[13]

Sunday, 10 June

At 10.30 we all went off (in our posh clothes – vomit) to Johnny and Melanie Ashby's confirmation and communion.[14] We had a one and a half hour service. Really exciting and thrilling. But we went back to their house for a big buffet wiv loads of other people. I had melon, wine, turkey wings, crisps, salmon roll, cheese'n'pineapple, Coke, lemonade, beer, punch, a straw-berry off the top of the gateau (don't tell Mum or anyone), loads of fresh fruit salad. It was luvly. I didn't have no tea. Belch. Both nans and paps came home from their hols yesterday. We saw them both. I got some chocs from N+P Collins and from N+P Reg = four Jersey postcards, a sick bag from the plane[15] and £2. Ace. Bed = late. Belch.

Friday, 22 June

It didn't rain much today. O good. Had pakt lunch as yewshal. Exams on Munday as well, too, in addition to, also. Nan baby-satted because we are babies. Saw Monty Python film *Now Fer Summat Completely Diffrant* till 12.30. My ankle hurts. Dohh! My

---

13. Lyrics from 'Into The Valley' by The Skids.
14. More arcane religiosity: veils and candles. It was like another world to us pagans.
15. Some kind of joke. We took it with us on our next long car journey though.

brain aches. I wish I was a prawn. I wish I was a Northumbrian anteater on Wednesdays. Silly boy silly boy.

Saturday, 23 June

There waz an exhibition on at art college. It was a crack. Yes. I bought a new racer bike. No I didn't buy it. Dad did. It's a Raleigh GT Super 5. Five gears. GT brakes. It's so brilliant and good and fast and spiny.[16] I also got three new dart flight barrels and this fortnight's *Smash Hits*. It's king. Devo: are we not spiny?

Sunday, 1 July

We dun the poster board up:
1. Generation X (mine)
2. Johnny Rotten (mine)
3. *Orca* (mine)
4. Boomtown Rats (mine)
5. *Moonraker* (Si's)
6. *CHiPS* (Si's)
7. Skids (mine)
8. *CHiPS*
9. *CHiPS* (both Si's).

Pritty good. It was sunny today. We made Sooty a new guinea pig run. Listened to the Top 40. Tubeway Army no. 1. Clash is back to 25, but Pistols are 24. Ace. Ruts are coming up as well. Silly boy – pardon.[17]

Saturday, 7 July

My new poster set-up:

---

16. I have affectedly adopted 'spiny' as an adjective meaning good – it derives from the Pirhana Brothers sketch in *Monty Python*: 'Dinsdale was convinced he was being watched by a giant hedgehog whom he referred to as "Spiny Norman". Normally Spiny Norman was wont to be about twelve feet from snout to tail.' I liked the Gilliam drawing of him in the *Big Red Book*.

17. One of our playground catch-phrases of the time was 'I heard that! Pardon?', testament to writer Peter Tinniswood, from whose BBC sitcom *I Didn't Know You Cared* (1975–79) it came. The character who said it was deaf Uncle Staveley, played by Bert Palmer, then Leslie Sarony in the final series.

1. Generation X
2. Johnny
3. *Orca*
4. *Moonraker*
5. *CHiPS*
6. drawing of Skids
7. Cotswold Wildlife Park postcard
8. *CHiPS*
9. *CHiPS*
10. Skids

I got the Skids poster from this fornight's *Smash Hits* mag. It's got words to: The Ruts, Sex Pistols etc. It's too ace. Plus ... up town, I bought two singles: 'C'Mon Everybody' by Sid Vicious (S Pistols) and 'Babylon's Burning' by the Ruts. They're 2 spiny and good. Plus, I've put up a poster of the Rats in place of ELO.[18]

Saw *Benny Hill*. Bed = 10.00. Babylon's burning. C'mon everybody! Hoooo, c'mon everybody. I wish I was a blakhed wiv anxiety, usin' mah mind. (Sponsored by Bernard Tosimov.)

Sunday, 15 July *WALES*

It was luvly and sunny and hot and glint. We went to Llanbedrog for the day. I got really burnt arms and legs. I bought the paperback *Coma*. It is so spiny. Mr Williams put a bit of rope up over a tree out the back for a swing thing. Apey gougey.[19] We went for a long walk after a egg n chipz tea to Pistyll beach. It was very warm all day. My legs are stingin'. I wish I was a lump in some rice pudding.

Monday, 16 July

I wish I was a trout. We went to Pwllheli for dinner. I bought a £2.00 All-American Frisbee. Had cold beef rolls for dinner on de beach. Read a lot more of *Coma*. Got really sunburnt. Luvly and hot tho'. Had a walk across Morfa Nefyn beach to a pub for crisps and Coke. We walk'd bak to the car cross de golfy course

---

18. With which the transformation from square to punk rocker is complete.
19. Just trying on a couple more irritating made-up adjectives for size.

and I had a beefburger in batter from a chip shop. Everybody else had chipz. Bed = 10.00 + John Peel.

Friday, 20 July
Rode to Nefyn garage with Dad to get his oil filter fixed. Went to Pwllheli for dinner. Had sams and crisps and cake. Also Melissa and I had Wimpys. I had a cheeseburger with tonz of onions. Mmmmm. Played cards and had scraps on the ropes with Si. Ace larf. Sent postcard to Kev. Bed = 10.00. Bought Paul Daniels Magic Cards.

Friday, 27 July
Went to Pwllheli in de morning. Went on penny arcade in fair. Lost all my pennies. So wot if I did, you twonk.[20] Still hot. Went home. Left Wales at 3.15. Arrived home at 9.00. Not bad time. Great journey. No pukin'. Got *Smash Hits* at service station. Got poster of Sting; words to 'Death Disco', 'Harmony in my Head', 'Here Comes the Summer' and Boomtown Rats' no. 1 'I Don't Like Mondays'.

Wednesday, 1 August
Went up Nan and Pap Collins' for dindins + tea. Lovely food:
    Meat, potatoes, gooseberry pie = dins
    Chips, bacon, egg, ice cream, cake = tea
Got some ointment and plasters for my toe. Went up town wiv Mum, Janice and Dean. Had a can of 7Up and got some Bubble Yum. Went to library. I got a vampire film book and various books about jellyfish, my latest in-subject. Saw *Cornynation St, Benny 'Ill*, documenstrual about video dating system. Bed = 10.00. Yes well.

Thursday, 2 August
This morning I went to Dr Costain (the chiropodist) about my ingrown toenail. I could tell you about the local anaesthetic he put in my toe, or the rubber tourniquet to stop the blood, or

---

20. You can't blame me for this one: I heard Compo say it on *Last of the Summer Wine*.

how he cut my toe when it waz numb, or how he sliced off the bit of excess flesh with a knife, or how he cut the jutting-out piece of nail, or how when he undid the tourniquet the blood gushed out, or how much dressing he piled onto my toe, or how swollen it waz or how it made me feel a bit 'off' after dinner. But I won't.

Paul Bush came after lunch. We had a wander to the paper shop. Paul bought a couple of music papers. *Top of the Popz.* 'Don't Like Mundays' no. 1. It's a bit mediocre. Bed = 10.00. My toe is bin bleedin' but Dr Costain dressed it with loads of stuff.

Friday, 3 August

I had my toe redressed wiv bandage, gauze and plasters. I could tell you how Dr (Simon) Costain plucked the bits of old gauze out of my toe wiv tweezers. Dat's an ooch.

Dad took Si and me to pics to see *Porridge.* Ace crak film. Real glish.[21] Starrin' Ron Barker, Rich Beckinsale etc. Grate! Also got Aug *Film Review* wiv *Arabian Adventure* (mediocre), *The Champ* (boring), *Fuck Rodgers* (weedy) etc. But it is an ace mag. I am a film fanatic. I love info on new films. Real spiny.

Saturday, 4 August

Got two singles at town. 'Here Comes the Summer' Undertones. 'Hersham Boys' Sham 69's farewell single. They're ace.

Up our house tonight we had Nan Mabel and Pap Reg's Ruby Wedding party. Loads of people came including Dean. We all had a larf. Bit of dancing. Lods of records. Lods of drink. Lods of food. Fresh fruit salad, turkey, sossy rolls, cheesecake and a Ruby Wedding cake that was gorgeously tasty and glish.

At 12.15 me and Si (sneakily) watched *The Mummy* late nite horror film in our bedroom. Really ace, scary, good, spiny. Till 1.30. Starring Chris Lee, Pete Cushing. Real good.

---

21. One of mine. Perhaps I should have mastered the English language before I started adding to it.

Wednesday, 8 August

Today I had my ingrown toenail done at the chiropodist's. It was a proper op. Dr Si Costain and his nurse and Dr Brenda Costain all wore masks, hats and hygiene gowns. I had a strip of nail cut out under local anesthetic (LA). I watched ... I've kept the cut-off bit of nail. Not too much blood. Two injections. It was okay.

Nice tee at Nanz. Chips (tons) and bacon.

Sunday, 12 August

Alfred Hitchcock (my idol)'s birthday (80th), so on BBC *39 Steps*. Really good film, ever such a good plot. I missed *To Catch a Thief* but on TV at 11.00 *Psycho*. I'm writing this at 10.30. Did me and Si watch it all? If so ... any good?

Ace. Shower scene ace. Dead detective ace. Corpse of mother ace. Very tense. 10/10

Saturday, 15 September

Went to art skool. All de lads went eg. Louis, Paul, Freak, Tony etc. Did sketchin'. I went up Kev Bailey's fo' dinner. Saw Phil, Leigh, Martin, Matthew etc. We had salad. We rode all round Parklands. Plus: we went up Paul Freeman's house.[22] Kev gave me a Sex Pistols reflector badge. Itz ace. Plus: we had a loada gos avec Kev's air rifle. Ace larf.

Saw *Wot's Up Doc?* on TV. It was a king crak-up. Leeds drew 1–1 to Liverpool.

Tuesday, 2 October

Usual day at school. Phil's birfday. Bit of homework. Bill Jeyes has had a skinhead.[23] Saw *Last of the Summer Wine*. Thank you for inviting me into your home.

---

22. Paul Freeman was a key punk figure. He unwittingly became my musical mentor, as he had a boxful of ultra-cool singles, from Dr Feelgood's 'Milk And Alcohol' in white vinyl to something by Cowboys International in clear. And he had cowhorn handlebars.
23. Now he looked like a true thug. I wouldn't be joining him on this particular journey. This was hardcore.

Friday, 5 October
Yes. Si Triculja has also had a skinhead.[24] Mr Robbins has gived us more chemistry homework. So we've started R.A.R. Rock Against Robbins. Saw *Horse of the Year* on TV.

Sunday, 21 October
I've got an ulcer. Saw *Roots* (1913). Buggles are no. 1.

Tuesday, 30 October
Saw *Star Games, Grange Hill, Summer Wine.* Saw *Not the 9.00 News.* No homework. Jim Pursey's radio show now 8.00–9.50, then J Peel. Listened to the end of Jim. Had Starjets, Members. John had The Damned ('Love Song' and 'Machine Gun Etiquette').

Sunday, 4 November
Roots: Alex had married Nan and had two kids, Billy and Lydia, but they've left Alex at the end of the prog. Made two Damned badges.

Monday, 5 November
No h/w. Too sacred. Went to see *Coma* at Lings with Auntie Margaret[25] ('AA' cert), starring Genevieve Bujold, Michael Douglas, Richard Widmark, Lois Chiles etc. Boy it waz an ace film. Good nasty bits eg. dead bodies in plastic bags in the freezer, maintenance man getting electrocuted, operations, autopsy, suspended bodies, great 'AA' stuff.

Saturday, 10 November
Got *Coma* soundtrack from record library. Leeds lost 3–0 at Coventry. Got the College fx 80 Casio calculator. It is 2 ace. £15.95. Sines, cosines, squares, brackets, cubes, memory,

---

24. One by one they fell – Gaz went under the clippers next. Lee Masters showed that he had a mind of his own after all by abstaining. I admired him for that.
25. Quite how this arose is a bit murky, but once I'd turned fourteen, Margaret must have rashly promised to take me to a 'AA' at the pictures – she said she liked scary movies, but had no-one to go with. I held her to it, and we went to see *Coma*, a middle-aged woman and a teenage boy. It was as odd as if Dad had taken our cousin Jane to the cinema.

inflatable life raft etc. I also got the 'Bodysnatchers' *Mad* mag. Got some new gloves.

Thursday, 15 November
Done me 60 yards. I am the Man From Atlantis. *TOTP* crap. Dr Hook no. 1 oh God. It's so bo-o-o-oring. Saw *Futtock's End*. Miss Bermuda is Miss World. Miss UK (Carolyn Seaward) 2nd.

Wednesday, 21 November
Went on careers trips. Our group went to Tootals clothes factory. Great larf. Old women on the machines etc. Me, Craig, Si and Lee = only boys in our group. We wandered round and nipped in the Cobblers for something to do.

Roy, Dad and me left at 5.20 for Wembley to see England v Bulgaria. Very foggy. So foggy in fact the match was postponed. We found out just as we got there. Drove all the way back. The match is supposed to be tomorrow instead. Will we go?

Thursday, 22 November
England v Bulgaria with Dad and Roy in Roy's car. Ace match. We won it 2–0. Dave Watson (1st half), Glenn Hoddle (2nd half). We were in the stands at the very front behind the safety barrier. Team:
1. Ray Clemence (Liverpool)
2. Viv Anderson (Forest)
3. Kenny Sansom (Palace)
4. Phil Thompson (Liverpool)
5. Kev Reeves (Norwich)
6. Ray Wilkins (Man U)
7. Dave Watson (Southampton)
8. Glenn Hoddle (Spurs)
9. Trev Francis (Notts Forest)
10. Ray Kennedy (Liverpool)
11. Tony Woodcock (Forest)

Ace atmosphere at Wembley. Great inside. Got rosette and two programmes. Great goal by Hoddle. There's only one team in Eur-ope.

Saturday, 8 December

Got my photoz back. Went Christmas chopin (shoppin'). Got torch and two badges for Si, *How Green Was My Valley* for Nan M, *Boys From Brazil* for Pap C, Catherine Cookson book for Nan C. whisky liqueurs for Pap R,[26] tights for Mum. Plus a 'Coronation St' *Mad* mag for me. And a Sex Pistols badge. Rather ace. Good day's chopin I think. I've rap'd up all my prezzies. Leeds drew 1–1 to Man U (wankers). Connor scored.

Tuesday, 11 December

Disco at school. What an ace disco. Me and Andy Howkins went as Undertones eg. rolled up jeans and DM boots. Loads of other punks eg. Paul Freeman, Si, Mark etc. Went wiv Craig McKenna and left me bike up his house. About five punk records eg. Tourists,[27] Sham, Skids and more. And Si and me wore our Harrington jackets inside out ie. tartan. Loads of mods up there. Madness etc. Few smoochy records at the end. And I had a smooch avec Cindy Offord. I had my hands full. Aaaaaahhhhhh. I'm in a trance now. O Cindy.[28]

Thursday, 13 December

Still secretly (nearly) in love with Cindy. Because of an ace design for a Xmas card I did for Mervyn at Dad's work he gave me a *little* reward. They've printed out loads of cards for all their clients and I got one and a £5 record voucher (spend it on Sat).

Had wanky hard Maths 1 exam. Put up my Sham poster. Had all 4th year cross-country. It was rather longue to say the least. I came 128th out of 180 boys. I am so nackered. Uncle Brian baby-sitted. Did two posters for the school bookshop. Wagged swimmin'.[29]

---

26. I always bought whisky liqueurs for Pap Reg.
27. The Tourists? Punk? What a generous door policy I was operating.
28. She would come to regret letting me slow-dance with her, the lovely Cindy Offord. I foolishly took it as encouragement and mooned over her for years, on and off. She never let me near her again.
29. From Jonathan Green's *Dictionary Of Slang* (I knew it would be in there!):
Wag/wag it/off vb. [mid-19C+] to play truant (cf. BUNK OFF; PLAY THE WAG). [HOP THE WAG] Don't be too impressed – I was too much of a scaredy-cat to wag it much.

Sunday, 16 December

Went up both Nans. Chemistry revision. Saw *EBC1*. Must see Cindy tomorrow. Ask her out?

Thursday, 20 December

Got 65% in art. Got 63% in French. And considerably less in maths. Saw *TOTP* avec Skids record of whom I bought on November 16. You see I know a good thing when I first hear it. And *Blinkety Wank* and *Dawson Watch*.

Scored three goals in water polo for our team in swimmin'. Drew teachers on the blackboard in French.[30] Must ask Cindy out tomorrow. Please. I *must*.

Friday, 21 December

Got a Christmas card from Cindy, that beautiful girl I asked out today. Yes I actually asked her to go out wiv me. She wants time to think about it,[31] so she will tell me when she next sees me. Soon I hope.

My other secret passion along with Cindy is sugared dates. They are as lovely as Cindy. I had a whole bowlful tonight. They were delicious. Got Christmas *NME*. It's really ace.

Last day of term. Left school at 3.00. Craig came round tonight. We listened to the Dickies album. He lent me 'Pretty Vacant' and 'Ever Fallen in Love' by Pistols and Buzzcocks. It snowed. Not really fluffy. Enuff to settle and freeze. Got 83% biology and 73% chemistry.

I really did ask Cindy out. Got cards from Cindy, Wally, Si, Glen, Pete. They won the dustbin on *3-2-1*. Ace, magic, at last.

---

30. This act of artistic crowd-pleasing happened with the full approval of our teacher, Miss Szkopek. What a sport she must have been. I even drew her as a big curly-permed ball with a pair of large, round glasses on and 'peg' trousers sticking out the bottom and she let me get away with it.

31. 'I'll think about it.' How those words retrospectively burn a hole in my heart. How many girls told me they were going to think about it? And why did I believe them? Cindy Offord didn't need to think about it. She knew.

Tuesday, 25 December

Grate Christmas Day. My presents: super quality bristle dart board, Leeds dart flights, *Monty Python's Life of Brian* LP, *Life of Brian* book, book of the film of *Alien*, desk tidy, 24 quality pencils, new page-a-day diary, giant drawing pad, Jasper Carrott book, book of graffiti, Skids badge, Undertones badge, Radio 1 diary, complicated game, dart sharpener, squash ball, bike clips, comb, ace Undertones t-shirt, pencil sharpener, *2nd Clapperboard Quiz Book*, £4.50 in vouchers, Matchmakers, Dymo label printer.[32] Everybody came today.

---

32. ... And no Lego.

twelve

Uncle Punk

London calling to the faraway towns
Now that war is declared, and battle come down.
The Clash, 'London Calling' (1979)

In his definitive chronicle of punk, *England's Dreaming*, Jon Savage is perfectly clear about what happened in 1979: 'Punk was over. Humpty Dumpty had fallen off the wall and there was no way of piecing him together.'

He pinpoints the death of punk to 4 May, the day the Conservatives swept to power under Margaret Thatcher, an event logged in my 1979 diary, as we have seen, with the positively Shavian insight, 'Oh. Hmm. New Prime Minister. A woman. Ooh dear.'

What I didn't note in my diary that day was the death of punk. For though historically and culturally, Savage is spot on, he speaks only for London. For Northampton and the other 'faraway towns' to which Joe Strummer might have been calling, punk had just arrived.

Though they soldiered on in name, the Sex Pistols had effectively ceased to exist when Johnny Rotten walked offstage at the Winterland Ballroom in San Francisco on 14 January 1978;[1] and when Sid Vicious died of a heroin overdose on 2 February 1979, there really was no piecing together punk's founding fathers.

---

1. 'Ever get the feeling you've been cheated?' One of the great lines of the twentieth century, though it rarely makes those dictionaries of quotations.

Fortuitously for those of us who were just turning 14 and living in the provinces, Sex Pistols product did not dry up. Death for them was not the end. My first ever punk single, purchased on 27 March 1979, was 'Something Else' by the Sex Pistols, a cover of the 1959 Eddie Cochran song and a Number Three smash.

Its 'video', taken from Julien Temple's *Great Rock'n'Roll Swindle* movie (released later that year), featured Sid Vicious getting out of bed in some off-white pants, cupping his bollocks, sneering in a mirror, getting dressed and bombing down some country lanes on his motorbike (he was sure fine lookin', man). On *Top of the Pops*, Jimmy Savile felt moved to warn the nation that riding without a helmet is dangerous. So was taking heroin and *possibly* stabbing your girlfriend (although it could have been the drug-dealer).

A punk Johnny-come-lately I may have been, but I was hooked into the Pistols universe there and then, dimly aware that it existed only in memorial. I remember Vicious's death, if only for the fact that Jo Gosling wore a black armband to school the Monday after, in doing so confirming her status as coolest kid in the playground. (I bet they made her take it off.) Back in February I can't say I'd shed a tear for Sid – in fact, on the day of his overdose, Stuart Skelton gave me an ELO pin-up and I received two back issues of *Mad* through the post – but I loved him now.

Thus it was that punk came in the front door on 27 March 1979, and the Electric Light Orchestra were bundled out the back. It was no less than a conversion, as decisive as seeing the light, and very timely, as being 14 years old means being a rebel, and here was my ride.

* * *

Punk had entered my consciousness before 'Something Else' and its handsome picture sleeve. It was out there. To my credit, I had bought 'Rat Trap' by The Boomtown Rats in November '78 and 'Heart Of Glass' by Blondie in February '79 – which at least shows a flash of new wave sympathy – but I had also bought singles by Racey and Violinski during the same period. My diary makes no record of it, but I *must* have been aware of the Pistols' 'God Save The Queen' in 1977, even in my royalist pomp. Surely *John Craven's Newsround* did some kind of report ...

As a rule, while punk was sweeping the nation in 1976, 1977 and 1978, I was busy elsewhere: glueing Airfix models together, playing with Matchbox cars and listening to *Grease*. Clearly, my age was a factor. As was the hard reality that all the major punk tours passed Northampton by, in favour of more glamorous places like Leicester and Birmingham.[2] So I have two alibis.

Records show that when the Buzzcocks joined The Damned and The Vibrators on the bill at the 100 Club punk festival on 21 September 1976, I was chuffed at getting two Corona Fizzical stickers off Martin Soards. When Steve Jones called Bill Grundy a 'fucking rotter' on live TV, 1 December 1976, I was busy making a Christmas card for Mum's squash coach. While The Clash were sending masonry flying on the White Riot tour in May 1977, I was learning a simple tune on the xylophone in rehearsal for a special form assembly.[3]

On 7 January 1978, at a late Christmas party round at Nan and Pap Collins's, the kids put on an elaborate show for the grownups: Simon, Melissa and I, plus cousins Jane and Paul. I have a fuzzy memory of this DIY extravaganza – I camply wore one of Nan's dresses and sang 'Hey Big Spender' at one point – but my diary entry tells us that I also did an 'impression' of someone called 'Uncle Punk'. I've no idea who this character is. Perhaps I made him up. I know impersonating him involved wearing my black PVC jacket (purchased from the Kays catalogue during my

---

2. Northampton is 'not a big college town' (to use the Spinal Tap vernacular). These days of course, the Roadmender has established itself as an itinerary staple for medium-sized bands, but it wasn't even a venue when I lived there, just a pub in a very bad location. The first ever gig I attended was U2 and Altered Images in the refectory at Nene College of Further Education (Park Campus) on 20 January 1981, a rare opportunity to catch a national tour in town (they had just released *Boy* and I'm proud to say I caught them when you could get close enough to smell Bono). In February, again thanks to the NCFE (perhaps they had an unusually hip ents sec that year), I saw Classix Nouveaux and Theatre Of Hate at the County Ground, and in 1982 I caught local legends Bauhaus at Lings Forum. But my most significant big gigs involved driving or being driven to other towns: The Cure, Siouxsie & The Banshees, Echo & The Bunnymen. How I envy people who grew up in *proper* places like Leicester and Nottingham.
3. I can still play it. D, D, D, E, D, F, G, A, A, B, A, B, C, D, A, A, G, A, G, F, D ... I think. Try it. If it sounds like 'The Floral Dance', I am Evelyn Glennie and I claim my £5.

Fonz phase) and sticking my hair up in some way. I used Melissa's toy guitar for rocking effect, and I must have sung something punky. Did I pretend to spit? Wear a safety pin? If only camcorders had been around to record what seems to be my very first acknowledgement of punk.

In December that year I wrote a facile parody of a punk lyric in my diary ('Let's all gob on a diary, lads/It's the latest craze'), accompanied by a cartoon of an imaginary group, Pete Pungent and the Snotrags (this is very much the time of Kenny Everett's Sid Snot and Gizzard Puke). It seems I was more aware of punk as per parodies and cheap gags on TV than I was as a potential source of personal insurrection or head-turning music.

But all that changed in March 1979, thanks largely to *Smash Hits*, which I had just started showing an interest in. Stuart Skelton, he of the ELO poster gift, bought some issues to school and I was instantly captivated by the magazine's unique selling point: the song words. Prior to D-day (or P-day) I took a keen interest in obtaining the lyrics to 'Sound of the Suburbs' by The Members and 'Lucky Number' by Lene Lovitch (sort of punk, certainly screechy and something Nan would bristle at on *Top of the Pops*). On 23 March I took down the names of all the kids I considered to be punks at a school disco: Bill, Lee and Si, of course, although not Gaz (I think he was more of a soul boy), plus three others, Jon, Paul and Mark. A line was drawn on the dancefloor. The DJ played the Pistols and the Skids that night; the tide was turning. I think Si wore his V-neck jumper without a T-shirt underneath, which struck me as punk in the extreme. And then, on 27 March, I gave myself to Sid.

Praise be.

As well as 'Something Else' I got 'Everybody's Happy Nowadays' by the Buzzcocks, again in fetching pic sleeve, which is something punk singles had over non-punk singles in those grey days. Art was intrinsic to the movement.

Never mind that my dad actually bought my two punk singles for me – from a trendy record shop called Revolver in Wellingborough (where his office was). That's not the point. He also bought me my first singles case that day too, a starter pack for the aspiring punk rocker. Dad bought many of my punk singles for me – it was easier for him to slip out at lunchtime than it was for me to get into town after school. I think he quite liked going in there in his suit with the crazy names of my singles on a piece of paper and handing it to the greaser behind the counter. I hope they treated him with the respect he deserved.[4]

In future weeks, whenever I'd saved up sufficient pocket money, I expanded my collection with seven-inchers by Squeeze, Sham 69, The Dickies, The Clash, The Ruts, Tubeway Army, The Skids and The Undertones, all the while perfecting their logos for reproduction on folders and exercise books. John Peel quickly became my late-night guru, listened to, as is traditional, with a single earpiece under the bedcovers. What myriad delights I heard there beneath the candlewick, from The Slits to The Dixie Cups.

By the time of the next school disco in July, I considered myself a card-carrying punk, and pogoed with the best of them – but I had one important step yet to take: the haircut. I wore cap-sleeved T-shirts, straight-leg jeans, and the regulation Harrington jacket (black, zip-up, tartan lining) but my hair was strictly pre-punk, flicked at the sides and parted. On 17 August, another landmark day, I asked Carol to cut my hair short enough for it to stick up on top. She did. The drawing in my diary suggests a modest crop, but getting it up off my earlobes was a mini-revolution.

Of course in these enlightened post-Gary Rhodes times, spiky hair is *nothing*. Everybody's got it. But in 1979, I was a true non-conformist for wearing my hair – let's face it – *fluffy*. There's a photo of me in the back garden in September, ostensibly modelling a batch of homemade punk badges (Ruts, Sham 69, Buzzcocks, the Virgin records logo), but in my maroon V-neck and jeans and spiky-top I do look quite edgy. Mum put up with it valiantly – well, it was her mate Carol who was styling me! And anyway this, as it transpired, was kids' stuff, hairwise.

So that was it. Transformation complete in the space of six months. No more proof were needed that I was a punk. I looked like one, I had loads of punk singles, I hated Abba, I had posters

---

4. Dad's finest hour was asking for a 12-inch ('The Bunker') by The Bollock Brothers.

of the Skids and Generation X up on the bedroom pin-board, I jumped up and down and kicked out at discos, and I had the *New Musical Express* delivered every Thursday. Nan Mabel was beside herself with worry. She assumed the next step would be a safety pin through my cheek and my immediate arrest. She'd obviously got me mixed up with Uncle Punk.

'You ain't one of these punks are you?' Nan would say.

'Yeah,' I would reply.

'Of course he's not,' Mum would interject.

* * *

I don't wish to make my metamorphosis seem glib in retrospect. If it seems to be all about wearing the right clothes and buying the right singles, it was. (I decorated a lampshade at the time with all the correct punk logos, although including AC/DC showed a measure of confusion.) I now appreciate punk as a cultural paradigm shift and a necessary wave of disenfranchised youthful defiance in the face of ineffectual party politics and social disintegration, not to mention an enema for the music industry, but aged 14 in Northampton, it was more about badges. I'd love to talk up my allegiance as something truly seditionary but I was just a kid with pocket money. There were, however, no gigs in town for me *not* to go to (or none that I knew about); and punks didn't even hang around the town centre in 1979. There was no scene, just a few pockets of attitude and violent dancing at youth clubs. But punk was important to me because it was my first push for individuality. Not everyone fancied themselves a punk; most kept their flicks and danced to disco records. It was my first taste of tribalism and identity.

It also gave rise in me a genuine mania for music: slavishly following the Top 40, spending hours fingering the racks in record shops, forming friendships over the arm of a hot record player, and eventually going to gigs. I continued buying the *NME* without fail every week until I was well into my thirties. Through early-Eighties *NME* writers like Paul Morley, Barney Hoskyns and Ian Penman and later Stuart Cosgrove and Sean O'Hagan I became interested in philosophy and hip literature, and eventually left-wing politics. I still buy records avidly – albums not singles, CDs not vinyl, but I pore over the sleeves just like I used to. And I still own every record I ever bought *and* the inaugural singles case Dad bought me over 20 years ago.

My blinkered devotion to punk, or what were already its dying embers, was broadened by necessity and experimentation. I bought into the multiracial storm of 2-Tone, became intoxicated by the early 12-inches (mainly Sparks and disco) and subsequently fell for New Romanticism. In 1981 I grew my spiky hair out into a lavish fringe and replaced the maroon V-neck with those fancy cavalry-style shirts that did up over one side, risking calls of 'poof'. Music and fashion now dictated my life. A healthy state of affairs for the normal teenager.

The punk ethic ('This is a chord. This is another. This is a third. Now form a band') even worked its clarion magic. I formed a modest two-piece band in January 1980 with Pete Sawtell called D.D.T. He had a guitar, an amp and the required three chords; I had nothing but sufficient bluster to sing The Undertones' 'You've Got My Number' into a tape recorder. Pete taught me how to tap out the rhythm with a tyre lever on a singles case and a drummer was born. We wrote a song called 'Past Tense' (Pete stole the riff from 'ESP' by the Buzzcocks, and I can even remember the first line: 'It's no use running down Memory Lane'), and by recruiting Craig McKenna on bass (he couldn't play one, but then neither could The Clash's Paul Simonon to start with) we were able to turn our bedroom daydream into reality.

I tutored myself long and hard in the art of drumming, using two rulers on a vinyl-covered stool, and in August 1980 talked Mum and Dad into letting me buy a second-hand snare drum and cymbal. After this the three of us took that most important step for any band: we got Dave Griffiths to take photographs of us. We began 1981 as The Brightest View, named after a 999 album track. We lacked only a vocalist.

Dave had a crack but it didn't work out. In February, my parents went beyond the call of duty and bought me a full Premier drum kit for £200 second-hand. What were they thinking of? That it would keep me off the streets? We built up a set list (Pete was the musical brains of the operation), and enjoyed sporadic 'recording sessions' in the extension at Winsford Way until, by letting Hayley's brother Vaughan replace Dave on vocals and rhythm guitar, we gained access to a mobile classroom at the NSB (where Vaughan went). Nothing much happened beyond a few enthusiastic C60s, but Mum and Dad allowed me to keep my drums up permanently in my new bedroom and I improved my rolls and paradiddles daily. (In May, I had moved in to the new extension-on-top-of-the-extension – independence from Simon and bunk beds at last, and not a moment too soon, hormonally speaking.)

In October Vaughan was out (he sold his guitar), and Jo Gosling the armband girl was in. First practice: Craig's kitchen. (The band wasn't just keeping us off the mean streets of Northampton, it was keeping us in the house – a small price to pay for the humbly amplified, Jam and 999 influenced racket various parents and neighbours had to put up with.)

A flight of fancy had, in two years, turned into a way of life, an expensive hobby. (I had promised to pay Dad back the £200 in instalments from my first – and last – Saturday job at Sainsbury's, even though I was only on £1.21 an hour, £14 a week. I fear I still owe him about £100.) The Brightest View had suddenly become a vehicle for four teenage rock'n'roll fantasies. In 1982, our big year, we changed our name to Late Heroes, then Absolute Heroes,[5] and made our live debut on 20 March at the Marina Bar in Billing (a private party, of course, but the smell of the greasepaint was the same and the blokes who hired us the PA got us our second gig supporting the Antibodies at the Black Lion pub a week later).

All this – the band, the hair, the drum kit, the Saturday job, the way of life – can be traced back to the day I saw 'Something Else' on *Top of the Pops*, and Jimmy Savile, the man who had ignored my letter about meeting Giles all those years ago, warned the nation not to ride a motorbike without proper protection. I thought, 'Fuck you, hippy!' and went out and got myself a decent haircut. If I'd *had* a motorbike I would have ridden it without a helmet all the way to Pete's house in Weston Way.

---

5. In combined tribute to The Jam's 'Absolute Beginners' and David Bowie's "*Heroes*". You see where we were coming from?

War was declared – but not the scary kind – and battle came down, all the way to Billing. I was a boy in 1979. Three years later I was a man. Alright, an older boy, but I was wearing clothes *I'd* chosen, not Mum, and Carol cut my hair how *I* wanted it, not Mum. I had passed through the white-hot crucible of punk and I had emerged stronger, harder, more individual, more motivated and more rhythmic. I was now ... Andy.

Andrew – he dead. Ooh dear.

thirteen

Ma Favourite Programme

Guilt is important. Otherwise you're capable of terrible things.
Woody Allen, *Broadway Danny Rose* (1984)

I have spent a lot of my adult life wracked with guilt, and I must say it has stopped me doing a lot of terrible things. Some of this guilt is prospective – if I do x I know I'll feel guilty about it so I won't do it (drop litter, park the car thoughtlessly, send a nasty email); some of it is long-distance retrospective – I wish I hadn't done x in the past (pulled the wings off daddy-longlegs, thrown those curtains out that belonged to our landlady, stupidly introduced Julie as 'the wife' once); and the remainder is global – if I do x, it will contribute to the ills of an already knackered planet (use aluminium-based deodorant, drive round the corner, ignore beggars). That's a lot of guilt for someone with no religious leanings. But I would rather feel guilty than not give a monkey's.

It is, of course, only the retrospective guilt that need concern us here. The really pointless kind. So I wilfully tortured insects – what normal child doesn't? At least it didn't extend to vertebrates, birds, pets. We could even file it under healthy curiosity, methodically plucking the legs off crane flies to see what would happen. It's no worse than industrialised vivisection and that's organised, supported and carried out by adults. Life's too short – albeit not as short as a crane fly's – to feel guilty about something cruel you did as a child. Of course we all look back and wish we were better human beings when we were in wellies, but the mind takes time to form. I grew up with a lot of silly attitudes that have been refined and even turned on their head by the years.

I sometimes think we are all born fascists and murderers, it's just that some of us thankfully grow out of it. For me, this is the true meaning of civilisation. For what is right-wing thinking if not straightforward selfishness? (Look at the way parenthood disfigures many a good liberal, turning them back into a blinkered Tory reactionary.) Adult xenophobia and racism are merely extensions of the childhood suspicion meted out to a kid who wears glasses. Steven Ambrose (*not his real name*) was the New Kid at middle school – he had the audacity to turn up mid-term in 1977, wearing thick National Health specs and using a pronounced limp in a built-up area.

Here is the welcome I extended to him, from my diary:

Monday: We had a new boy in our class – Steven Ambrose.
              Methinks he is a twat.

Tuesday: This new kid is a twat.

Wednesday: This new kid is really loon.

Thursday: Made jam tarts in cookery. Well you ought to
              have seen the new kid's efforts. Ha ha.

Ha ha. These words are accompanied by malicious cartoons of the New Kid with his tongue sticking out and hands fixed in classic 'spaz' mode. Flies buzz around my little drawing of his rubbish jam tarts. I'm sure Steven was alright really. Slightly eccentric. Gangly. He did nothing to harm me or affect my holidays and yet I seem to have been boiling over with hostility towards him. I was, like most kids, wary of that which I did not know. I was inadvertently displaying the classic fear of difference that lay at the heart of the Third Reich. I had rejected Steven Ambrose for no better reason than not really knowing him. And for his glasses. Next stop, a subscription to

Eugenics Week and the annexation of the Sudetenland. Ha ha.

Alright, a bit extreme, but I kind of wish I'd seen the bigger picture. My worldview during those delicate teenage years left a lot to be desired. My worldview in fact had very little 'world' in it. Let's have a look through the inverted telescope of small-mindedness once again. There's a bit of all of us in here.

* * *

Northampton was a strictly white bread town in the Seventies. The estates of Abington Vale presented a sea of pale faces, likewise the three schools I went to. The Leslies lived over the back, as we have established, and their daughter Angela was the only black kid in my class at primary school. There was also Alana, an Asian girl (I can't be any more specific than that), Kim Gupta, Wyn Murphy (Welsh) and that's it for the lively ethnic gumbo.

What I will say is that race was never an issue. I was born in the year of the first Race Relations Act and they would have been proud of me. Angela and Alana (and later Nina and Maria and Ketna), they were just girls in my school. There was a black kid in my Saturday morning art class, Louis – again, no issue. He was just Louis. Bearing in mind the Caucasian bias of the landscape, I grew up commendably colour-blind. I suppose I could've been more *interested* in the fact that Kim's parents had presumably settled here in the Fifties or Sixties – I might have learned something – but instead I just regarded him as another kid to play with.

Not being a big industrial centre – outside of shoes and lifts – immigration to Northampton was anything but large scale (Birmingham, Wolverhampton and Coventry were more needy of extra hands). Anyway, we had all those overspill cockneys to house first. But none of this made me suspicious of non-whites. I was obviously more offended by people with glasses or a funny walk.

Casual racism came in the form of lazy talk: woggies, blackies and nig-nogs. Pap Collins used these terms the most,[1] but they

---

1. Nan and Pap Collins lived in a part of town that used to serve the factories. I expect they saw the first immigrants in the Fifties and Sixties as a threat. Nan never said anything offensive, but Pap's claim about Butch barking at woggies didn't even impress me as a tiny kid.

were occasionally heard in our house too, spoken matter-of-factly and without any overt violence. I will make no woolly defence of that here. I'm afraid *Love Thy Neighbour* made it alright. I say 'afraid' only because it became such a soft target during the revisionist Eighties – along with Benny Hill, *Mind Your Language* and Jim Davidson – and I'd love to be able to talk it away as a sign of the times like writer and co-creator Vince Powell is often called upon to do now on television, but I can't. We loved that programme and it ran for four years. We all knew that Eddie was ever the honky loser and Bill the sambo victor in their little turf wars, but that doesn't make it alright. Thanks to Eddie, we didn't mind our language.

Because there were rarely any black kids around to offend, we used the bad words with abandon, even 'nigger', although never *at* anyone. They weren't used as terms of abuse, merely said without thought or care (which can be just as dangerous of course). We parroted Jim Davidson's [2] impression of a West Indian, Chalky, but again, not to mock. It was good fun to shake your head vigorously and make that noise with your lips. A boy called John Godfrey, quite a wag, became the centre of attention on the coach home after the French trip with his note-perfect Chalky. Although it pains me to relate (that retroactive guilt again), my diary speaks of 'doing nigger impressions'. The irony of this thoughtless idiom is that, aged 12, I learned all about the black experience, watching *Roots*.

The 12-hour epic mini-series based on Alex Haley's book was first shown in 1977, but when it was repeated in 1978 I saw every episode and hung on its every development, tracing the bloodline of African slave Kunta Kinte through Kizzy, Chicken George, Tildy and Tom. This was some powerful education. They say half the American population watched the final episode and many whites did so through a kind of national guilt. Well, not me – I watched guiltlessly, with an obsessive interest in the plight of the slaves. And the punchline is ...

---

2. This was 1978, so we must have been aware of the up-and-coming Davidson and his trademark routines from the ITV sketch show *What's On Next?* (1976–78) – he didn't get his own show until 1979.

Roots, so my diary tells us, was 'ma favourite programme'. On 24 October, I write, without a hint of irony, 'Just saw de final episode ob *Roots*. It wuz de gratest programme of all time.'

Surely 'ob all time'?

This though was my phonetic tribute to the black diaspora, to civil rights, to race relations.[3] Kunta Kinte was my new hero, and I would prove it by talking – and writing – just like him, just as I had previously done with the Fonz. I drew good likenesses of the *Roots* characters from memory, just as I had done with the cast of *The Poseidon Adventure*, the drivers of *Wacky Races* and – hey! – the Harlem Globe Trotters before that. I knew more about where Alex Haley's ancestors had come from than I did about my own. I understood the bigotry and violence and segregation and yet I couldn't quite square that with my own demeaning use of the word 'ob'.

I had a long way to go. We all did. Bloody hell, they only shut the *Black & White Minstrel Show* down in 1978.

* * *

So I wasn't a racist, just confused. I was a rampant homophobe though. Everybody was. Poof, queer, poofter, woofter, homo, mo, bummer, bum chum, bender ... these were all genuinely felt terms of abuse at school, and as stinging an insult a boy could use on another boy (we never considered that there could be female poofs). At upper school, when being a poof started to mean more than being a pansy, the playground folk devil was Noel Collier. He was an older boy, a sixth-former, who had the reputation for being a bum chum. The traditional response to passing him in the corridor was to pretend he had touched your rear end (bum bandit, shirt lifter, turd burglar) and whip him aside while jerking your body away from the clear and present danger. There was a whipping sound that went with this pantomime and it was something

---

3. Another stylistic precedent was Ugandan despot Idi Amin, the subject of a humorous, fictional column in *Punch*, collected in a book which Uncle Jim introduced me to, and which I got for Christmas in 1975. This was written phonetically – dis, dat and so on – and I thought it was tremendously funny. It explains the pre-*Roots* presence of 'de' in my diaries. Again, you can wish it away all you like, but this was the Seventies: a confused and confusing time for all in the so-called New Commonwealth.

like *cccchhhw-tcherrrr*! Sort of a throat-clearing rising to pursed lips
and the sound of steam being let off; a bigoted *Ivor the Engine*. I
have no idea where this came from, but it was the universally
recognised fanfare of homophobia at Weston Favell.

Unlike casual and even accidental racism, the demonisation of
poofs was deep-seated in the family (and may well linger, albeit in
a less vehement, more suburban way). Nan Mabel and my mum
were the worst offenders, talking about someone (always male)
being 'a bit that way' or 'a bit funny' or 'one of them'. What they
were scared of, I don't know, but a slave to convention will always
have many enemies. As far as Mum was concerned, of all the
crimes I could have committed in my teenage years, turning out
gay would have been the most heinous – worse than being on
drugs, getting someone pregnant or even having my ear pierced.

It's no wonder then that the combination of this blind ortho-
doxy at home and the constant stereotyping of homosexuals on
TV (John Inman, Larry Grayson, Dick Emery) established in my
mind the most Neanderthal attitudes to sexual preference. I bet
Noel Collier wasn't gay. He probably glanced the wrong way in the
showers once. Stock insults grew from the tiniest acorns. I know he
didn't deserve the mockery of the lower years, that's for sure, and
I really hope he went on to live a gay life, as in happy.

I did a lot of my learning, good and bad, in front of the television.
Roots may have taught me that black people had had a rough time of
it, but not all telly was so educational. Mike Yarwood taught me that
all politicians were buffoons, which wasn't such a bad grounding, but
at the same time *It Ain't Half Hot Mum* taught me that anyone effeminate was a poof and therefore inferior in some way to other men,
and Indian people wobbled their heads and said oh deary me. It's
getting on for a worldview, but hardly sophisticated.

I thank *Mad* magazine for dragging me out of the mire. I started
getting this monthly fix of US satire in 1977,[4] although it was the

---

4. Mostly for the movie spoofs, which continue to delight me to this day, especially the
Seventies ones ('The Poopsidedown Adventure', 'The Ecchorcist', 'Rockhead', 'Airplot
'77') drawn by Mort Drucker, one of the most influential artists on my own drawing style.
The man's a god.

subsequent investigation of back issues from the late Sixties and early Seventies that really opened my eyes. Here, magazine by magazine, was a journey through America's most turbulent years – Vietnam, Watergate, civil rights – and from a left-leaning, hippy perspective. Here's what I learned from the jokes in *Mad*: the police are brutal, peace signs are good, smoking causes cancer, the environment is being destroyed by big cars and pollution, Nixon is a crook, drugs involving syringes are bad, drugs you smoke are good, and advertising is a confidence trick. Quite a difference from Dennis Healey saying 'Silly Billy' and Mr Humphries being free.

If only *Mad* had been enough to turn me into a 13-year-old libertarian. But influence on what I suppose we must call my politics, social and sexual, came from all quarters, and most of it was a long way from *Mad*'s informative insurgence. Puerile peer pressure at school was just as persuasive, and I accepted every playground convention without interrogation. When puberty set in, for instance, acne became an invitation for merciless 'micking' (the local vernacular for taking the mickey), even among friends: Dave Griffiths's problem skin put us into pun overdrive, adapting song titles like Paul McCartney's 'Pimply Having A Wonderful Cyst-Pus Time'.

Parents were also a source of related mockery, if they were too poor (which meant you were a 'tramp'), or too old, or, in my own mother's case, too young and glamorous. It got back to the kids at school that she had a black skirt with a split in it – very risqué! – and the subsequent baiting reflected this. The fact that my dad mumbled was also a target for mickery ('mumbly, grumbly dad!'). I took it like a man, just as Dave took his and Collier took his. At that age you're beholden to the most brutal form of natural selection: forge alliances with the strong and stamp on any sign of weakness, difference or oily skin – including your own.

During the punk purge, Gaz Smith (for no-one was immune from micking) was pilloried for having an Elvis record in his house. It was probably his parents' but that didn't matter. 'You luuuurve him,' went the taunt from a disloyal Si Triculja when Presley died. A reasonably well-respected kid with impressive Oxford bags (the kind with the pockets) called Andy was given the nickname

'Budgie' because his father bred them. Couldn't shake it. He was Budgie until he left that school.[5] Burns was christened Willy Wetpants after the long jump indiscretion. Mr Eales the music teacher was legendary for his hairpiece – kids would blow at it when he wasn't looking, and call him Wiggy. The fiery Mr Hughes had obviously had a brain operation – the scar was there to see – making him fair game. Compassion? Empathy? Benevolence? If it was too hard we couldn't understand it.

The catalogue of sins that fed the culture of micking was vast: hair, skin, clothes, voice, parents, physical imperfection, or any deviation from the norm, whatever that was. It's no wonder being a *cccchhhw-tcherrr* carried such an enormous penalty.

* * *

I'd love to say I rose above all this but I didn't. I was just a kid who wanted desperately to fit in. When my old mate Hirsty was deemed a poof, I could no longer mix with him. (Still, he's a vicar now, so I'm sure he'll forgive me.) At least I grew out of it eventually. Not everybody does. I know plenty of otherwise perfectly nice people in their thirties with intolerant, right-wing views, and they live in London, not the sticks.

I feel fortunate to have experienced enough real life since moving to the capital and soaking up true cosmopolitanism that *all* childhood prejudices have been cleansed. My deep love of hip hop today has echoes of my appreciation of *Roots* in 1978 – the black experience, in particular the urban American one, is foreign to me but exerts an irresistible allure. It's happened to many a white boy before me and since. When I rap along to The Wu-Tang Clan's 'Let My Niggas Live' in the car (all the while guilty as hell for burning up fossil fuels), it is an intense but private pleasure. 'Keep it that way,' says my wife.

Today, some of my best friends really are gay! But I never really

---

5. I hated Andy whatever-his-name-was. He deliberately 'spilled' water over a really good painting I was doing in art, out of jealousy one assumes. But then he was called Budgie by his *mates* and that must have led to a lot of pent-up bitterness. I screwed up the soggy artwork and methodically painted it again, but he was still called Budgie in the morning.

hated homosexuals at school, because frankly I had no idea what or who they were. I'd never met one. I thought they were like Dick Emery's Clarence and I'd never seen anyone like that. (Noel Collier didn't mince, wear floppy hats or carry a handbag.) I certainly hadn't entertained anything as specific as the notion of anal sex, Honky Tonks.

So I do feel needlessly guilty for some of the myopic and ill-informed prejudices I harboured as a teenager, but it's not as if I joined the NF or went queer-bashing, and just as every plate of soba noodles I eat today cancels out a Lord Toffingham lolly I consumed in my youth, so – I like to think – every enlightened thought I have in my thirties compensates for an unenlightened one I had in my teens.[6]

Anyway, the most insidious influence on me as a malleable adolescent wasn't *Love Thy Neighbour* or Si Triculja, it was my seemingly innocuous, laid-back Dad. When I approached voting age, he tried to blackmail me into becoming a Conservative by telling me that if Mrs Thatcher and the Tories were ousted, he would instantly lose his job, and wouldn't be able to afford to give me my monthly allowance any more. And I believed him. Because I believed everything, and we are all Tories until proven innocent.

---

6. I experienced a very odd strain of guilt at college. A girl I went out with whose parents were in the throes of a messy divorce made me feel guilty – deliberately or otherwise – for coming from an unbroken home. I realise now that all this unnecessary pain and hand-wringing was just part of being a tortured art student. We worried about nothing.

1980

Selected Extracts From My Diary

Another Boots page-a-day diary, oatmeal in colour and hand-decorated with a Joe Orton-style collage under transparent sticky-back plastic for protection. The collage features cut-out members of the almost-ran punk band 999 and their distinctive raffle-ticket logo, Marilyn Monroe, The Elephant Man, *Gene Hackman (now officially designated My Favourite Actor) and a Dymo label reading* 'ANDY COLLINS. BLOODY PRIVATE'. *I'm not sure it's sincere – the diary wasn't exactly secreted away under lock and key. I suspect it's just the self-consciousness of a 15-year-old.*

1980 is a car crash to look at, initially. Punk (still going in Northampton remember) dictates the design style and again, it's a glorified sketch book, much of it filled with variable-quality cartoons of film stars, punk heroes and my mates (clearly for the reader's benefit – bloody private indeed). Thankfully, things smarten up as the year progresses and punk subsides. Plus, the entries get longer again around August. No theories as to why.

Meanwhile, in-jokey school catch-phrases take over from Python quotes, and the real swearing begins …

Monday, 7 January

Got my record library order form back, which means I can go and get the Ruts LP I ordered before Christmas. Ace. Went up Craig's this morning.[1] Dad got me the Undertones album. It is really grate. Magic sleeve.

Saw *Question Of Sport, Give Us A Clue, Coronation Street, In The Family.* Saw *Thunderbolt and Lightfoot* illegally. Clint film. Norty bits.[2]

Thursday, 24 January

Got *NME*. Ace. They had the best group in the world on *Nationweird* today ... yes, the Shadows. No, you ignorant twat, the Undertones. Them. They had live film of 'Get Over You'.

I made up the numbers in our inter-form rugby. We lost 14–8. Saw *Watch This Space*. Craig, Pete et me went up de Supacentre. Craig got the Specials EP and I got 'London Calling' by the Clash. Plus *Smash Shits*.

Tuesday, 29 January

Got my two ordered *Mad* back issues back. No. 179 = 'Moronic Woman'. No. 182 = 'The Shootiest'. Ace stuff.

Went up Pete's tonight. Been trying out our Undertones 're-mix'. Rhythm guitar = Pete. Lead guitar = Pete. Vocals and Undertone knowledge = moi. Drums? = me if poss.

Friday, 1 February

2 much h/w. Went up Pete's for another nearly-recording session. We've ditched copying the Undertones and we're writing our own stuff. I've gotta come up with the lyrix. Pete's gotta come up with the muzic. I'm on vocals, Pete's on guitar. Name? Dunno. The Tramps? Alcatraz? The Beakys? The Comatose Villains?

Tuesday, 7 February

What the hell can we call our group (me + Pete)? Got it ... Frenzy?

fren'zy n. fury, delirious excitement. – frenzied a.

---

1. Craig McKenna, soon-to-be bassist with The Brightest View and Absolute Heroes, was new to school and Northampton, having moved here from Watford (though his family were Scottish). He had almost translucent Gallic skin which reddened frequently, and blond hair eventually swept into an impressive wedge. His parents were the first people to own a new-fangled video recorder – certainly in my orbit, possibly the whole country. They seemed to be well-off – they lived in new cul-de-sac Kestrel Close (where my upwardly mobile parents moved in 1983). They had a dishwasher too! And their garden was full of dogshit, deposited by their three yappy terriers. Craig had an effortless cool about him, despite the redness, and was the first among us to get a legitimate girlfriend: Sarah Wadsworth.
2. My first glimpse of pubic hair in a film.

Yes! Must be. What say Pete? I'll ask him tomorrow. Did another recording-nearly session. Working on a number ritt by me, 'Past Tense'. Good I tell you. Frenzy?

Wednesday, 8 February
Pete don't fully agree with Frenzy. A few we thought up today: The Zips (hmm); The Outlaws (oh dear); Riot Control (like much); The Stereotypes (hmm); Psycho (oh dear); Enforcer (like much); The Bit-Parts (hmm).

2 much homework. Had shitty 'glamour' careers video.[3] Got Stiff Little Fingers' new new new release, 'At The Edge'. Jolly good it is too. Went up Craig's. Saw *Coronation St, Benny Hill* (rather norty). Had hare wash. Listening to John Peel, whose wife's having a baby and Mikey Read is doing de show for him. Clash etc.

Thursday, 7 February
I'm just writing some rather interesting lyrics for a coupla new songs for us ... me and Pete. Yes, our actual, agreed-on-for-the-time-being name is D.D.T.

Yes ... D.D.T. Well, we like it. Erm ... dichloro diphenyl trichloroethane (insecticide).

Craig came roond. A bitov h/w. Specials no. 1. Melissa got 'Captain Beaky Freaky'. Badminton in games. Pricey and Ager had a great larf scrap. Had hair cut/spike.

Sunday, 10 February
Did my *Smash Hits* Specials album competition entry. Rather hopeful. Only six winners. Had to design 2-Tone man for record of choice. I did 'Smash It Up'. You never know ...

Saw *Airport*. Rather good film actually. First two thirds not so good; last third = excito.

Thursday, 14 February
Went to see *Invasion of the Bodysnatchers* with Paul Garner, Pete

---

3. I wish I could see that video today – now that I have a 'glamour' career hem-hem.

and Brian at the Film Society up College of FE.[4] Only a quid to get in, not many people, good enough screen, no strict age restrictions – obviously, as it was a very worthy 'X'. Only made last year. Not an old film at all. Don Sutherland, Brooke Adams, Len Nimoy, Veronica Cartwright etc. Really good'n'gory. Nice pod scenes, rather horrific, creepy and ace. Birds Eye peas, sweet as the moment when the pod went POP!

Tuesday, 26 February

Paul came down.[5] We have compiled the 100 Best People in the World. Gene H is friggin' well in there.

Saturday, 1 March

Yes it's nearly my birthday. So as a birthday treat Dad paid for me, Craig and Paul to go to the ABC to see *Nightwing* 'AA' with Dave Warner etc. and nasty vampire bats and bitten-up people and blood and big caves and Indian territories and a lady run over by a jeep and great s. effects and blood and teeth and bats squeaking and good. Plus *Billion Dollar Threat* which was good for a larf.

And Simon is in a real much-sulko mood. He has laid there on his bed since 8.30 and it's now 9.30. What a queer. Nan and Pap baby-sattedified. Saw *Tales of the Unexzzpected* about people turning into bees. Zzzzz.

---

4. The NCFE Film Club contributed greatly to my expanding mania for cinema. Not only did it show key X-rated American films to a then 15-year-old enthusiast (*Invasion of the Bodysnatchers, Godfather Part II, Apocalypse Now, The Warriors*), but subtitled ones too: French, Japanese, Hungarian, Cuban, German. My film-going companions were always Paul Garner and aforementioned Nene College cohorts Neil Stuart and David Freak.

5. Paul Garner was perhaps my most important friend in the fourth and fifth year, art buddy and film buddy (he was as obsessed with Charlton Heston as I was with Gene Hackman). Though he existed outside of the cooler orbit of Craig and Pete and the band, our friendship attained a higher plane through all the hours we spent together. We went on telly together, appeared in the paper together, drew published cartoons together. Paul actually went on to forge a career in commercial art, storyboarding and the like, and I bump into him a lot. A fine chap, with creativity coursing through his veins and a mordant sense of humour (he became convinced he was a werewolf during his diploma year at Nene).

Tuesday, 4 March

Yes it wuz my birthday. For a start I got £8.50 – because Nan's fiver went towards a book ... *The Illustrated Encyclopedia of the World's Great Movie Stars and Their Films* (£7.95). Really ace. Melissa got me a great, bolus-shaped rubber and an ace ruler. Si got me the *Rocky/Rocky II* fotonovel. Too ace for words. And Mum'n'Dad got me an *x* quid Hitachi radio/cassette avec aerial, cassette player and recorder, FM, bass, treble, volume, four channels, earpiece, mains socket or batteries etc. It is tooo good.

Went up Paul's. Going to buy blank cassette, *Nightwing* and *Heaven Can Wait* fotonovels, a Dickies single, *Alien* movie book?, two *Mad* mags.

Wednesday, 5 March

Dad didn't get home till late last night but I found out dis morning that he had bought me the Dickies single 'Fan Mail' yesterday. It's in red vinyl and with a spesh fold-out free colour 21"x14" poster. The single und the poster are rather goodo.

Still a loada anticlimax-type trouble brewin' between WFUS, NSB, NSG, Lings, Trinity, Thom A Beckett etc. Everyone gangs up and goes home. But it gets the teachers and cops out. Never anythink happens. Know what I mean?

I tell yoo this radio wot I got too ace. I'm listenin' to Jonathan Peel now. Had nice supper. Coffee and cow sandwich. Did you know I can't draw Robert Redford? Jacqueline Bisset is nice enough to put a poster up of her today. I can draw my mate Gene.

Craig come down. Did our intriguing Jane Austen h/w. Who is Jane Austen to inconvenience us?

Friday, 7 March

Went up Creeeegie's house. He was up the Centre with Andy Bonner.[6] I sat and watched TV with his mum till 8.00, then us three had a larf in his room when they came back. Craig bought *Smash Hits* for me because I have come in the top six in the 2-Tone competition. My entry's bin printed. It's really good to see

---

6. Mate of Craig's. Had a lot of disco records.

my name in the mag in print. I'll be getting a Specials album. Goodo. Got *Bodysnatchers* fotonovel. Ace.

Saturday, 8 March

Paul und me went town. He got a magic *M*A*S*H* poster and some pencils and I got three black pens, drawing book, blank cassette, Siouxsie and the Banshees LP from r. library.

Chron & Echo sent a coupla blokes down art skool this morning because our classes have got one week to live. Bleedin' education cuts. Took photos of our class and just me.

Matish Neil lent me lods of *Mad*s inc. *French Connection, Cuckoo's Nest.* Watching *Tales of the Unexplainable.*

Tuesday, 11 March

Craig is still going out wiv Sarah. Paul and me did our mafs h/w. My photo and Dad's ed cuts letter waz in the *Chronic & Eccho.* Ace photo of moi. Paul's Dad got me the original to keep. Ace. Also Tony, Dave and Louis. (Paul, Neil, Jeff, Simon cut off!)

Saw *Grollywood* about directors. Went oop Paul's.

Thursday, 13 March

Had some cheese on toast tonight. 'March 13th and all's well.' 10.12 and John Peel is playing 'You' by Delta 5. It is so ace, ace, ace. I am listening to John Peel. I *did* go up Paul's and we *did* have a laugh. They *are* playing 'Going Underground' by Jam on John Peel. At this moment in time.

I *can't* draw Hackeline Bisset. They *are* now playing the Slits on JP. I *haven't* read *Alien* completely yet. My old diareary *does* make Paul crack. Tucker Jenkins *is* a bottom lip.

Mum n Dad *did* go to parunts evening tonight. 10.00 and all's well. I say, this Slits record 'In The Beginning There Was Rhythm' is rather goodo. But now JP's playin' Flexys Midway Bummers (Dexys Midnight Runners). My toe isn't swollen. It was last year though. Bed = 10.00-ish. What does ish mean?

Friday, 21 March

Boring day. (Got my biology book wot I paid for at school.) But it waz a gud laugh tonight. I rode up Pete's. Pete and me rode up Craig's. Craig, Pete and me nackered ourselves riding up Dave's. Dave, Craig, Pete and me went round Howkins'.[7] Howkins, Dave, Craig, Pete and me then went round Matt's.[8] Later we went round Howkins' again and ended up back at Dave's till 9.00. Ace.

Thursday, 3 April

Went up Craig's s'morning. Went up Craig's s'afternoon and tonight. Where ... did ... you ... get ... that ... blank expression ... on your face.

Craig, Pete, Andy and me went off to the Girl Guides (don't let that put you off) + Fanciers FC Disco at the Fanciers Club. It was a real good place. Also went: Cindy, Sarah, Jo Gosling, Lisa ... They played mostly good music (Specials, Beat, Madness) but too much disco. But whoo cares. There was no proper slow dance at the end, but I'm probably seeing Lisa again.[9] I know her number. We didn't get the chance to dance, but me and Howkins sat with her for 45% of the night (7.30– 10.30). Craig made it up with Sarah. Howkins really *likes* me for being slightly luckier with Lisa than him. Shit, I'm sorry Howkins.

Sunday, 6 April

Nan got me my Easter present – a pack of Matchmakers. Pretty appropriate. Lisa came down this afternoon. Great. She came down at 2.30. We went up Craig's later and I walked her home to the Arbours.

Recorded 'Gangsters', UB40, Selecter, 'Echo Beach', 'Poison

---

7. Andy Howkins, later nicknamed Howx, then Honx, because it was a funny word, and he was a funny boy. Stocky, Undertones fan (he actually went to London to see them play) self-effacing to the last and he had a table tennis table in his garage.

8. Matthew/Matt/Matty Allen, with whom I struck up a deep and unexpected kinship in art and history. The first of our lot to get hairs on his chin, obsessive about Monty Python's 'Embarrassment' sketch and the drawings of *Mad* artist Don Martin (in particular the phonetic sound effect 'Geeen!'), rode a scooter, played an acoustic guitar and dug Emerson, Lake & Palmer. Great guy. Became a postman.

9. See Chapter 14.

Ivy'. All ace. God, Lisa is nice. Did some to my *Poseidon Adventure* picture. What record reminds me of Lisa? 'Nite Club'? 'Teenage Kicks'?

Tales of Unexplainable = 'Fat Chance'.

Saturday, 12 April

Leeds 0–1 to Crystal Palace. Oh bum. Me + Paul rode all the way up Neil's and Neil wasn't at Neil's. So we returned. It killed us that bloody ride.

Last *Tiswas*: John Peel, Beat, Specials, Bodysnatchers. Led Zep. Rainbow, Al Minter etc.

Lisa's this afternoon. Got ace photocopy of our 'Top 100 People' off Paul. It is so big. And goodo. Lisa, Dave, me, Andy all went round Craig's tonight. Did a few *Smash Hits* crosswords and Howkins nearly jumped out of the window. And we listened to records and I walked Lisa home. Romantic Interlude. Got 2 Pentels.

Monday, 14 April

Shit I've been spelling Liza's name wrong for the last 11 days. Disgusting! Liza with a 'Z'. OK? Seen Liza tonight. Went round Craig's + Pete + Dave + Andy. Walked Liza home. Romantic Interlude. Saw Liza at school as well. No h/w. Saw *Halls of Anger* + Jeff Bridges. Blax + whites school movie. Ace. And *Film 80* – *Tom Horn, Empire Strikes Blecch, Starting Over* etc.

Friday, 18 April

Andy 4 Liza. Seen Liza at school. Did self blood tests in biology. Jab. I'm blood group 'O'. What an average-o kid. And tonight Mr Merrick took 15 of us to Solihull[10] ice-skating, inc. me, Liza, Pete, Craig, Mick, Paul Smith etc. It was a really good larf even though me + Liza were not quite ace on skates. The ice got really wet later on. We went in the minibus. Also had chips at 9.45. Got back in the minibus (Romantic Interlude) at 11.35. Ace.

---

10. I told you how barren Northampton was in those days. We had to go 50 miles to find an ice rink.

Wednesday, 30 April

I'm writing this at about 12.00 as I've just watched a tribute to Sir Alfred Hitchcock (RIP). He died yesterday. Ace film clips were on it. Woshed my hare. Went up Liza's tonight. Shit this torch is running out. (I'm writing this under the bed covers by the way.) The Undertones are at no. 11 in the charts. Great. Liza 4 Andy.

Saturday, 3 May

Sports Report ... Last day of season: Liverpool beat Aston Villa 4–1 (Cohen, Kennedy, Johnson x 2), clinching the League Championship. Man Utd lost to Leeds 2–0 (Hird [pen.] 76th min, Parlane 14th min) – *Match Of Day*. Ace. So Man Utd are 2nd, Ipswich 3rd. Watford beat Burnley 4–0 (four goals 1st half) and end up two from bottom three in Division 2. Bye bye to Bolton + Derby + somebody else from Div 1. And up come Leicester City from 2 to 1. Grimsby come back up into 2 from 3.

Aberdeen won the Scottish League. Celtic 2nd, St Mirren 3rd. Where were Rangers? Portsmouth beat Cobblers 2–0 here and so the fans left our peaceful little town alone as their win means they rise into Div 3. Liverpool still got one game in hand as well (Middlesboro').

BBC1 Goal of the Season: (results next Sat.)

My choice:

1. (H) Justin Fashanu
2. (J) Terry McDermott
3. (K) Ray Kennedy

(You are a witness to the fact that I'm right.)

Leeds (no order): Lukic, Hird, Stevenson, Flynn, Greenhoff, Madeley, Parlane, Cherry, Graham, Harris, Connor (sub). No more 'bring me the head of Jimmy Adamson'.

Saturday, 10 May

AM went down town with Dave, Craig, Andy and Pete. Pete bought 'Living on an Island', Andy got some disco 12", Dave and Craig went clothes shopping, I got *Smash Hits* and got two LPs from the record library, *At the Chelsea Nightclub* by Members and *The Biggest Prize in Sport* by 999. That album is really good. 999 are ace. Pete agrees entirely. Me + Pete've ordered *Separates* by 999 from the libry.

This afternoon me and Pete went up Craig's to watch the greatest Cockney rip-off ie. the 1980 FA Cup Final: Arsenal + West Ham. There was only one fucking goal. Devonshire through Pat Jennings' big hands, shot by Cross, rebound, and goal by Brooking headed off Pearson's shot. John Lyle was happy. 1–0.

Shit Celtic beat Rangers 1–0. Craig says that Jimmy Hill talks through his arse.

All of us (eg. moi, Liza, Pete, Craig, Dave, Andy, Howkins, Matt) went to the Colts Preservation Disco at Lodge Farm. Also there: Cindy, Fiona Brown, Liz H, Davenports etc.

Monday, 16 June

Well. Now, for me and Paul it's 'crap yourself time'. We're going on telly *live* on Friday. On *Look East*, all about drawing, cartoons, caricatures etc. Dad, Paul's Dad + us are driving to BBC Norwich on Friday midday. We've got to collect loads of drawings together. Live? Worry. Went Paul's tonight.

Wednesday, 18 June

Worry, shit, crap, nervous, worry, worry. Got four photos of *Look East* team to caricature, to practise for Friday. Went Paul's. Finished self-portrait. Had photos took (me and Paul) for *Mercury & Herald* and *Chronic & Echo*. Fun!? Worry! Nervous!

Friday, 20 June

No crap brick nervous worry any more. Paul and me got picture in *Chronic* advertising our *Look East* appearance. Got home from school at 10.30 and left Northampton at 12.15 in Dad's car with Paul and Paul's Dad. Arrived Norwich at 3.15 and went into BHS for a scone and Coke and into WHSmith's to kill time. Went BBC East studios at 4.00 and met Ian Masters for a chat. Took loads of pictures into the actual recording place and we sort of talked Ian M through a few bits of our work eg. my self-portrait, Paul's Clint picture, my *Psicko* front page, Paul's *Ben-Hur*. Take 2 worked. Couldn't use anything white. No white drawings or anything.

Watched our un-live bit at 4.45, and then drew our Tony Scase and Ian Masters caricature pictures up in the drinks room. Drinks, everyone offered us drinks. Spoke to and got autographs off: Ian Masters, Judi Lines, Tony Scase, Bob Bufton and Roger Maynard. It was really fun. Did our live bit at 6.10.

Burned home after burgerish dinner at 7.15. Got back 10.00. Me and Paul got back our Tony and Ian pictures (respectively). Mum and Mrs Garner said that the programme was OK. Gonna see the video of it at Craig's tomorrow. We get paid you know! Fun!!!!

Friday, 27 June
999: 'Eyes in the dark become flashing lamps.'
F = fun thing. *UF* = unfun thing.
F I had all the afternoon off school.
UF Because I had to go to the dentist's.
UF I had three tooths out.
UF Gas pain!
F It didn't take long and I didn't puke or anything.
F I ate loads of food and did some more to my *Poseidon* spoof.
F Mum made a really fun flan! (eg. flan and real strawberries everywhere + jelly + cream.)
F I had three slices at various times.
F My teef (ex) have stopped bleeding.
F Jon Billingham,[11] Dave, Craig and me went up the school to see their production of *The Mikado*.
F Matty and Liza were in it.
F Saw Cindy on the way home. She wants me to show people round on the English open evening with her. Fun.
F John (next-door) took five photos of me + Paul on TV. Ace prints. He's given them to me.

---

11. The same Jon who showed us a video of *Deep Throat* when we were in sixth form (and his parents were out). It certainly put *Thunderbolt and Lightfoot* in the shade.

F Got £8.00 appearance (BBC *Look East*) sent to me + £38 expenses for Dad. He's giving me £15 and Paul £5. FU-UN.

Saturday, 28 June

Money money acting funny anything you gotta do.[12]
Whole total = £8 + £38 = £46
Whole money for me = £8 + £15 = £23
Money for Paul = £5
Money left for Dad = £46 − (£5 + £23)

$$= 46 - 28$$
$$= £18$$

Money still left for me to spend
= £23 − (£10 to put in bank + £3.69 999 LP)
= £23 − £13.69
= £9.31, which is equivalent to: two singles, a bottle of ink, *Mad.*

Tuesday, 15 July

Me and Matty went on the Science Museum trip. It was a good laugh. We went in the Natural History Museum as well. We saw the insects, whale, human biology etc. We both fell asleep on the way back. Fun salad tea. Shower and ...

3rd + 4th Year Activity Day Disco in school hall. Went: moi, Craig, Pete, Matt, Dave, Howks, Andy Bonner, Liza, Jo, Cindy, Fiona, Liz H, Spratty, Andy Manton, Jenny, Monroe, Tanya, DD, loads of 3rd year girls. It was fun but there was only one slow record. Mehhhh! as C McK would say. Some exceptional music played: Dead Kennedys, Chords, Police, 'Jump to the Beat', Jam, Joy Division.

Saturday, 9 August *HOLS*

Came to Jersey ... Left our house at 7.05 indy morning. We burned off in the car (only three pee stops) for four hours to Weymouth. A port. We drove onto the Seasink ferry (Sealink then, sorry) called the *Earl Godwin* for some weirdo reason and we had a 'first time on a ferry for four fifths of us' – only one

---

12. It is, of course, a 999 lyric.

throwing up (Dad) – loads of packed-up food – wandering around – nice weather 70% – four hour journey to Guernsey (spellt wrong). We ran into a thick fog bank at 5.00 and had annoying, Melissa-worrying, two-minute-interval foghorn blasts. That's when Dad released some crisps and grapes from his bowels[13] onto 'B' deck.

Waited for passenger unloading/loading at Geurnsey (spelt rong) half hour, and the *Earl Godwin* burned off to Jersey (one and a half hours). Did you know I got sunburnt just lazing on 'C' deck in the wind and sun for half hour. God. Who needs nice weather and holidays if you tan in the Channel?

Arrived at Jerz 8.45-ish. Really ace hotel eg. the Merton – first floor, massive dining lounge, late meal on arrival salad/coffee, gigantico swimming pool (residents only – us), ace bar, supa-clean. Love it. Si, Liss and me got our own room (or 'rum' as Pete S would say). Goodo beds.

FACT: I will spend and send (postcards) all f'night.

FACT: Dad smelt of puke all day and had to change.

FACT: Paul is not smelling of puke or on a ferry (I think).

God, there was a nice girl on the ferry. (From Parklands no less.)

Sunday, 10 August

The food is goodo in this un-slummish hotel eg. menus:

Brekky = fruit juice, corn flakes, bacon, egg, tea.

Luncheon = Scotch (Craig) broth, veal salad, apple turnover, coff.

Dinner = egg mimosa, tom soup, roast chick, lem sorbet, cheese, biscs, coff.[14]

---

13. Not strictly his bowels, more like his stomach, since that's where half-digested food comes from.

14. We were knocked out by the hotel experience as you can see. It was a bold, sophisticated new era for us after a lifetime of self-catering in Llithfaen. Looking back on the Merton, it was far from posh – more an oversized, 'affordable' establishment for old folks and families whose dining hall was like the world's biggest canteen, but the idea of *waiter* service and occasional soups with French names made us feel as if we were at the Hotel Du Cap in Cannes, and we lapped up every minute of it.

Fun food. Dad had a shower. Good. Walked and sat upon Gorey beach. Gorey? What an uncool name for a beach. Went in the 'residentz only' pool s'afternoon. It's big. Massif 15ft diving board (unused by moi), 15ft deep end, 5ft, 3ft, 2ft, slide, deckchairs (not in the pool), pretty warm etc. I got super-red tanned. What a burn. Christ I am burnt. God the itch.

Sat down in the bar after a town-walk tonight for a couple of hours and three beers. Some grannies ballroom danced. There was this really Morris-man-dancing weirdo trying to disco tonight. I want to punch him.

Wednesday, 13 August

Gave my film into the hotel developing service. Be ready by tomoro morn. Fun food: f juice, corn f, boiled eggz, tea. Minestrone, plaice, Bakewell tart. Mushroom soup, Florida cocktail, grilled ham, vanilla slice + cassata denise, c+b, coff.

AM town. Fort Regent – massif sports/leisure etc. complex thing sort of. Became holiday members eg. little photos of us to put on membershit cards. They came out really badly. Dad was looking up; Liss had Dad's belly in her ear; Si had a curtain on his head; I was leaning over, no expression; Mum just stared into space. Fine ...

PM hot. Sat around swimming pool all aftnoon. Tonight: watched Joey Kaye Laughter Show cabaret in ballroom, then watched OAPs dancing. When four fiths of our family disappeared I went down to sit with a load of other kids (five nice girls) from 11.00 till midnight. Disco tomoro.

Saturday, 16 August

Went to a second-hand bookshop and dug out three paperbacks: *Alien* (16p), *Marathon Man* (16p), *Day of the Locust* (10p). Funshop. Food: f juice, c flakes, toast, tea. St Germain soup, ham salad, Madeira sponge + apricot sauce. *Soup de jardinier* (gardener soup), roast veal + sauté pots, mandarin flan, coff. Really nice food.

Leeds lost to Aston Villa 2–1 (Terry Connors) at home. 'Adamson out.'

AM town and pool.

PM Corbiere Lighthouse walk. It was pretty shitty considering wot it was sposed to be. Just walking. It was hot tho'. Then sat by the pool till dinner.

Si + me sat with the remainders of yesterday's lot. Four ninths (but the best two ninths) + Keith + Lorraine. It was just ballrooming etc. I bought three drinks. My God, one wasn't even for *me*. It was for Paula. Born 14th March 1966. Castlefield, High Wycombe, Bucks.[15]

Monday, 18 August

Average day. Went St Ouens PM. Pool AM. Nice wevva. Menus: (see last Monday except for:)

2. Mock turtle soup, cod, blackb tart.

Why are you so worried about what I eat anyway? Went town smorning. My camera wot I dropped in a bloody rock pool Saturday is completely dead according to the Boots expert. They'll have a go at developing the film that's in it but I bought another camera (+ flash + film), same as ex-camera which Dad will pay for with insurance claim dough. Good business this insurance game int it?

Also bought *Breaking Glass* Hazel O'Connor album (£3.00) Boots. Can't play it but I can look at the cover till 23rd.

Paula and Jackie went out again so moi + Si sat with Lisa and her bloody mate (her Dad bought us two ciders each) who disappeared at 11.00. Danced with two new girls, Karen and a fat one. Not as nice as Paula.

Thursday 21 August

Went Fort Reject (Regent – sorry). Played mini-golf and generally wasted money in amusement arcade. Godknowshowmuch. Went

---

15. My first Holiday Romance: a quick snog after hours in the TV room on her last night, which led to furious letter-writing and, in 1981, two visits to Northampton, where Paula and I pretended to be boyfriend and girlfriend. It was ultimately pretty chaste – we were only 15 – indeed, it was the saucy promises she made in her letters about what we would do after her 16th birthday that scared me off. No more letters. No more visits.

to discover Portelet Bay, some Frenchsoundingbloodyname beach and St Ouens (Owens, Oooens, O.N.s, Wons, Oo-ons, Ouens?) It was nothot. Bit windy but dry.

Menus: see last Thurs except:

2. Celery soup, steak chasseur, steam jam sponge.

Tonight, disco, brilliant music. Danced two slow ones with Lisa. Sat + danced with: Lisa, Deb, Liss, Paula, Jackie, Ashley, Tony in general. 'Went out with' Paula from 1.00am–1.34am.

Stayed up (too) bloody late. Had one and a half pts cider, one pt lager (and a packet of crisps please). Got hot and nackered and 1.00–1.34 was the best bit of the holiday.

Saturday, 23 August

Had an early breakfast eg. tea and toast. Set off from the Merton 7.00. Sealink (*Caledonian Princess*) left St Helier harber (spellt write) 8.00. Ship didn't hit icebergs or blow up or even turn over. Pity, I might've met Gene Hackman. Met the Welsh couple + kidz who came over to Jerz with us, Mr and Mrs Thomas, would you believe?

Ate all the way home till 4.00. Piled into the car and didn't get lost at Newbury and stopped at a Wimpy. God I love Wimpys. Home at 9.00-ish for more food. Chips and fish cake from chip shop. Got three *Film Review*s among the pile of 'should have been cancelled' *Chronic*s + bills + school report and Pete n Craig postcards etc.

From that ace hol I've gained:

A very experienced food palate, a liking for fish, a H O'Connor LP, Diana Ross single, tan, 8 paperbax, some Dad sick on my Harrington, 64 photos, two *Smash Hits*, Paula's address, two sugar lumps, a new camera, 14 diary filled pages.

And lost:

About £14. ~~My virginity~~.

Friday, 29 August

Dad took me and Pete round somebody-who-put-an-advert-in-*Chron*'s house. It was Steve Morris and he sold me (£30) snare drum (Hayman skin) on Premier stand, tom tom (Prem skin), cymbal + Prem stand and two stix. I love it. But the neighbours probably don't. I like drums.

I am a filmgoer. Might go to film – *Amityville* – if I can grow six inches tonight. Strain.

Friday, 5 September

Shit, I can't go to Wembley. Shit, I can't get any good shoes. Shit, I can't get any new jeans. Shit, I've only got a quid spare cash. Shit, Mum n Dad keep going on at me. Shit.

Monday, 8 September

Ha ha Jimmy Adamson has resigned from Leeds. Ha ha. We don't care, you big-headed pillock with massif ears! Who will bring Leeds back to supreme power? Bremner, Clarke, Hackman, Lorimer, Hoffman or Charlton (Jack not Heston, Paul).

Bet Gene has never heard of Leeds United Football Club.

Wednesday, 1 October

Went to Farm[16] disco 7.30–10.45 with Craig and Andy. Pete didn't turn up. Lots of fun people there: Dawn and Lisa and Kate and Karen and John and Dick and Mick and Mick and Leigh and Andy M. and Tanya and Carly and Zoe, Tracy and Julie and Jo and Terry has had a Jam spike and Neil and a friend of Mick's and Louise and Cindy and Jane and Toyah and etc. Music was fun. Diana George Jam Whispers etc. there was some ace light-type lights, strobe, flashings, smoke bombs ... smoke bombs? Yes. Danced and sweated for 58% (approx) of night and my hair was dripping down my cap-sleeve neck. I left before the end in order to not get garroted by Dad after arriving 11.30 yestday. Everyone (approx) wore baggy trousers eg. Carly a good example. My God! Home at 10.55. No beheading by Dad. I am liquid at the moment. You could drown a hamster with the sweat in my baseball boots. Tired.

---

16. The Farm was a converted barn up Booth Lane that housed the youth club.

Saturday, 4 October

Dave and Paul and Neil came down smorning and Dave bought four singles, one of whom I borrowed eg. 'Rock And Roll' by Human League. I'm into it man. I wanna side part my hair and wear thin black ties and button-down collar black shirts and black baggies.[17]

Wednesday, 29 October

The following things are wrong with me:
I eat too much junk food.
I haven't done Dad's office a Xmas card yet.
I have only seen eight Gene films.
I sometimes get spots on my legs.
My teeth are crooked.
I want to go out with a girl from another county.
I laughed at a prison officer on BBC with Paul.[18]
I can only swim 100 metres.
I played terrible at squash on Tuesday.
I was late for *Pressure*. [19]
I missed *Covenant With Death* (Geno) yonx ago.
I don't eat enough vegetables.
I am not going out with anyone.
I have forgotten Paula's phone number.
I pick faults with myself.

Thursday, 20 November

Dad's birthday. I got him a *Mayfair*. Good present. Mmmmmmmmm. I have just tasted something as nice as the tastes of malt bread, yogurt, ginger beer, Drifters, dry roasted peanuts all mixed together ie. one of Dad's sherry liqueurs.

---

17. The day – for me, not Jon Savage – that punk died. Long live The Human League.
18. The prison officer we laughed at was on the documentary series *Strangeways*. I don't know what was so funny.
19. *Pressure* was a gritty, low-budget 1974 British film about the black community in South London, with particular emphasis on Rastafarianism and sound systems. The Film Club showed it. More education for me ('There really should have been subtitles,' I wrote in my diary).

Mmmm. I scored in hockey and a ball hit me on the head. Hockey is ace.

Saturday, 22 November
So! It was Kristin who transplanted a square inch of JR with a square inch of lead. Kristin, JR's sister-in-law, is now JR's sister-in-Strangeways. Thanx, *Chronicle*, for letting the secret out at 6pm. Mates. Haha, if you thort it was Sue Ellen.

Monday, 24 November
Why does everyone keep dying on me this year? Alf Hitch, Stevie, Mae West, Hattie Jacques, lead singer of Ruts, L.S. of Joy Division, George Raft, Peter Sellers, Yootha Joyce etc. Saw *Film 80*. Barry Normal hates *The Island* and *Awakening*.

Wednesday, 25 December
Ace stuff: new drum sticks, Python album, *Not 9.00 News* LP, *Holy Grail* book, *Guinness Film Book*, *Golden Turkey Awards* book, inks + brush, talc, scarf, felt tips, *Elephant Man*,[20] *French Connection*,[21] *Graffiti 2*, rubber, record box, biros, glue, razors, diary, sweat shirt, Merry Christmas.

---

20. Making-of book.
21. The original novel by Robin Moore.

fourteen

I'm Not in Love

Another girl in the neighbourhood
Wish she was mine – she looks so good
The Undertones, 'Teenage Kicks' (1979)

Here then are my O-level results:

English Lit	C	English Lang	B
Art	C	Maths	D
Biology	B	Chemistry	C
History	U	French	C/B (written/oral)

Not great are they? Hardly an exhibition match. Pete, for instance, got A grades in all three sciences, and Richard Ford got *four* As – mind you, Fordie was the kind of square who wore his school rugby top *out of school.* Three years earlier I had walked away from middle school the anointed one, top of the form, Mr Hundred Per Cent. Now I was merely scraping through my exams (and in the case of history, failing miserably[1]). These results by the way have nothing to

---

1. Actually I have an alibi for history. Our teacher Mrs Horrocks thought she could crack the exam code, and using past papers, had worked out exactly which essay subjects would come up. She advised us which bits to concentrate on in our revision and, by the same token, which bits to ignore. On the day, it turned out she was completely wrong, and loads of us did badly. 'U' by the way is 'ungraded', which was the equivalent of the exam board coming round and slapping you in the face at the Bold Dragoon. They say Mrs Horrocks was in floods of guilty tears when the results came in, which is why I've changed her name.

do with getting a few questions wrong in front of the hard kids – by the time I sat my O-levels in the fifth year, I had put that pimp-rolling pantomime well behind me. Bill, Lee, Si and Gaz weren't in any of my option groups anyway, and since they would all be leaving school at the first opportunity to join the nearest scrapheap I couldn't have cared less what they thought any more. No, these below-par grades squarely reflect the performance of a distracted boy. It seems my academic brilliance was history and here's why.

O-levels come at precisely the wrong time (or they did for me anyway). You're 16. You're waking up to the world. If you're a boy, testosterone production is now in overdrive, not to mention luteinising hormone (hey, I got a B in biology). Secondary sex characteristics rear their ugly head and, unless you are at the NSB, girls hove into view in a big way, sometimes obscuring everything else, including the sky, and certainly taking the urgency out of homework, revision and the Industrial Revolution.

I first noticed the opposite sex in 1977, aged 13, which is pretty much by the book. You might say that my first sexual act was buying Rebecca Warren some fudge from Wales. (The crushing disappointment of her response was certainly a useful lesson in this regard.)

I will now call Hayley my first girlfriend without inverted commas, the culmination in 1978 of an intensive campaign of 'chatting up' and 'asking out' at school. She was my first French kiss, as we used to say demurely in those days: the kind where you bang teeth and try to convince yourself this is hot stuff. But like all apprentice relationships, it didn't exactly run deep. I don't even remember it officially ending, although I did experience for the first time that nagging tied-down feeling during the French trip, where very little French kissing actually took place. Well, we had been 'going out' for a week – I expect the magic had gone.

After the Hayley watershed (the main consequence of which was a lasting friendship with her supercool older brother Vaughan), I enjoyed an entirely unrepresentative rally of girl-friends that summer – although not one of these nursery-slope liaisons went beyond hanging around awkwardly and perhaps the engraving of initials on the see-saw. I was asked out by a girl called

Louise at school. She scared the life out of me because she had 'a reputation' (possibly fictional) but I said yes. It lasted a week, and I'm not sure I even kissed her. (I didn't. I didn't kiss her.) She packed *me* in, which was only fair, as she'd started it. Without stopping to check the time I immediately dallied with a girl called Rebecca (not Warren, another one – was she really a vicar's daughter?), who I kissed at a youth club disco that finished at 9.15 p.m. Then I went on holiday to Wales, forgot all about her (no fudge), and 'chucked' her on my return with this tremendous act of backpedalling in my diary on 11 August: 'I chucked Rebecca. Well I chucked her ages ago but I told her tonight.' (Women love a bastard.) I chucked her down the field, which is where most of these torrid events took place. Where else were we supposed to go?

Then I hit what would have been my first girlfriend drought – so soon! – which neatly and not unconnectedly coincided with going to the new school, where my self-confidence took its first beating.

A grand total of no girlfriends in 1979; one in 1980; and one in 1981 (or one-and-a-half if you include 1980's Holiday Romance, Paula from High Wycombe, who came to Northampton twice). Mind you, *not* having a girlfriend is more of an exam killer than having one at that age. The fancying, the stalking, the longing, the fretting, the sighing, the asking out, the rebuff, these are what take up all the headspace and breaktime.

The key females in my life throughout 1979 were Kris Monroe, Sabrina Duncan and Kelly Garrett, better known as Charlie's Angels. I watched a documentary on TV about Marilyn Monroe in August that year, and her famous early nude shots against the red background imprinted themselves on my mind, unhelpfully in the circumstances. The out-of-the-blue smooch with Cindy Offord at the end of the year would be my only unimagined contact with the opposite gender, and we all know how far that got me.

I'll think about it ...

When, on 3 April 1980 I seemed to impress Liza at the Girl Guides and Fanciers FC disco (she was a year younger, but like all girls, seemed a year older) I couldn't quite believe my good fortune, and our subsequent 'going out' lasted a creditable stretch, through the rest of April and into May. Six weeks all told, during which I walked her home a lot, and invented a code for our chaste, no-hands brand of snogging in my diary ('romantic interlude') – the first time I had ever hidden anything from its pages! I also wrote her name many, many times in all sorts of different pens, albeit spelt incorrectly for the first 11 days (it is written Liza but pronounced Lisa).

What did I learn from this great leap forward? Loyalty, I suppose. The pitfalls of trying to integrate a girlfriend into your regular circle of mates (Liza and I spent much of our quality time with Craig, Pete, Honx, Matty, Andy Bonner and Dave, listening to things like *The Specials* LP and 'A Forest' by The Cure). But the most important lesson of Liza was the one relationships save up till last, the lesson of rejection. I'd had a pretty easy ride for my first 15 years in this regard. Anita Barker's mocking of my stabilisers was a knock-back, but it all happened so fast I didn't have far to fall, and Tina Woods choosing Mark Walsh over me in the days before Hayley was a blow. But this was kids' stuff. When your other half instigates the termination of a relationship after six whole weeks it stings. I didn't love her, even when at the height of my junior fixation I wrote 'ANDY 4 LIZA' with my Dymo label-maker, but I thought she was awfully pretty with her freckles and when she chucked me on Tuesday, 13 May I was temporarily devastated.

You can tell by the way I pretend not to be devastated in my diary:

> Yeh well I'm not going out wiv Liza any more anyway. But it's nothing to shit yourself about. If she fancies some bigheaded wanker from Lings it's her hard luck.

Of course it was my hard luck – because she'd got in first. She packed me in on the playing fields at school, having sent out a misread early warning signal two days prior when she revealed that she didn't like my beloved 999. I vowed on Tuesday, 13 May never to be chucked again.

This proved surprisingly easy for the next 16 months. I didn't get another girlfriend until September 1981.

* * *

Some girls will, some girls won't, some girls need a lot of loving and some girls don't, as Racey so memorably sang, and I so memorably half-found out over the next 16 months. To be fair to myself (well somebody has to), I did discover The Holiday Romance during my first drought, thanks to the improved sociability of staying in a hotel rather than a farmhouse. For my dalliance with Paula of High Wycombe we have H. Adams of Wellingborough to thank. This was my dad's insurance firm, who rewarded his ten years' loyal service in 1980 with a directorship, hence the upturn in our family's financial circumstances and the seismic cultural shift that summer from North Wales to the Channel Islands. (We couldn't afford to fly there and hire a car, but give us time.[2])

The fumbling courtship rituals at the Merton Hotel were made all the more artificial – and convenient – by the sheer scarcity of kids staying there at any one time. A sprawling holiday camp of a place, it was still a magnet for the elderly in 1980, with bingo on Tuesdays and ballroom dancing every night except for Thursdays when there was a disco with a DJ who had mistaken his job title for dress code. All residents between the ages of 10 and 18 would form a breakaway republic in the ballroom in order to get away from their parents and exploit the generous bar policy of serving anyone who could see over it. Every year throughout my mid-to-late teens, each Merton week would be immortalised in snapshot: a motley line-up of Debbies and Daves from places as far afield as Portsmouth, Liverpool, Redhill and Manchester, sticking their thumbs up around a table of empties, the flash reflecting in the head-height glass panels of the balcony above. In a good week, there might be anything up to a dozen of us, checking each other out over illicit halves of cider with an eye on the main chance (i.e. a slow dance on Thursday – with parents watching from the balcony – and perhaps a French kiss in the TV room).

This siege mentality was like being in a group of survivors after a plane crash – somebody was *bound* to get off with somebody else

---

2. Significantly, it was Nan Mabel and Pap Reg – ever the jet-setting, colour-telly-pioneering sophisticates – who went out and road-tested Jersey and the Merton for us. And they flew. And they hired a car. Definitely working for the CIA.

eventually, especially with the scent of the barman's apron so high in our young nostrils. (Where else but in an old persons' hotel ballroom could an ecosystem of hormonally altered teens enjoy this kind of autonomy, especially the younger among us? It was like going to the same youth club every night, with exactly the same 11 people, except they served Pernod and instead of getting a lift home, you got a *lift* home.)

Hence: Paula, who, like Liza was a year younger but seemed a year older. It being my first Holiday Romance (actually I never got much better at them), I took our one snog in the TV room – the kind where the younger kids watch – very seriously indeed and we agreed to write. It wasn't boyfriend–girlfriend but seeing as how I couldn't get anyone to go out with me in Northampton, I remained steadfastly loyal by default to Paula across those 70-odd miles for the duration of our fruity correspondence. And she did come down for my 16th birthday party, which was something of an honour for her.

But it all ended in tears after her second and, as it turned out, final visit in July (we sat and watched Prince Charles marry Lady Di on the telly, which was probably an omen). When Paula got back to High Wycombe, she wrote that letter with the all-too-fruity suggestions concerning what we would do when she turned 16 on 14 March 1982. I panicked, and chucked her by return of post, thus at least sticking to the anti-chucking legislation laid down on Tuesday, 13 May 1980.

I had moved on apace with Paula, but I wasn't ready for any really rude stuff. Luckily for me, none would be forthcoming.

* * *

Know this: I'm not going to talk about anything as intimate as losing my virginity – partly to protect the memory and the other party involved, and also because if you wanted to read about sex you'd have picked up a novel by Edwina Currie. Suffice to say, I lost my virginity statistically very late, when I was 18 in fact – long after most of my peers – but true to form, it left me with neither emotional scars nor a sense of deep self-loathing as it occurred after a measured, patient run-up within what was my first actual, serious, long-term relationship,[3] and not up against a wall or with the local loose woman à la those *Porky's* films.

My trajectory of development up to this pivotal point was a sort of very low curve that suddenly jerks upwards, as it were. Even when I started to get girlfriends more regularly these weren't exactly steamy affairs. I don't know why but I was very timid about female anatomy. I could reproduce the textbook diagram of a woman's reproductive organs but not from life. I wouldn't say I had a full-scale hang-up, I just didn't fancy going there. Not just yet.

I went out with a couple of girls who were more, shall we say, gung-ho than I and all it did was bring the chucking date forward. Jo P, my one proper *local* girlfriend of 1981 and not to be confused with Jo G the singer in our band, lasted just under two weeks. She gave me my first love bite at Neil Stuart's party, which was a warning shot that I was out of my depth from day one.

It dawns on me that I may be flattering these formative liaisons by calling them 'relationships' – they are more like dress rehearsals, basic training. As teenagers, we flit restlessly from one partner to the next like bees between stamens, and that's as it should be – there'll be plenty of time for commitment, self-assembly furniture and arguing later. I say that for as long as you still think of it as 'going out with', you're not in a relationship, you're just kissing the same person on a regular basis and scratching initials into playground apparatus.

I went out with Rebecca (neither Warren nor the vicar's daughter, a third one) for a full month. She was the first girlfriend I'd had with an imagined weight problem and I dealt with it very

---

3. Another Jo, but not just another Jo. A 15-year-old girl from the NSG (Northampton School for Girls), we were together for 296 days, from December 1982 to October 1983 (thus I am skipping ahead a bit by mentioning it). It was the first relationship that behaved like one: it evolved, bedded in, developed catch-phrases and I didn't get bored. Who am I now to say that just because we were under 18 we didn't love each other? If we thought we did, we did. It was certainly the most mature coupling of my life so far – a very good, steadying influence on my luteinising hormones – and even though there was a lot of other stuff ongoing in my life (the usual: band, films, drawing, hair), we did spend a lot of time together for those ten months, and even had the odd row, usually borne out of Jo feeling she was throwing away her 16th year in a long-term relationship. She was two years younger and yet somehow still seemed a year older.

intuitively by not noticing or caring. A slight girl as I remember her, she wrote this in my diary on the day we started going out, 'Hi! I am not fat. I am obese.' This was so far from the truth it simply did not compute, and I didn't take it seriously at all. I was too busy listening to 'Nowhere Girl' by B-Movie, experimenting with auburn hair dye and planning Absolute Heroes' next live gig. Rebecca would have been my Falklands War girlfriend if I'd taken much notice of what was going on in the South Atlantic but I'm ashamed to say I was distracted again. I actually packed her in before the Royal Navy Task Force even recaptured South Georgia. Rejoice, rejoice. I'm sure she did.

I developed a system in 1982: I marked the beginning and the end of each relationship in my diary with coloured triangles. Thus, Rebecca was a lime-coloured triangle (28 days); Wendy[4] was an orange triangle (25 days); Sarah – who I'm embarrassed to say I don't remember, but she's there in the book – a yellow triangle (10 days); Caroline, a pale blue one (her mum was one of our teachers at school – I think it's called playing with fire – a misleading 46 days as I was away in Jersey for 14 of those); Lynn, red (a misleading 63 days since she was 1982's Holiday Romance, and we only saw each other once afterwards – I took the coach all the way to Manchester so I must've been keen); Carol, brown (the dampest squib of them all, six days); and Fiona, pink (24 days). A pattern was emerging, one made up of multicoloured and in some cases overlapping triangles. My life had become a Venn diagram.

I don't want this chapter to become a meaningless roll-call of girls' names (Rebecca followed by Rebecca followed by Rebecca), nor am I aiming to come across like some auburn-haired Casanova '82. It is after all like a big game of musical chairs at that age. The truth is, I couldn't find anybody I wanted to stay with for longer than 28 days. I got bored with them; they presumably got bored with me too, it's just that I always got in first with the P45 phone

---

4. Interestingly, my mum's favourite of all my teen girlfriends. Perhaps because Wendy actually spoke to her. What a spin doctor she was. Great big spiky hair too, which ought to have doomed her relationship with Mum from the start but didn't. Had a laugh like a honking seal.

call. I did occasionally pack a girl in face to face, but Fiona, for instance, I deliberately called while *Grease* was on telly so she'd be keen to get off the phone and back to John Travolta.

* * *

What did this string of brief, surprisingly chaste relationships teach me? Well, that I could get girlfriends (I did fancy myself a bit, but then I was in a band). That I was easily bored. That ultimately I preferred my male friends to any girl (the real quality time I spent in 1982 was with Pete and Craig and Matty and Vaughan, and a five-day biology field trip to Exmouth was more notable as a quasi-homoerotic male-bonding session than as a girl-hunt). Lust was something I saved up for pop stars and film actresses. I saw little crossover between the objects of sexual desire I cut out of magazines and the girls at school.

I'm needlessly ashamed to say I started compiling 'Horn Charts' in my diary, and here we see unattainable women like Bo Derek, Catherine Deneuve, Ann-Margret, Suzanne Dando, Lesley Ash, Keren Woodward, Denise the dark haired one out of Tight Fit, and Axa, the pneumatic she-warrior in a *Sun* cartoon strip, fighting it out for the top spot. (I would have paid most of my pocket money to actually see them do that.) Girls at school didn't as a rule get a look-in. They were all too attainable. Like all boys in a band with a girl singer, I always fancied Jo G from behind my tom toms, but she was officially not for asking out, and we all kept a professional distance. Hence the allure, I guess. She may as well have been Keren Woodward.

So what was happening? What were girlfriends for? What was the point of awarding them the first coloured triangle, when I was already envisaging their second one?

I think I went out with girls in 1982 because:

(a) I thought I ought to, and
(b) I could.

During the previous lean years, I had filled all the no-girlfriend time with much more important and rewarding stuff: drawing caricatures with Paul Garner; learning the drums and forming the band with Pete and Craig; growing a floppy New Romantic fringe; watching as many films as I humanly could; and collecting Sainsbury's trolleys from as far afield as the Mayor Hold car park in my clip-on brown tie. Even in 1982, the Year of the Triangle, I kept up the band, the films, the drawing, and the hair. I wrote *Not the Sixth Form Revue*, which we performed for three nights at school; I passed my driving test first go (and dented the bumper of Mum's Metro the *day after*); I made endless humorous and elaborate tapes for my friends' birthdays featuring Pythonesque sketches, sound effects and spoof songs; and of course, I found time to turn my diary into a work of art, a surrogate water cooler around which the whole gang would gather. BLOODY PRIVATE!

If I'm honest, girlfriends were way down my list of priorities, even when I had one. There were bursts of uncontrolled over-reaction when a new triangle appeared (the diary is full of heady and harmless nonsense like 'I am going out with wonderful Rebecca ... God, Paula's beautiful ... Where will I be tomorrow? I'll tell you: Manchester with the girl of my dreams ... etc.'), but at the end of the day I think I would have traded any of them in for Vaughan or Pete or Craig.

I was at least building up an impressive repertoire of ex-girlfriends, which made me feel terribly experienced and worldly. Another landmark in late '82: I mistakenly called Liza an 'old flame' in front of her in the Bold Dragoon pub and she slapped me round the face. I thought old flame simply meant ex-girlfriend, but she took it as an implication that she was on the back burner and at least it got me my first slap, which I must have earned by then (for ending it with Caroline by showing her photos of Lynn if nothing else). But because we all moved in the same social circles – Absolute Heroes gigs, Willowtree[5] discos, the sixth-form

---

5. A regular party venue at the famous Billing Aquadrome, a caravan site near some water. Other party venues of choice at the time: the Sturtridge Pavilion (in deepest town), the Marina Bar (also at the Aquadrome), Opus II (town), Dallington Squash Club (miles away), the Regents (can't remember) and the Masonic Hall (near Nene College – luckily, they let girls in).

common room, Alan's flat and the Bold – it was impossible to avoid exes. We just had to get on with each other, there was no room for lingering resentment.

However, despite the teen anguish, we weren't in love, any of us. We were just messing about. I ended up with crap O-level results and some seriously worrying school reports in the sixth form[6] not because of girls, but because of the band, the films, the drawing, and the hair.

Oh, and *being gay*, but that deserves its own chapter.

---

6. My reports from the end of the lower-sixth, July 1982, horrify me now to look at. 'Time is running out for Andy,' warns my form teacher Mr Chennels. 'He seems to think that by some good stroke of fortune he is bound to land on his feet – I hope he wakes up soon.' Mrs Pearson suggests I remember that 'biology is not creative or arising from within, but learned, remembered and recounted as required'. Mr Coppock predicts that 'unless improvements are made, next June could be something of a nightmare'. Mr Gilbert worries in English about my 'lack of note-taking', while even in art, Mr Mutton says he lives in 'anticipation of wonderful things which seem increasingly unlikely'. I know. I was pissing it all away, wasn't I? That's what happens when you give the best years of your life to rock'n'roll.

1981

Selected Extracts From My Diary

A pattern is now set. Another Boots page-a-day diary, this time burgundy, and another collage under transparent sticky-back plastic: U2, Gene Hackman, Dustin Hoffman, the logos of Duran Duran, Premier ('1st in percussion'), Film Review *magazine and a Sainsbury's price label for ironic effect.*

So it's films, more films, post-punk music, being in a band and getting a job. This is the most colourful and best-kept diary so far, a riot of felt-tip, Caran D'Ache pencil and caricatures drawn elsewhere, cut out and stuck in with Pritt. Paul Garner had by now started a similarly styled journal and we would constantly compare them, hence the attention to upkeep and visuals. (And hence the erosion of honest text – because the diary has become an amateur film review and art gallery, I start to get behind with it. Entries are filled in days later. The immediacy is gone. It's a sad day.)

Hey, I wish you could see the pretty drawings, because the actual words now fall into second place, and great swathes are just movie reviews – dull third-party reading indeed. (Day one, 1 January, is dominated by a lengthy dissection of Papillon *– rated four and a half stars in case you're interested – and that's how the year ends, with two reviews filling 28 December,* The Thirty-Nine Steps *and* The Battle of Midway.*)*

The list of favourite people in the now traditional self-questionnaire at the front includes the Elephant Man and Barry Norman.

Sunday, 18 January
Undepressing things:
The Blue Lagoon is on next week.[1]

My birthday is in 44 days.

We are going to see U2 *live*.

Paula is probably coming.

I am definitely getting a new room.

I am definitely getting a new room.

My sore throat's gone.

I am certainly getting a new room.

A new room! And it'll be 10 foot by 10 foot and I'm helping to design it and have my own colour scheme and record player and I can paint something on one wall[2] and I'll just sit on my bed in it and admire the four walls and door. I could say 'ace'. But I won't. (It gets me very irritated.)

Monday, 19 January

If they can free hostages why can't they buy me a video?[3]

Thursday, 26 February

On the way home from Dave F's this morning the police force decided to stop me and look in my bag etc. I assume, as they said, 'Sorry, mate,' when they stopped frisking me, I am not the Trinity Ripper.[4]

Paul Bush (long lost Grendon-inhabiter) came down after lunch. He is into Rush, Peter Gabriel, pilchards on toast and drums. His sister's going out with the lead singer of a group of whom the drummer's going out with the bassist's sister and his brother's engaged to Paul's *other* sister. Got that? No I'm fine.

---

1. I was *so* into films, I would watch anything. I actually went to see *The Blue Lagoon* twice, once at the ABC in January and once at Lings in March, which was stupid as it only counted as one film in my running total. (I must have really wanted to see Brooke Shields's body-double topless.)

2. I ended up doing a painting on my door. Of me.

3. The 52 US embassy staff held captive by Iranian students in Teheran for 444 days, released just as Ronald Reagan was inaugurated (the Ayatollah wanted to humiliate the outgoing President Carter by delaying the hostages' departure from Teheran Airport). But I *really* wanted a video.

4. Trinity was the area where Neil Stuart and Dave Freak lived. There was no Ripper there, I was merely making a point about the *pigs*.

Friday, 27 February

The Brightest View had recording session number two at Winsford 'Living Room' Studios. We put sound on tape from 10.30 till 5.10. Ace. We did 'No Smoke', 'They Said', 'Dropout', 'Mirror Mirror', 'Average Girl' and 'No Penalties'.[5] What a day. Good results. Sorry. Modesty. Positive results. Last *Grange Ill* of series. Cry. It continues not. I had some beautiful fried potatoes today.

Monday, 30 March

Depression (temporary). Don't worry. Woke up in a rather depressed state of mind. Rode up Craig's depressed and nearly finished Art CSE depressed.

However after tea I made Paula a sort-of-late-birthday card and stayed in and collected up £3 to get Paula a sort-of-late-birthday present record voucher and did all my homework and washed my hair and wrote my application to Sainsbury's and ate an orange and a yogurt and found out that Craig is now going out with Rebecca Fourthyear.[6] Ace.

Somebody's had a gunfight with Mr Reagan in America. Big news. He's alive.

Monday, 6 April

I *could* say: 'One-six for the breaker on the side, bring it back, come on. Can you give me a nine on your rough twenty, good buddy? What's your handle? That's a big four and you've got Hi-Hat here, Hi-Hat. Can you give me a ten thiry-six 'cos there's a lot of wallies bleeding over this channel. Pick a number, breaker. Roger-D, and it's a ten-ten till we do it again, Polo.' But I won't. Went Vaughan's. Mucked

---

5. Hard-hitting social commentaries about, respectively, smoking, authority, apathy, vanity, homogeny and football violence. Cheers.
6. The sweet Liverpudlian who cut hair, liked Japan and imagined she was 'obese' (she wasn't). As we have established I went out with her for a whole month in 1982. It's like a soap opera.

about on his CB. Got tickets for *Peer Gynt*. Small amounts of homework.[7]

Friday, 1 May

I think Vic is there. My room is under an epidemic of fun at the moment ie. today, its wonderful interior met a brand new bed plus all the burgundy topping, my once garage-bound drum kit, three shelves, a dartboard and a Spandau Ballet poster. O wow. (Oh shut up about your room, Andy.) Bin invited to John Lewis's party. O good. How Blitzy[8] shall I turn up? Oh my God the Human League's new single[9] is revolutionary! Oh, calm me down, someone.

Wednesday, 13 May

Video. Well it's here. Yes, it is here. It exists and it's ours and I love it. A Philips job[10] with loads of cute black buttons all over it. Ooh, the little cassettes just pop out automatically and ask you to record *Coronation St* and FA Cup[11] on them. Oh God, how ace and grey and real. I don't even care that we didn't practice tonight. Instead I went with Craig, Dave etc. to watch Cindy leg about in a Lings-ish athletix meeting,[12] and I piled over her house to pick up my French oral sheets (good excuse). It took me nearly three hours to pick them up.

Friday, 29 May

Andy Collins ... you know him as pupil of Weston Favell

---

7. 'Small' meant large in our sarcastic world. Do you follow?

8. As in, how like the androgynous trend-setters who went to clubs such as the Blitz in London would I dress? The answer, on the night, was not very. I wore one of Mum's scarves as a neckerchief but under a large coat. I slipped the neckerchief off.

9. 'Sound of the Crowd'. It *was* pretty damn good.

10. The Philips 2000 system (with two-sided tapes): first casualty in the VCR wars, and Dad had *bought* rather than rented it. We eventually replaced it with ... a BetaMax.

11. Replay: Spurs v Man City, 3–2.

12. The Lings leisure centre with the little cinema attached also had an athletics track.

Upper School, ex-member of NCFE Film Club, drummer with Brightest View, drawer of caricatures and O-level candidate 46100 10045. Well now ... Andy Collins the employee of J Sainsbury Ltd. Earned my first three or four quid by watching nice films, having a tour of behind-the-scenes Sainsbury's, trying out my little box-opening utensils and having a cup of tea. Skin-tight overall[13] (I'm getting a new one don't worry).

Wednesday, 12 August *JERSEY*
Ow my legs! Owowow. How can it be unbelievably hot for four days running? Who cares! *Orca* is one cool book. Our waiter calls Melissa 'Peach Melba', Pap 'Mr Smith'. Me 'John' or 'Steve McQueen'. Cool catering. Corn flakes – bacon tomato – minestrone – plaice peas chips – Bakewell tart ice cream more ice cream – soup – Virginia ham pineapple sauce – sherry trifle – beautiful.

OK, so 'ace' got on our nerves. Well 'cool' is beginning to push its luck. *For Your Eyes Only* on Sunday perhaps. JJ Stewart Show was a laugh. The best Merton cabaret I've seen. JJ was a really horny bloke playing his mixture of trombones, trumpets etc. suggestive chat all the way through. I think I've had about 16 ciders so far this holiday.[14]

Tuesday, 18 August
Went on a shit walk to Corbiere.
Si won (wait for it ...) 40 quid on the bingo. Lucky. What a job! Air pistol shop here we come. Lucky!

Wednesday, 2 September
Yes! 6th form! Yes here I am – in the WFUS lower sixth! I'm in Mr Chennells' form (promising) and I'm doing my three As – Art Eng Bio. Haven't got my cool 'distinctive blazer' yet.

---

13. More sarcasm.
14. I did much of my formative drinking at the Merton Hotel. Because our parents always knew where we were, they turned a blind eye.

I'm in no great hurry. I'm really into the sixth. I don't think Craig is! Some people are hard to please.

Saturday, 12 September

This man gets in the way of my life sometimes.[15] Unpredictable!!

'Be a Deputy Manager' Part 1:

8.20am 'You will be sacked if you do not work constantly. Collect trolleys at your tea break. DIE or LEAVE.'

18.06pm 'Well done, lads. You've done an excellent job. KISS.'

Got an xtra 50p in me wage packet today (why? who cares?) so I had a Britvic 55 for tea break. Classy, eh?

Gaw, I had a real workout on my drums today. Lovely. I'm going to get into real 35mm photography. Bad tragic news: Leeds ****ing lost 4–0 to Coventry. Jackie Bisset[16] is in love with a ****ing Russian ballet dancer twat. Cry!!

On a lighter note ... £14.50. Hahahahahaha.

Thursday, 17 September

Rubik's fucking Cube can turn an average human being into an uncontrollably violent, axe-wielding madman can't it? Aha – I got a copy of the instructions. The *instructions* can turn an average human being into an uncontrollably violent, axe-wielding madman!! It says, 'Now you will have an even number of U sides facing upwards.' LIKE HELL! I tried it about a dozen times and I NEVER EVER ended up with an even number. (Add 'fucking' between each word there.)

How to really solve a Rubik's Cube.

1. Chuck the bugger away.
2. Go to bed.

---

15. The deputy manager at Sainsbury's was the pantomime villain Mr Eccleston (he even had a moustache). We all hated him, but then he was the boss, and when you're a worker (like I was pretending to be for the 18 weeks I was employed by Sainsbury's), you hate the boss.

16. As in the film star Jacqueline Bisset, whom I fancied.

I didn't watch *Telefon*. [17]
a) it looks suspiciously like an 'A'
b) it clashes with everything
c) bor-ing.
TOTP was relative bolox.

Monday, 19 October

Yes it's true! ITV have got *Close Encounters* for Christmas. My God no. Yes yes yes! Words I say a lot lately: twang – wonderful – bum – cool – into. Don't ask why. (I think) I saw exactly 83 films in 1980. I have seen 77 this year so far (I think). [18] Interestin' eh?

Saturday, 28 November

Round-up time: Obsession of the week: Cindy/Dustin Hoffman. Record of the week: 'Visions of China' Japan. Great Expectation of the week: fancy dress party. Hint of the week: I've spent £4 on Paul's Xmas pressie (that was ruthless, sorry). Dr Who of the week: Patrick Troughton. Sex Object of the week: Janet Ellis (*Jigsaw*). Haircut of the week: John Taylor/Robert Redford. That was good wasn't it?

Friday, 25 December

The day after *Poseidon Adventure*. [19] Otherwise known as Christmas Day. Ingredients: half a ton of relations, a surprisingly large pile of presents and too much food. Present highlights: some fun boots, [20] a beautiful Bo Derek calendar, *The Directory of Film Stars*, [21] and the 'I Could Be Happy' twelve-

---

17. A Charles Bronson thriller directed by Don Siegel in 1977. You see, it was an event if I *didn't* watch a film.
18. My final total for 1981 would be 121 films seen. In 1982 it was 144, and 1983 a storming 175. I have never stopped being proud of myself for this intense self-education.
19. *The Poseidon Adventure* 'premiered' on TV as we know in 1979, but it was on again on Christmas Eve this year – the third time I had seen it.
20. These boots were all the rage during the New Romantic years: black and sort of velvety, you tucked your pleated trousers into them (and then had to keep re-tucking them all night). Commendably effeminate though for a provincial lad.
21. Actually *The Illustrated Directory of Film Stars* by David Quinlan.

inch. Also received: *Hedgehog Sandwich* (not literally), [22] *Ripping Yarns*, record box, some personally printed letter-heads, Quality Street (for a change!), felt tips, various useful things like scissors, pens and vodka liqueurs, *Horror Stories*, Duran Duran single, some cassettes, some macho *Playboy* talc etc. Family present: toaster sandwich thing. Not a bad haul, eh? I love my boots and Bo Derek.

Wednesday, 30 December
1981 was the year of ... the new room, my first gig, Jo P, parties, Jack Nicholson, hair dye, [23] Altered Images, The Brightest View, *Rainbow*, 6th form, O-levels, *Ad-lib*, [24] Sainsbury's, Jersey, Charles and Di, Paula, vodka, *Hitchhikers' Guide*, The Video, Pernod, white Christmas, fun and *drums*!

---

22. The second *Not the Nine O'Clock News* LP.
23. I had by now started to experiment with tints and dyes supplied by Carol. The sort other people can only detect if you stand under a bright light. (One such tint coincided with night-time carol singing so I was able to impress the others by shining a torch onto my hair all evening.)
24. In time-honoured sixth-form fashion, we discovered irony round about now and watched certain kids' shows religiously, like *Rainbow* – every lunch hour – and this, *Ad-Lib*, a suitably ropey ITV teatime magazine show with Duncan Goodhew among its gang of upbeat presenters (also actors Tilly Vosborough, Dave Nunn and Oona Kirsch). These were the *Supermarket Sweep* and *Neighbours* of our day.

fifteen

Alan's Flat

Just because you're gay,
I won't turn you away
If you stick around,
I'm sure that we can find some common ground
Billy Bragg, 'Sexuality' (1991)

The dream is over
John Lennon, 'God' (1970)

The flashpoint came in the summer of '82 and had it not been for all that dyed New Romantic hair in my eyes I would have seen it a mile off. My relationship with Mum and Dad was coming to a head. The honeymoon was almost up.

I was, in the immortal words of Viv Savage,[1] having a good time *all the time*: gigging, writing, rehearsing and enjoying the first modicum of local fame with Absolute Heroes, making highly wrought birthday cards and tapes for all my mates, and notching up seemingly endless parties at the Willowtree function room; Mum and Dad were understandably concerned that I had taken my eye off the academic ball. I had actually kicked it over a fence.

My bloodless O-level grades were enough to clinch me a place in the sixth form, but – as I found out in term one – A-levels seem

---

1. Keyboard player, Spinal Tap.

timed not just to run counter to your galloping hormones, but also to coincide with the age of the provisional driving licence, almost-legal drinking and Saturday jobs. Indeed, merely *being* in the sixth form with all its perks (common room, kettle, tuck shop, study periods, 'distinctive blazer') creates precisely the wrong environment for work. It did for me anyway.

The problem underlying all this was easy to see. I'd decided by now that I really could do art for a living (despite the stingy C they gave me for my O-level – a sign that I was misunderstood, obviously). My naïve childhood jotter fantasy had found a precedent: there were art colleges, I'd discovered. While my peers were thinking about university places in Bath and Bristol, I pinned my hopes on studying art. (I know what you're thinking: studying art = oxymoron. And, as someone who spent four years doing it, I can't really argue.) Of course, you can't just do art A-level and spend the rest of the time eating Aeros from the tuck shop and organising the revue. So I took English, because I liked writing, and – to make up the numbers – biology, one of my few Bs, which did at least involve a bit of drawing (aorta and xylems and mitochondria mostly).

My whole attitude was wrong from the day I first donned the maroon blazer: I was doing one subject I truly cared about – but thought I was so good at already I didn't need to put any further effort in; a second subject I liked but was only taking as a fall-back ('At least get English, then you can always be a journalist if the art career falls through,' said my parents, clearly out of their minds); and a third subject which was the equivalent of the *Guinness Book of Names*, the sort of tome I took out of the library simply because you were allowed four and there were no others about vampire films or Tony Hancock.

Mr Chennells was bang on when he wrote at the end of my first year, 'He seems to think that by some good stroke of fortune he is bound to land on his feet.' I did think that: I *lived* by that rule. My first 17 years on earth had seemed like one long 'good stroke of fortune' (I wonder if he meant to type 'stroke of good fortune'?). I blame my parents for this sense of enormous well-being. They were the ones who had brought me up in an atmosphere of fun, freedom, farmhouses and fish fingers. I figured this was what life was going to be like for the foreseeable future: drawing cartoons, putting triangles in my diary and playing a drum kit which I hadn't even paid for. Apart from the wobbly start at Weston Favell, the U in history, and perhaps my ingrown toenail, life had been pretty sweet for Andy Collins. (FANS ... AUTOGRAPHS LATER!) Where was the evidence that I couldn't surf through the next few years?

On 4 March 1982, my 17th birthday (whereupon I erroneously wrote 'I am a man!' in my diary), I was a massively confident, energetic and happy human being. My horoscope from the paper that day was telling: 'Your solar chart looks positively divine. There is little that I can guard you against, except maybe a bit of waste and extravagance. Apart from that you are the life and soul of the party, and the year ahead of you looks delicious.'

Nothing about biology essays, you'll notice, but then horoscopes are a load of shit. Nevertheless I believed that the stars had aligned for me that day: I *was* the life and soul of the party, the year ahead *did* look delicious. Let me through, I'm a Pisces!

I had packed in my soul-destroying Sainsbury's job before Christmas – with Mum and Dad's blessing, I might add, as I'd protested it was interfering with my A-levels. (Well it was, but so would the Saturday activities I replaced it with: drinking, sleeping, and hanging around the Grosvenor Centre.) They bought me a Hitachi SDT-1000 faux-stack hi-fi for my birthday and I thanked them kindly, put it in my new bedroom and played my new Bauhaus and Gina X[2] albums on it. And what's more, the day after my birthday, Vaughan passed his driving test, a hugely significant pivot, as it freed him up to become my willing chauffeur in his second-hand red Viva aka the 'Bossmobile' (I called him the Boss, not because he looked anything like Bruce Springsteen, or indeed because he was the boss at the printers where he worked, but because I hero-worshipped him). Positively divine.

What could possibly go wrong?

* * *

---

2. Forgotten German diva, very much in the Grace Jones mould, and big at Northampton's only New Romantic nightclub, Das Bunker. I never went there (it was over-18s only) but Vaughan did – further fuel to the fire of my hero-worship. Alan even DJ'ed there.

Thus began a new period of my life where I no longer needed my dad, or anyone else's, to come and pick me up from parties. I was, thanks to Vaughan and the Test Centre at Gladstone Road, independent for the first time. Well, dependent on him but he didn't mind. He was only a year older than me (and still lived at home) but seemed about five years older with his car and his job, and this was where the floodgates opened.

Vaughan (or Vorno as we called him) introduced me to Alan Martin, another senior chap who was also in gainful employment. Better than that, he worked at Our Price records in town, which seemed to be just about the coolest job anyone could have aside from being Barry Norman or Jacqueline Bisset's ballet-dancing husband. (Alan owned a full-size cardboard cut-out Gary Numan and everything.) An occasional DJ, he was part of the local rock scene: although Our Price was a chainstore, individual branches still had character in those days, and Alan's was a noted hangout. As a result he seemed to know everybody. A gregarious bear of a man with Seventies hair and a Toyah fixation, he was interested in Absolute Heroes and came to see us rehearse in the school hall with a view to becoming our manager (this was before our first gig). We initially called him Mr R Price, for a joke, but were secretly flattered that a man who worked in a record shop was interested in us. He was also an inveterate giggler and hard not to like.

He stopped giggling briefly a month later when his parents effectively threw him out of the house. I was unlucky enough to be a spectator at this cathartic moment in Alan's life (Vorno had driven us round there). I guess the row had been brewing for some time, but on this particular balmy evening, Alan and his equally bearlike Mum had such a steaming head-to-head he ended up storming out, with both parents screaming obscenities at him as the Bossmobile pulled out of Poppyfield Court[3] at high speed. I must admit I was quite shocked at the expletives they came out

---

3. Don't be fooled by the fragrant, rural street names. They're all like that in the eastern estates. Alan's subsequent Blackthorn flat was in a street called Great Meadow, Wendy lived in Sidebrook Court, Jo in West Priors Court and so on. It makes Northampton sound like a village in *Morse*.

with, which just shows what a sheltered home life I must have led. But then Alan did live in Lings.

At least he used to. The next thing we knew – and I think you may be ahead of me here – Alan had moved into a flat in nearby Blackthorn. He was officially the first friend I'd ever had who didn't live with his mum and dad. So now, right in the middle of my A-levels, I had one mate with a car and another with a flat. It was a recipe for the best of times and the worst of times.

Alan's flat became mythic almost immediately. He shared it with a bloke called Nigel, and it became a magnet for a whole host of us who lived with our parents. Don't start thinking Jonathan King at the Walton Hop – we were most of us aged around 17 and 18, and Alan and Nigel were only 19 going on 20. No luring went on. We loved it there, and Alan and Nigel had to clear up the cups when the rest of us had driven off into the night (or been driven off, by guess who). Alan's flat was a place where you could open a tin of Birds Devonshire custard and eat it all with a spoon. The place also acted like a miniature singles bar, serving instant coffee, Marmite, Rice Krispies and mushy peas at all hours, and playing musical selections from the collection of, well, a man who worked in a record shop. And cardboard Gary Numan was there to watch over us.

When the flat started to become a scene, Alan wrote a message to me in my diary: 'Why, you young fool, you'll end up like me and Nigel if you come up much more ... BLOODY PERVERTED!!!' He didn't mean it literally, although if Mum had happened to glance at my journal she'd have seen from my little cartoons that a typical Saturday night round Alan's might involve Nigel administering a home-made tattoo to someone called Phil with a sewing needle and some ink, or Nigel shaving off all his body hair. To make matters more suspect – for Mum anyway – I slept over a few times. Eek.

Slap bang in the middle of all this sleaze, Mum and Dad went to a school parents' evening (I think we can see where this is heading) ... the kind that culminates in a serious 'chat' on their return. 'They made me admit I'm a lazy sod,' says my diary for 21 April, and you should read the next bit in an over-sincere American accent: 'Admitting it to them was admitting it to *me.*' I vowed to pull my socks up. The next day I stayed in and caught up on my

English essays and copied up a backlog of biology notes and did some life drawing and went to bed at 9.45 p.m.

And the day after that I went back to Alan's flat.

Actually, there were two Alan's flats, just like there were two Miss Ellies on *Dallas*. The Blackthorn one, over in the eastern wilds of Northampton, lasted for about six weeks. Then, tragically, Alan moved back in with his parents, which was seen by all as a moral defeat, mainly because we'd have nowhere to go and eat tinned food and do silly stuff on beanbags. In July, he did the decent thing and moved into a second flat, much closer to the town centre and thus even more of a refuge for passing waifs and strays. ('This flat will be full of me for a long time,' I wrote on the day he moved in, just in case Mum was reading and feared that she might have wrested me from Alan's sinister clutches.)

Alan now shared with a guy called Martin, who may or may not have been gay (he had a moustache – he was). There was a feeling that Alan himself might be gay – he didn't have a girlfriend in the whole time I knew him.[1] This was the early Eighties: dabbling with bisexuality was all the rage. Certainly one or two gay-seeming types started to enter the expanded flat orbit now that it was in a more cosmopolitan (for Northampton) spot. Considering what a default homophobe I had been in my early-to-mid teens I am proud to say that by now, with my horizons stretched, I couldn't care less about anyone's sexual preference. I didn't feel preyed upon and if these slightly camp people were gay or bi, they were also a right good laugh. Plus, there were always plenty of girls around.

Significantly though, none of these girls was my *girlfriend*. I'd briefly been out with Wendy, whom I met through the flat dating agency, back in June, but we seemed to make better friends than a couple and were happier parted and flirtatious than tied-down and anxious. But Mum hadn't forgiven me for finishing with Wendy, and she was out to get me.

---

4. Alan is now married with two kids and lives in New Zealand. He's very keen for my mum to know this. 'You should tell her that I'm now leading a very respectable lifestyle as the manager of a newspaper, I have my own business, I own a house with a harbour view, I no longer drink and I spent three years as a youth worker!'

One night I came home from the flat, around 11 p.m., and said this rather provocative thing to Mum and Dad, who were still up, watching telly:

'God, I think I was one of the only people at the flat tonight who wasn't gay!'

Light the gay touchpaper and stand well back ...

This was Mum's signal to snap. Even though I had made it clear in my assessment of the evening that I *wasn't* gay, she took it to mean that I had – as she had long suspected – been sucked into a den of iniquity and could 'go a bit funny' at any moment. She genuinely thought I was about to end up BLOODY PERVERTED, and for my own sake – to save my soul – she laid into me.

Mum had sat passively back and watched for five months as I'd become a brainwashed, work-shy bum-slave of Alan and his evil cohorts. Now she was mad as hell and she wasn't going to take it any more. Can you picture Michael Jackson hanging on to those two trees in the video for 'Earth Song'? The bit where the wind almost knocks him off his feet and it's a bit like the end of the world? It was actually a bit like the Collins front room that night, although I don't think Jacko's sexuality has ever been in as much doubt as mine was. The combined browbeating I got from Mum and Dad made parents' evening seem like a soothing damp cloth on my face.

They tried to ban me from visiting Alan's flat. I wasn't having any of that. Mum, who always led these assaults from the front, threw at me my poor performance at school (which I couldn't argue with – they'd read the 'good stroke of fortune' report), my stupid auburn hair (now tending to stick upwards with backcombing and spray), my clothes (tending towards old black T-shirts, rolled-up jeans, sailing pumps and no socks to even pull up) and even my approaching driving test (lessons paid for by them). For this ethical, mental and sartorial decline she blamed, among others, Absolute Heroes ('They're never going to get you anywhere!' – or was it just, 'They're never going to get anywhere'?), Vorno (for driving me astray), and Alan, the great Satan at the centre of this inferno. To adapt *The Poseidon Adventure* tagline: Hell, backside up.

Mum worked part-time as a secretary at Lings Upper School on the other side of the tracks (or the other side of Weston Favell

Centre). She *knew* about ex-pupil Alan Martin. What she knew about him she wasn't prepared to divulge, but it put her on the moral high ground. She seemed to know him better than I did, even though – as they were quick to point out – I spent most of my life at his flat while he tickled my chin and fed me grapes. I knew him to be a voluble, hospitable and generous pillar of the rock community. I saw no marauding shirt-lifter. He was my mate, and the manager of our band. *And* I liked girls.

However, rather than dissuade my parents of my homosexuality while in the dock, I rather cruelly left it up in the air. Like many a musician before and after me, I rather enjoyed this new game of being sexually ambiguous. Was I or wasn't I? We'll be right back after these massages.

* * *

Let's look at the evidence: since meeting Alan, I had fouled up my end-of-year exams and let off a worry-bomb among my school-teachers; I had stayed out all night a couple of times (although never without Mum and Dad knowing exactly where I was); my hair had become incrementally more auburn and as such effeminate to more conventional eyes; and the band had played half a dozen gigs, most of them at a fairly rough pub in town called the Black Lion.[5] During that period I had brought home four girlfriends, although admittedly only about once per girlfriend. But since when had an inability to keep a girlfriend meant latent homosexual tendencies? Perhaps I was just a bit crap at keeping them.

It may be unfashionable to say so, but I don't think I have a homosexual bone in my body. I've never *had* a homosexual bone in my body either. When Alan once climbed into bed with me in the middle of the night, I simply got out and slept on the floor. Well, I *was* sleeping in his bed, and he *had* been an over-garrulous

---

5. We played the Black Lion a great deal, but it was one of the only halfway decent live venues in Northampton at that time. It was all function rooms and pubs. For the record – and this means a lot to me – Absolute Heroes also played the Marina Bar, the Sturtridge Pavilion, the Paradise Club, Dallington Squash Club, the County Ground and the Five Bells. And Daventry Youth Centre, our only out-of-town gig. Thanks for letting me share that with you.

host in offering to sleep on the settee that night. I think he wanted his bed back. Fair enough.

I quite liked the cachet of seeming on the verge of an alternative lifestyle to my parents. It gave me an air of well-travelled mystery around the house. We went on our annual holiday to Jersey two weeks after the 'Earth Song' lecture, and I think Mum and Dad were glad to have me close at hand again and under the same roof for a fortnight. For those two weeks I happily regressed back to being the wide-eyed, brown-haired boy of the year previous. I befriended Lynn, the girl from Manchester whom I later went up to see, and I certainly looked heterosexual from where Mum and Dad were sitting, up on the balcony. (It's ironic really that the year before, unbeknown to my parents, when I had the Spandau Ballet fringe and the shirts buttoned up one side, some kids at the Merton had shouted 'Poof!' at me in the coffee lounge.)

Back in Northampton, for as long as the Lynn thing trickled on, I think Mum and Dad relaxed a little. They certainly refrained from shouting 'Poof!' at me on the stairs. Lynn at least kept my mind occupied for a lovelorn few weeks, and although I didn't stop going to Alan's flat, it stopped being my second home.

I went back to school and tried in earnest to avert next June's nightmare (the one Mr Coppock had predicted 'unless improvements are made'). There was a riotous party round at the flat for Alan's 20th birthday, starting at 5.20p.m. – and on a Wednesday too – but I spent most evenings at home when we weren't gigging.

I don't know if the novelty of Alan's flat had worn off. He was still Absolute Heroes' manager (for which he took 0 per cent of our earnings I might add) and we still saw him a lot, but it was around then that pub culture took hold for the first time. This was after all the school year during which upper sixth-formers turned 18.

I spent more time at the Bold Dragoon pub up in Weston Favell village than I had ever done at Alan's flat, but my parents didn't seem to mind, even during the week, and even though it involved me drinking Fosters (quite an urbane choice in 1982, by the way). I can only assume they felt that going to the pub was more 'normal' than hanging out behind locked doors with home tattooists. What harm could possibly come to me drinking illegally in a village pub beyond choking on a domino or falling into the open fire? The Bold became our new hangout, the hard-but-fair landlord getting more and more agitated every time one of our group celebrated his or her 18th in there. 'Is that the last one?' he would ask. Yes, we would lie.

Mum and Dad gave me a top-up lecture a month into term, and Mum flew off the handle and said two inflammatory things to me:

'I wouldn't be very proud if you got a D at A-level!'

And:

'I reckon *I* could get an E at A-level!'

I felt affronted by these remarks. Getting any kind of A-level was actually a lot harder than Mum thought, and it's all very easy to *talk* about getting one at the breakfast table, but not so easy to spend two years doing the essays and the projects and the note-taking. More pressingly, I could well foresee getting a D or an E so I wanted to create an atmosphere in which all passes were good passes.

But through it all they never once grounded me, as American parents say (and do). In fact, I was encouraged to borrow Mum's Mini Metro in which to drive to the Bold. I suppose it stopped me boozing, which was a good thing, but I'll never forget Dad taking me to one side that November and having a manly chat:

'Borrow Mum's car whenever you like,' he said. 'You could use it to give a lift home *to a girl.*'

A girl! Is that not priceless? They were trying to buy back my heterosexuality with petrol. However, I took his advice to heart and drove a new Bold regular called Della back to her house that very night. Nothing came of it – she lived on one of the eastern estates and there was a hole in the kitchen wall where her older brother had punched it during a family row. Della was not for me. But I appreciated Dad's offer all the same. (It's significant that Vorno faded from view somewhat once I'd passed my test, but not completely – I wasn't that mercenary.)

Mum admits today that me turning out gay would have been her worst nightmare, although I suspect only because of what the neighbours would say. If I'd got a girl pregnant around this turbulent time I think Dad would have patted me on the back. That's something I suppose.

* * *

So my brush with gayness had passed without incident. At Christmas I met and fell for Jo – where else but at a week-long Christmas party at Alan's flat? – and entered my first long-term relationship. But I still looked a fright and would do for quite some time. My hair expanded outwards and skywards through committed back-combing and upside-down blow-drying; it also got auburner; my turn-ups rose higher up my sockless legs, as did the sleeves of my second-hand dress jacket (this was the Eighties). I actually looked more and more effeminate as 1983 wore on,[6] but I had a long-term female girlfriend on my arm, so how could Mum and Dad complain? They did, but how could they?

I drove Jo everywhere, which meant I wasn't getting pissed, and even though they couldn't have known it for sure, I wasn't on drugs. I never even saw or smelt a drug in Northampton – not to my knowledge anyway – until much later when a guy called Pete Hepworth[7] on my art foundation course at Nene College offered me a puff of his joint on the Racecourse. It made me giggle for half an hour, but I never pestered him for any more. So much for getting hooked.

Don't forget I had never smoked. I'd come home with my donkey jacket reeking of fags on many occasions but it wasn't my smoke – and I think Mum actually believed that. She'd given up years before, although she briefly and inexplicably took to having the odd More cigarette on holiday (the kind made of chocolatey brown paper). I called her bluff one year by demanding she give me one. She did. I smoked it reasonably convincingly. It was bloody horrible. No More, thanks.

So despite appearances, I had turned out alright really. I never paid them back for the drum kit, even when Absolute Heroes brought home some door money from the Black Lion, but at least I never threatened to have my ear pierced, not once. It was a good

---

6. Some hard kids actually punched me in the side of the head for looking a poof on the racecourse after a party in 1984. I was with the distinctly heterosexual-looking Simon that night, who, like the good infantryman he was, suggested we run like hell. I can only assume he thought I might fight like a girl and didn't fancy the odds.

7. He wasn't called Hepworth but that's what we called him (after learning about the sculptress Barbara Hepworth). This was art school, you squares.

year for Mum and Dad, 1983: in June the Tories got back in (low taxes, therefore my allowance was safe!), and in July we moved upmarket into a new house with three toilets in the village (into the cul-de-sac where Craig's family lived, staggering distance from the Bold).

Simon was about to start a promising career in the army, while I had gained a place at nearby Nene to do my pre-degree foundation year (the first step on the road to legitimate higher education). This despite failing one of my A-levels as predicted by Mr Coppock. Biology. Nightmare. I got an O grade, which is the equivalent of having moved on not a jot in two years of study. (I know. Why didn't the exam board just come round and slap me in the face? They knew where I drank.) I blame my failure squarely on repeats of the first series of *The Young Ones*, albums by New Order,[8] George Clinton[9] and Wasted Youth,[10] the hot weather and the distraction of a general election. (Alright, maybe not the last one, but I could hardly blame Jo – she was studying concurrently for her O-levels. She passed all eight.)

I finished with Jo just before the start of my first term at Nene. I won't say I packed her in, that's for kids, but I did end it and for her own good – she was feeling her age, which was two years younger than me, don't forget. It turned out to be a dry run for the real, final split in October. Alan had by now moved out of his flat and bought a house in Southfields. I don't believe I ever even went there.

Thus began a clean slate, and the year that Mum and I really fell out.

---

8. *Power, Corruption and Lies* (Factory, 1982).
9. *Computer Games* (Capitol, 1982), Clinton's first solo album, the one containing 'Atomic Dog'. It was a new boy called Dave 'Newboy' Payne, from the white socks heartland of Essex, who introduced me to funk.
10. *The Beginning of the End* (Bridgehouse Records, 1982). Who remembers Wasted Youth? They were The Strokes of their day, albeit not American or successful. They weren't local and yet nobody outside of the Alan's flat scene seems to have heard of them (they're not even logged in Mick Mercer's book *Gothic Rock*). This album was reviewed in *Sounds* and described by a man called Jim Reid as 'quite possibly the worst record released this year. If you like your juvenile rock obsessions cloaked in New York leather ... then, mate, Wasted Youth are the boys for you.' Where do I sign?

sixteen

Wayward Up Lancaster

Everything seems to be up in the air at this point.
Talking Heads, 'Mind' (1979)

I wish you were going away, not Simon!
Mum to Andrew after a row, Sunday, 13 February 1983

Didn't really mean it – your loving Mum xx
Written without my knowledge in my diary on the same day

I'm not a parent and have no plans to be one, so I can never really know the clawing, bittersweet pain of seeing your children grow up and leave home. I was emotional enough when our two cats were spayed and had to stay at the vet's overnight, so I can at least hazard a guess at what it must be like. In 1983, aged 40 (funny age), Mum lost Simon to the British Army, and a year later, aged 41 (funnier age), she lost me to the weird and frightening world of art school. (So did Dad of course, aged 42 and 43, but as we've established he's a stoic individual with constant recourse to the bigger picture.) Her two boys, gone.

She and I had a row on the day I left. It was only right and proper that we did. We'd been at loggerheads ever since July's house-move. We lived in the genteel Weston Favell village now, where Mum foolishly imagined a better class of neighbour to be twitching the net curtains. If I may say so, she developed ideas above her station the moment her feet hit the gravel drive. She made the commonest of errors – equating money with class. In fact, the residents of Kestrel Close were just like the residents of Winsford Way: white-collar wage slaves made good. (If 'good' can be measured by length of gravel drive.) These weren't posh people, and nor were we.

Of course, reactionary relatives like Nan Mabel would say, 'Ooh, *very* posh!' when they saw the new house, in the same way that Cilla Black says, 'Ooh *very* posh!' when a contestant on *Blind Date* reveals that he or she works for a PR company. I'm afraid Mum took the 'very posh' literally. And because she was now apparently landed gentry (even though she worked as a school secretary), my ever-worsening appearance became an unbearable thorn in her side. It wasn't what *she* thought of the army trousers and Oxfam macs I wore to Nene College, or the fingerless gloves I wore at the dinner table, it was the barons and baronesses with the binoculars who lived either side of us.

I sympathise with Mum now of course. I looked quite dreadful in 1983–84, although not as bad as Paul Garner who often came to call for me in the mornings (he had effectively adopted the 'look' of a Vietnam war veteran combined with werewolf Eddie Quist from the film *The Howling*). I have no idea what the residents of Kestrel Close actually thought of me, or him, because these people didn't exactly spend a lot of time chit-chatting over the garden fence, forming Young Wives groups or accompanying each other down the welfare. Unlike the good folks of Winsford Way and Ashbox Close, they kept themselves to themselves.

So, this final school year was agony for Mum, and as a result, second-degree agony for Dad. When it came to taking sides in a domestic firefight he rightly took Mum's and backed up her hysterical all-out attacks with more restrained low-level cover. But he and I had some important bonding sessions that year – he accompanied me on the train to London to look round Chelsea (the only parent there that day), and he drove me back to the college with my bulging portfolios for the interview. Mum wouldn't have been seen in public with me. Thus she and I grew detached in our new detached house, and when Kevin Pearce – a schoolfriend of Simon's at a loose end after he'd joined the army – filled the vacancy left by long-term girlfriend Jo in October, a regimen of furtive hairstyling took hold.[1] At weekends I would drive to Kevin's parents' house and in his bedroom – to the sound of Death Cult, SPK[2] or the Bunnymen's 'Killing Moon' – we would backcomb our hair into rock-hard Robert Smith haystacks using gallons of Boots hairspray.[3] Kevin's mum turned a blind eye, even though they too lived in a cul-de-sac.

Off we would go into town, fully sculpted, to hang out at whichever wine bar allowed in weirdos that week and drink black-currant and lemonade (me, because I was driving, and Kev out of moral support – and because it seemed like a very gothic thing to drink). Our hair would not move. It was fixed. And by the time I rolled in, Mum and Dad were in bed. In the morning it would be flattened by sleep and they were none the wiser. I had no wish to cause trouble you see.

The row we had on the day I left home was about clothes. Mum forbade me from packing some item of clothing – it could have been my army trousers, the dirty blue mac with the ripped lining, or just something second-hand and painty – and I touchéed her. 'As of tomorrow,' I said. 'I can wear anything! You won't even *know* what I'm wearing!'

She withdrew in tears. Not because I was right and could indeed from then on wear a clown costume and a Carmen Miranda fruit hat, but because she was heartbroken that I was leaving home. She was about to relinquish her maternal role irrevocably, and effectively cut out a part of her own femininity, casting it

---

1. Having resisted Mum's attempts to turn Simon and I into twins all my life, I saw no irony in the fact that Kevin and I wore exactly the same clothes and had exactly the same hair when we went into town.
2. Minor industrial noise band, most famous for 'Metal Dance' and not being Einsturzende Neubaten.
3. Also Harmony, Country Born, Bristows and Sunsilk.

aside for ever. One of her chief functions on earth – one to which she had devoted 19 of her 41 years – was over, done with, gone. I was too fat-headed to see it. (I think I understand women better now, but it took another ten years of pain to get there.)

Dad set me straight and I felt bad. (I already felt bad but for different reasons.) I packed the offending piece of rag anyway and Mum gave me a kiss on the doorstep when I left. It was probably our first mother-and-son kiss since 1978 (kissing Hayley had made kissing Mum seem all wrong so I stopped). The whole unnecessary blow-up was a learning experience, and a healing one. After my first homesick week of college I put Mum and Dad at Number One in my People Charts.[4]

Morrissey only got to Number Four.

* * *

So that was the end, beautiful friend. I was no longer resident of my mum and dad's house or a citizen of Northampton. They kept my bedroom for me, left the Smiths pictures Blu-Tacked to the walls like the grieving parents of a murder victim, and I duly returned every holiday (because the halls of residence chucked us out), and played at being my pre-college self, hitting the town with Kevin and going to the Bold, and occasionally, if our leave coincided, seeing Simon. But I was, as predicted, a visitor. Overspill.

After I left, Northampton town centre grew more and more violent and unwelcoming (I'm sure it's improved since the J.D. Wetherspoon revolution) – an irony that was completely lost on Nan Mabel, who remained convinced until her dying day that London was more threatening. Even when I graduated from Chelsea in 1987 and became a freelance illustrator she whittled – was I getting enough work down in London? Yes I was. Why couldn't I move back to Northampton and get a job here? Because I didn't want to work in Sainsbury's, Nan. Again, looking back, I can sympathise with her plight: she had lost two out

---

4. 'For being there.'

of four grandchildren to the wider world and that hadn't been part of the plan. Families stay close in Northampton. (Ironically, when Simon left the army he moved back to Northampton with his young family; I'm the only one still missing in action.) What Nan hadn't spotted was that we *were* close. Miles on a motorway sign have nothing to do with it. I always felt close to my family – we just never said the words. (Of course I still do, and we still don't.)

If I am a product of my parents and grandparents, they should all be pretty pleased with themselves. I may not be in the market for supplying grandchildren but Simon and Melissa have been industrious enough in that regard. I am happy and healthy. I have what the Weston Favell careers officer would have deemed a 'glamour' job. London made a man and a socialist of me, and my first job in journalism showed me the world – or at least its airport lounges and hotel lobbies.

If I was looking for a scene to tie up Act One of my story dramatically I suppose a funeral might do it. Halfway through my college years, Mick Spratt, a key figure in the sixth-form social circle, was killed in a car accident. We all assembled, *Big Chill* style, back in Northampton for his funeral: Craig, Jo G, the two Neils, the two Daves, Honx, Lis, Liz, Hetty. It was a happy-sad occasion, remembering this much-loved, laugh-a-minute member of our gang and lamenting his premature loss, but it was also the day we all realised we were no longer in the sixth form. Without the distinctive blazers – or even our early Eighties uniform of big coats and wedgey fringes – we had become indistinct from one another.

It was too soon for the school reunion, that's all. We were all still finding ourselves at various seats of learning, or in Craig and Jo G's case, within the local job market. When the wake was over, we all returned to our study bedrooms in Hatfield and the north and moved on.

Or there's the funeral of Pap Reg, which occurred halfway through writing this book. For me, the star of that particular wake was Auntie Jean, Nan Mabel's younger sister (Great Auntie Jean, strictly speaking, although we've never known her as such). She held court in the front room at Kestrel Close, the spitting image of Nan – broad Northampton accent, unrendered consonants, steeped in the old ways, loud and funny, intentionally or otherwise (it was hard to tell, as it had been with Nan). Jean spoke ardently about her own family, ticking off the current whereabouts of her grandchildren in the same way Nan Mabel probably used to (*'air* Andrew's in London, *air* Simon's in the army ...'), and when she revealed that one of them has multiple piercings while the other has 'gone wayward up Lancaster' everything fell into place for me – why I love Northampton and why I love my family so much.

First of all, 'gone wayward' simply means he is living in sin with his partner, something still clearly frowned upon by the surviving matriarchs of the family. Secondly, this lad has committed no greater crime than to move to Lancaster, but is nonetheless considered both exotic and disloyal for it in the same breath. But most of all, it was the way Auntie Jean's words made me smile broadly. (She really is a great Auntie.) Wayward up Lancaster! What a tragedy it will be when Estuary English and *Home and Away* have wiped this accent out. These, I thought, are *my people*. They made me; I am cut from the same shoe leather.

I suddenly became ashamed and melancholy that I had so methodically shed the accent (now that really *is* wayward). Northampton, I accepted in that moment of clarity in Mum's 'posh' front room, exerts just as much of a romantic, storybook pull on my heart as, say, Ireland does to its scattered descendants and Bow Bells do to all those displaced Londoners living in Milton Keynes.

The welfare, the field, Abington Park, the market square, the Mayor Hold car park, Pap's allotment, the Willowtree, the Bold, the Farm, Alan's flat, Weston Mill – this used to be my playground. If I grew up normal in the Seventies, it's because Northampton isn't just anytown, it's my town. My *kind* of town. No matter what the season, Northampton will always exist in the dull, flat colours of an Instamatic photograph, and will pulsate to the great tunes of Bauhaus and perhaps 'In Dulce Jubilo' by Mike Oldfield.

I don't believe in God, but I believe that God is in the details.

I didn't lose my innocence in Northampton, I left it. Even North Wales, my geographical significant other, felt like Northampton with extra sheep because I experienced it with Mum, Dad, Simon and Melissa – and sometimes Nan and Pap – and anywhere we went, we always took Northampton with us. It rained in Wales just like it rained at home, we still ate sausages and fried potatoes and Mini-Rolls for tea and the whole fortnight smelt of Dad's Viva.

Although this book ends in 1984, my childhood ended in August 1980 when we set sail for Jersey on the *Earl Godwin*. (Lovely on the wa-ter!) That upturn in Dad's finances spelled the real end of innocence: from then on holidays meant posing at discos, family membership at the Fort Regent leisure complex and eating *soup de jardinier*. Wales meant having fun against all odds. In Jersey fun was part of the package. As Love And Rockets[5] so memorably sang, 'There is nothing less amusing than the amusement arcade.'

Denholm Elliot went from the Hotel du Lac to the Bangkok Hilton. We went from Mr and Mrs Williams's farmhouse to a Jersey hotel named after a borough in South London.

It may seem perverse to say it, but my Seventies ended in 1980. I think they must have started in 1970 too. Oh well. You can't force these things.

* * *

You'll remember that Mum dressed Simon and me as twins when we were growing up. It didn't work. You can't force these things. They encouraged me to take English A-level so that I could always become a journalist. That worked. They brought me up to look after my things and be nice to those around me and come home for my tea. That also worked.

Mum tried to indoctrinate me with mispronunciation of food-stuffs but I chose my own path. Dad tried to indoctrinate me with

---

5. The band that rose from the ashes of Bauhaus and enjoyed moderate success in America. This line is from 'Dog-End of a Day Gone By' a song on their first album, 1985's *Seventh Dream of Teenage Heaven*.

Thatcherite self-interest – for my own good, of course – but I failed him there, just as I had done by taking no interest in cricket. At the end of the day, my parents did very little moulding, allowing all three of us to follow our instincts – Simon into khaki, me also into khaki but as an art fashion statement, and Melissa into the bank. I'll bet they wouldn't do anything differently if they had the chance to go back and do it again – except perhaps Ilfracombe.